GARY SCARPA

LESSONS FROM THE STAGE

A life in the theater

Foreword by
Dartmouth Dean of Admissions,
Lee Coffin

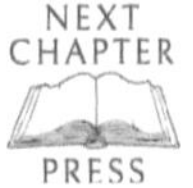

First edition

Book cover design by Mario Lampic

Author photo by Julia Gerace

Printed in the United States of America
Names: Scarpa, Gary, author
Title: Lessons from the Stage
Description: First edition / Next Chapter Press
Identifiers: ISBN: 978-1-7365146-5-8
Classification : Nonfiction; Theater

For more information about books by Gary Scarpa, visit www.garyscarpa.com

To Mom,
who nurtured and loved the performing artist in me

"How one sees, one does. How one does, one is."

- Ruth Asawa, American artist (1926 - 2013)

FOREWORD

MY LESSONS FROM THE STAGE

It was Sarah who made me do it.

Perhaps my very first lesson from the stage happened before I ever stepped onto one. I tried something new.

Sarah was my middle school bestie. She had older siblings, while I was the first in my house to arrive at "the high school," as Shelton High was known around town, so Sarah was my orientation guide. She was wise to the ways of those intimidating new hallways, and she had seen a flyer announcing auditions for the Drama Club's fall play.

"That sounds like fun," she said. "Let's do it."

I usually did what Sarah suggested, so I did it.

Sometimes, the border of one's comfort zone mimics a force field, and it holds you back. The stage taught me to be open to opportunity when it says hello. I learned to say "let's do it" when someone proposes something new. "New" is an adventure, and adventures are usually exciting. The stage certainly was!

That said, the freshman version of me had *no* expectation that I would make the cast in any kind of role. As I have tried to reconstruct that moment, it is lost to me. I have no recollection of that first audition nor my introduction to Gary and Fran Scarpa, the directors of the Drama Club at Shelton High School, who would become lifelong mentors and friends. Mr. Scarpa was the cool teacher – I had already learned that after a few weeks at the high school – and I am certain I would have been a ball of nerves as I walked into his room for that first-ever audition. I had no intention of making Drama Club one of the defining themes of my high school experience, nor did I have any ego attached to the outcome.

Sometimes, serendipity dances in your path. In a blink that I could never have recognized as "the moment" that it was for me, the Sarah-inspired audition led me somewhere unexpected. As I scanned the cast list on the bulletin board near my homeroom a few days after the audition, I saw...my name!

My stage debut in the fall of 1977 was as "Man with the Rifle" in *The Man Who Came to Dinner*. For the record, I was not a man ("man" being a *preposterous* description for a fourteen-year-old who weighed 100 pounds wet), my character was not invited to said dinner, and the rifle I carried as a prison guard was bigger than me. But my one line of spoken dialogue and my huge prop were not the point: I was in my first play. And there's another lesson. A part does not need to be huge for it to be impactful. I was introduced to theater, and that introduction shifted my path in a profound way. As Robert Frost famously wrote, "I took the one less traveled by, and that has made all the difference."

In my sports-centric hometown and certainly in my sports-centric family, the arts were not the obvious path for me. My dad wanted me to play football, but a huddle and shoulder pads were not in the cards for me. And there was a perception that the "cool kids" were not in Drama Club, a lesson to be wary of conventional wisdom and its (mis)perceptions.

As it turns out, the cool kids *were* in Drama Club. And they weren't alone. It was a rare space where the school's social cliques intermingled. The "drama kids" paired up with varsity athletes in a dance sequence, the cheerleaders worked with the set crew, and the honors nerds (myself included!) met peers with other talents and priorities. It was a real-life version of *The Breakfast Club*, and it would make an indelible imprint on my high school experience as well as the arc of my life beyond high school. I met the stage, and it embraced me. During high school, the Percy Kingsley Auditorium became a second home. I had found my people.

The Scarpas were the drama duo who changed my life. They met a skinny, quiet, fourteen-year-old freshman with braces, and their mentorship created a confident, gregarious person who thrived in front of an audience. Over the next nine years, I appeared in fourteen shows with Gary and Fran. Seven productions were at the high school, one was at a nearby girls' school where the moonlighting Scarpas imported a few boys for key roles, one was at a nearby community theater group, and several were staged through a youth-oriented summer theater company that the Scarpas founded.

From my unremarkable debut as "Man with the Rifle," I became President of Shelton's Drama Club during my senior year, and my classmates voted me Best Actor when senior superlatives were awarded. Neither outcome could have been forecast when I auditioned for my first play in 1977. Both happened.

I had a few lead roles, a few supporting parts, and a few gigs in the ensemble. I worked backstage as stage manager for a fourteenth production. Sometimes I got a callback for a lead role, and sometimes that role went to someone else. That was the way theater worked. I learned how to navigate disappointment, and I was taught that every part was important, whether I spoke, sang, pantomimed, or directed cues backstage. That's another lesson: I learned to embrace what I have and make the most of it. A cast is a team, and the team has the same goal. The lead needed the supporting parts and the production crew to lead in their own way.

Characters as diverse as Ali Hakim in *Oklahoma!* and Papa in *I Remember Mama* and Chino in *West Side Story* and Motel in *Fiddler on the Roof* trusted me to tell their story. As a sixteen-year-old who had just been released from his braces, I wore my grandfather's cardigan as I played a senile old man named Herbert in a one-scene performance in a cabaret. The multi-ethnic, multi-generational rainbow of my acting resume was another lesson for me – a gay, Catholic kid from suburban Connecticut – as I learned there are other ways of "being" than the one I knew. Through these roles, I met new "people." I got to "be" that person as every costume I wore and every accent I conjured transformed "Lee" into someone else. Every performance enhanced my own story as the lessons of a charming Persian peddler and a nervous Jewish tailor helped me grow.

The stage taught me so many things. Learning a script or a song or blocking or choreography or set design are not lessons one draws from American Lit or AP Biology, but those extracurricular lessons were as edifying as anything I encountered in a textbook. When I sang my first solo on a stage, it was as intimidating a moment as it was exciting to have earned such a spotlight. My duet – from *The Fantasticks* – helped me navigate stage fright and bolstered my self-confidence and poise. I had to hit my notes *and* stay focused in the moment even as I saw my grandmother smiling at me from the third row. Similarly, those unexpected moments when someone dropped a line or missed a cue, or when a prop malfunctioned at a critical moment of the story, were vivid lessons in quick thinking, in trusting myself to improvise as I moved the story back on track, forward.

Ultimately, I found my life's work in a different arena. I became a college admissions officer, and I have served as a Dean of Admissions at three colleges and an independent school over the past thirty years. But, as I reflect on my years as a high school and college-age performer, and on the roads I later traveled, I see a number of parallels. Indeed, I have used my many lessons from the stage *every* day of my career and in my adult life. Composure, teamwork, discipline, time management, courage (my first kiss on a stage as Ali Hakim was also one of my first kisses in *any* situation!) were welcome skills that I retain to this day. The stage requires confidence and poise; it instilled those traits in me.

Public speaking became my second nature, a clear and powerful lesson from the stage. As a college admissions officer – and, more recently, as a college admissions dean who hosts a college admissions podcast – I regularly speak in front of audiences big and small without notes. My experience in Drama Club empowered me to own my professional space, to "perform" with agility in whatever venue I confront, to tell a story with clarity and confidence, to annunciate my Ts, to engage my audience, to be charming or funny, and yes, to entertain. While I never imagined a professional acting career, the lessons from the stage are assets for *anyone* who must communicate in a macro way. Any lawyer in a courtroom, or politician on the campaign trail, or professor in a lecture hall must own the podium, too. The stage offers that preparation.

My time as an actor – regardless of the number of lines that I had or how much stage time there was for my character – taught me to own my piece of it. Every part counts. Collaboration is a critical skill in all settings, and I know how to own my piece of the puzzle. Theater reinforced the importance of collaboration onto my consciousness. It is as indelible as the confidence and poise I also came to embody.

I owe Sarah a huge debt of gratitude because Shelton's Drama Club was a game changer for me. It transformed that skinny, quiet boy into a gregarious (maybe still nerdy) extrovert whose high-profile career centered around public speaking and performance. In 1977, that trajectory would have seemed improbable at best and ridiculous by any sane prediction. And yet, it happened. Here I am, an Ivy League dean and a podcaster.

I often wonder what might have happened to me had I not seen my name on the cast list for *The Man Who Came to Dinner*. Would that outcome have produced a minor shrug in me as I turned away from the bulletin board and explored other opportunities in high school? Probably. And without my *tiny* presence in the play that fall, would I have auditioned later that year for *Fiddler on the Roof*, the spring musical? Maybe, but I suspect it is possible that my minor setback from that first audition would have dissuaded me from a second pass at the stage. Serendipity is real.

The lessons from the stage are tattooed on me. Had I missed those lessons, I wonder if my fourteen-year-old persona would have endured, uninterrupted by the intoxicating glow of a curtain call? (And would I have come to love show tunes?!) Without my lessons from the stage, would I now be Dartmouth's Dean of

Admissions? Maybe not. I'm not sure I would have gravitated towards such a public-facing role had the stage not taught me how to thrive in such a spotlight.

One lesson is vividly clear to me. I am who I am because I auditioned for a play in the fall of 1977 and I met Gary and Fran Scarpa. I took the path less traveled, and it led me someplace wonderful. And the lessons of that journey continue to teach and guide me almost a half-century after my accidental audition.

Lee Coffin
Shelton High School Class of 1981
Dean of Admissions and Financial Aid, Dartmouth College

PRESET

PRESET

When you think about the moment before a play begins, perhaps you envision a plush red curtain with tassels and gold-braided fringe hiding the mystery of what's on the stage. But just as often as not, the stage is *preset* with no curtain to be seen. The set for Act I, Scene 1 is sitting on the stage before you, dimly lit in a most aesthetic way, and you sit in the audience viewing it, reflecting and imagining what magic and mystery the play you are about to see holds for you. Let us think of this chapter as the *preset*. And let us, then, begin.

You hold in your hands a book about the theater. Or, more specifically, about the amateur theater. Professional theater may be mentioned on occasion as it suits my purpose, but this is a book primarily about amateur theater – of my experiences in that world over the better part of a half century.

Merriam-Webster defines an ***amateur*** in this way: *one who engages in a pursuit, study, science, or sport as a pastime rather than as a profession*. And: *one lacking in experience and competence in an art or science.*

My hope will be to dispel that second definition – and maybe the first as well. Of course, the word amateur comes from the Latin amātor, which means "lover, enthusiastic admirer, devotee."

I am all of those things, and I daresay most people who've

spent their lives in either the amateur or professional theater are as well.

In truth, I was often paid for my services, sometimes a very small amount, and other times slightly more than a very small amount. But the young people and adults whom I directed for more than four decades were not paid.

This is a story of how, during the summer of 1973, I fell in love with an art form and a girl, all in one fell swoop. It is a story of how I married the girl, starting a partnership in life and in theater, and of how we brought two girls into the world who grew up on the stage and became our partners in directing well before they turned twenty.

It is a story of how this woman and I would go on to mount more than two hundred productions over the course of forty-three years. To put that time frame in perspective, I will use a sports analogy (which I have done many times in directing plays and will no doubt do in this memoir). Using legendary college coaches as examples, UCLA's John Wooden coached for twenty-nine years; Tennessee's Pat Summitt coached for thirty-eight years; Indiana's Bobby Knight coached for forty-two years; and UCONN's Geno Auriemma is now beginning his forty-first year coaching as I work on this book.

Yes, this is a story of a lifetime on the stage. I expect that it will be something of a valentine to the world of theater, which was rewarding to us, to say the least. I will not paint us as something we were not, nor will I pretend our experiences were more (or less) than they were.

My goal is to tell our story in an interesting and creative way because the theatrical life was, for me, one of ultimate creativity.

This was our destiny...our journey...our legacy.

THE GOBLETS

In the corner of our dining room sits a kitschy table my wife Fran and I found at a secondhand shop. It is small and round with a glass top and a glazed, ceramic elephant as its base – the kind of elephant one might see at a wedding in India, complete with a colorful cloth draped over its back, with bells and bracelets, and painted toenails, topped off with decorative headwear – all of these adornments symbolizing good luck and prosperity. The elephant, as I understand it, is the sacred animal in Hindu culture.

This table serves as our coffee nook; a Nespresso machine, pods, and flavored syrups are not-so-neatly laid out on its glass surface. It also serves as something of a theatrical sacred memorial space for our family as photos of us are hung on the walls: a photo of Fran and me conversing in front of Shelton High School's stage when we were in our early twenties; a photo of me conducting a live orchestra during a dress rehearsal; another dress rehearsal shot of me conducting with my right hand while, in my left arm holding my three-year-old daughter Mia who is covering her ears, not because she doesn't like the orchestra but because she's spending this rehearsal in the orchestra pit with me, and it's loud; a photo of Fran, a bobby pin in her mouth, styling the hair of a kimono-clad Gina who, at four years old, is the only child cast member in *The Mikado*.

And there are more recent photos taken years later – the four of us posing for a family picture (Gina and Mia are adults here) at Center Stage on Center Street, the theater we founded in 2005; Fran and me in 2011, holding a wooden sign that says "Center Stage," outside the doors of our new location, a grade school in town where my mother and, eons later, both of our daughters and our grandson attended (our third location in less than a decade – we would call them Center Stage 1.0, 2.0, and 3.0); the four of us on the stage of the Shelton High School auditorium, a sea of a thousand orange seats serves as our backdrop; and the four of us again around 2017, during an open house for Center Stage's education program.

A cream colored shelf resides among the photo montage with three more nostalgic images. The center photo shows Fran and me toasting on our wedding day in 1976 with pewter goblets given to us by the first cast we directed. The goblets were inscribed with the words: "*The Music Man*, 1976." The goblets are gone now, somehow lost in the mayhem of more than four decades in the theater. To the left of our wedding photo is a picture of that first cast in full costume in the midst of performing the song, "Trouble." To the left of our wedding photo is a candid of our last production, a multi-generational, age-appropriate cast. In the center spaces between the three photos are two new pewter goblets, given to us by that last cast, inscribed with the words: "*The Music Man*, 1976" and "*I Remember Mama*, 2019," the two shows that were the bookends to a career in theater.

Yes, our coffee nook is a sacred space for us Scarpas because it reminds us that during that span of forty-three years, theater was our life, beginning with a pair of goblets, now lost, and ending with replacement goblets.

WHAT THIS BOOK IS

Lessons from the Stage is divided into two parts – Act I and Act II. In Act I, I will tell my story, but it is not only my story; it is my family's story, because had I not met my wife in a college play and married her, I don't believe I would have had this theatrical life. In turn, our children literally grew up in the theater, and as young adults, they both became our partners in creating theater. Besides being our story, it is also the story of the hundreds (even thousands) of talented and giving people who appeared in our shows and volunteered behind the scenes – who, in the process, became an amazing extended family for us. In life, there is the family of birth and the family of choice. We were fortunate to have both. So, ours is a story of theater and family and, in fact, life.

In Act II of *Lessons from the Stage*, I will draw upon the various components of preparing a play for performance and take a good look at each one, giving my perspective based on decades of practical experience. Act II will include many anecdotes and insights into the complex world of theater.

In both acts, there will be lessons that we learned along the way – lessons in creativity, teamwork, learning from our mistakes, problem solving, self-expression, confidence, making connections, perseverance, imagining the possibilities and so much more. Personally, I have never been involved in a pursuit where there were more lessons to be gleaned than in the wonderful world of theater.

WHAT THIS BOOK IS NOT

Lessons from the Stage is not a "how-to" manual. While I think that someone new to directing plays can benefit from it, I will not explain how to direct and produce a play.

It is not a forum for me to talk about the most talented people I've ever directed. It goes without saying that when you spend a lifetime directing plays, working with talented people is part and parcel of the experience. In fact, I will generally not mention actors by name. In the vast majority of cases where I reference an actor, I will use the name of the character he or she played, and my purpose will be other than to highlight the individual talent of the person, but rather to make a larger point of one kind or another.

Finally, this book is not a forum for me to thank the hundreds of people who volunteered behind the scenes. There were simply too many wonderful folks who helped us through the years to thank, and attempting to include them all wouldn't make for interesting reading. Our volunteers were selfless, enthusiastic participants in our pursuits, and we will be forever grateful to them for their incredible work.

Those backstage folks whom I will mention are people I feel were instrumental in helping us get started or assisting us in "upping" our game. Through the years, we were always striving to improve. Along the way, we were grateful to collaborate with people who could help us do that.

A DISCLAIMER

Casting has changed over the course of the last few decades, first slowly and then more quickly since the Covid pandemic. I grew up in an era where Caucasian actors like Audrey Hepburn played Native Americans in films about the Old West, where Yul Brynner and Rita Moreno (neither Asian) played the King and

Tuptim in the film version of *The King and I*, and where, years later, Jonathan Pryce played a Vietnamese hustler in the Broadway show, *Miss Saigon*.

Things have changed over the course of time, and we see now that such casting practices are no longer acceptable. Having directed in Shelton, Connecticut which had little diversity during our career, we mounted plays like *The King and I*, *West Side Story*, and *The Mikado* in an era which pre-dates the positive changes that are in practice today. It's important to note that we are in full support of today's casting conventions which assure that people of different races and ethnicities are given fair and equal opportunity and appropriate visibility and representation.

But I'd like to tell our story exactly as it occurred in the time period when we directed.

A FINAL THOUGHT

This work is simply one man's perspective about an art form. And there are many perspectives and many ways of doing things in theater as in all walks of life. While I shared this theatrical life with my wife and daughters, and while we came to work in the theater as a family, and while I believe we were mostly aligned on the subjects set down in this book, these words are the product of my thinking and mainly express my personal perspective on the topic and my unique memories about our life in the theater.

So, it looks like the audience is comfortably seated and it's almost time for "lights up," so, please direct your attention to the *stage* before you!

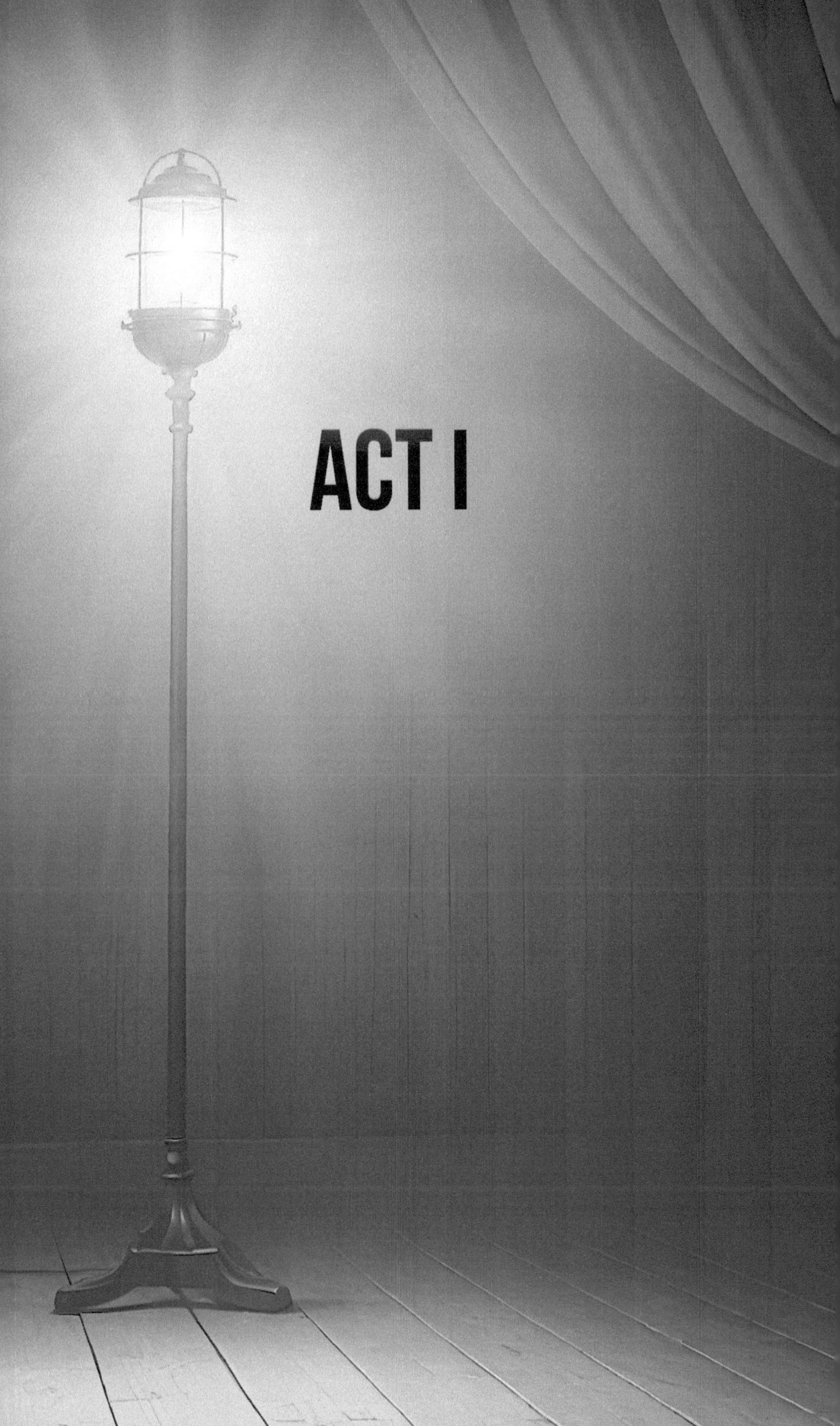

ACT I

ACT I, SCENE 1

STUDENT UNION, 1973

In the midst of the hustle and bustle of the student union, I sit drinking coffee with a group of people that have materialized. I say "materialized" because most of them are students I have recently met. It's a case of meeting someone in a class who knows someone who knows someone else, and before you know it, you have six or eight new friends.

One is a Vietnam vet who goes by the name of Duke. Bearded and burly, Duke could win a Jerry Garcia look-alike contest. There's something about me – my energy or my humor – that causes Duke to address me as "Scarpa the clown." It amuses him, and it doesn't bother me a bit.

Duke sits at the end of the table reading the college newspaper. He looks up, and over the din of silverware clinking and the buzz of dozens of mid-afternoon conversations between classes, he calls out, "Hey, Scarpa the clown, I got a question for you. Do you sing?"

"Actually, yes," I reply. "I grew up singing. In high school I played guitar and sang in a pretty good rock band. Why do you ask?"

Duke doesn't look up from the paper. "The theater department is holding auditions for a musical, The Boy Friend*. I think you should try out."*

I am utterly stunned, befuddled, mystified. There are at least a half dozen of us at the table. "Why me?" I ask. "Why would you single me out?"

"I don't know," Duke says. "I just think you'd be good at it!"

And so the seed was planted. Perhaps it was precisely the seed I needed to help me grow into the real me, the me I was destined to be.

As a college junior, even though I was an education major, I didn't picture myself teaching. Instead, I imagined a career as a writer. What that looked like and what shape it might take, I didn't know, but being a writer was in my heart. I was also looking for a big adventure. Having been pressured to go to a local college by my father, I very much wanted, even needed, to get away. I hoped to enter a graduate program in Creative Writing at an out-of-state college after graduating. In the spring of my junior year, I even purchased a book listing summer internship opportunities for college students in my effort to get away from home. But Duke's suggestion would change the course of my life. It's funny what can happen over a cup of bad coffee.

Not that there wasn't a precedent for my arrival on the theater scene, but the truth is, at the time, I knew almost nothing about live theater, having had only brief brushes with it.

DISCOVERED

Perhaps, I shouldn't have been surprised at Duke singling me out that day. I had been "discovered" a good many years before. As a child, I was identified by a local Scouting legend, Ed Strang, as having musical talent, and I began singing in Scout shows at the tender age of seven.

As a young man, Ed was credited with starting the first Cub

Scout pack in the country, Pack 3 Cub Scouts in Derby, Connecticut.

My older brother was a Cub Scout, and my parents and I would pick him up from the meetings. In the process, I sang along at rehearsals Ed was conducting for the annual Scout show. This show, which continues to be an annual event in the Lower Naugatuck Valley a century later was, at the time, known as a minstrel show, complete with end men in blackface, but Ed would, within a few years, change its name to a "gang show," given the racial tensions of the civil rights movement, and the end men would henceforth wear clown makeup instead of blackface. It's pretty eye-opening to reflect on the fact that performing in blackface was conventional during my lifetime.

LESSON:
It's funny what can happen over a cup of bad coffee.

In those years, this man who would change my life, the man behind Scouting in Derby, Connecticut, noticed me singing all the songs with the regular Scouts and asked my parents if I would sing for him. Ed, as everyone called him, including all Scouts, organized the show and served as master of ceremonies, or "interlocutor," as it was known in the minstrel show world. I wasn't yet old enough to be a Cub Scout, and before I knew it, at only seven years old I was featured in the show singing a duet, "Little Brown Jug," with the younger sister of one of the Cubs.

For the remainder of his life, Ed would call me the most talented boy who had ever performed in these shows – but don't get excited. Most of the boys were not very gifted.

Within a few years, I noticed a competitive spirit within me. Typically, Ed would have me open and close the show. When another good singer on the program would receive a nice round of applause, even at the tender age of nine or ten, I would think to myself, "I will be better than him! I will be better than him!"

My mother embraced the newfound discovery of my singing ability, practicing my songs with me and teaching me many of her favorites. As a young girl, she had shown singing talent herself, performing in local competitions at the Commodore Hull Movie Theater in Derby. In the process, she hoped to be "discovered."

I will never forget that some weeks after that first experience singing on stage, my second grade teacher, Sister St. Jude, told me she heard about my performance and asked if I'd like to sing a song to the class.

"What would you like to sing?" she asked.

I remember saying, "How about 'The Birth of the Blues' or 'Swanee'?" Imagine! A seven-year-old singing those songs.

After my impromptu performance, Sister St. Jude said, "You have a beautiful voice, Gary. Where do you think you got such a lovely singing voice?"

"Well," little me replied, "my mother helps me and so does my Scoutmaster."

"Yes, I'm sure they're very helpful," she replied, "in *learning* your songs, but who gave you that voice?"

I simply repeated my first answer. To me, she seemed a bit dense.

It was not so obvious to me at seven years old, but the answer she was looking for was that *God* had blessed me with my musical talent.

To this day, though, I still attribute my gifts as a performer to my mother. With her guidance, I became quite a little showman. She would have me practice my solos while she washed the dishes.

I'd stand in the corner of the kitchen of our small apartment and belt out my song.

After I hit the last note, Mom would say, "Do it again."

So, I'd sing it again, only to be told, "Do it again, but better."

After a third or fourth repeat of the song, I'd feel frustrated, and ask, "Why do I have to do it again? What was wrong with it?"

Mom would shrug and say, "I don't know. Just do it better."

In one sense, I knew it was a little game we were playing, but in another, in my effort to please her, I'd try harder each and every time. You can see why I was confused by Sister St. Jude's implication that God was responsible for my talent when, to me, it was obviously my mother who was responsible.

I would go on, during those early years, not only to sing in Scout shows, but school shows. I also often sang with dance bands at family weddings when aunts and uncles would urge me to do a solo. I would confer with the band members, and before I knew it, like a miniature Frank Sinatra, I was at the microphone singing my heart out, comfortable performing with a group of musicians I hadn't had a minute's rehearsal with.

LESSON:
I still attribute my gifts as a performer to my mother. With her guidance, I became quite a little showman.

In those years, I was repeatedly approached by adults who had seen me perform who asked if I took voice lessons. It was something I would have loved to do, but my family didn't know of a voice teacher and probably felt it was an extravagance. I would one day realize that if they had looked for one, they very likely would have found my future wife's parents, renowned voice teachers in New Haven.

A friend recently asked me how I understood myself as a grade school student. Did I identify as an athlete? A student? Giving the question great thought, I said, "I most identified as a singer."

NO TO SHAKESPEARE, WILDER, AND WEBBER

But theater? I'm not certain that my first-generation Italian American parents were familiar with the world of Broadway. If they were, perhaps it seemed like another extravagance to them. We didn't go on family vacations, so I suppose they weren't about to take me on day trips to New York's Great White Way. None of my many friends, as far as I know, had ever attended theatrical productions when we were kids in the 1950s and 1960s, unlike the young people who would later pass through my doors, for whom attending Broadway plays would become a staple of their theatrical development.

Most of my childhood travel adventures came via the Boy

Scouting movement. As a Scout, I visited New York City several times, but a Broadway show was not on the itinerary. Our trip consisted of stops at the Ripley's Believe It or Not! Museum, the Museum of Natural History, and Radio City Music Hall where we enjoyed a show featuring the Rockettes and a major motion picture. Close, but not Broadway exactly. What I remember most about the Radio City shows was sitting in the first row on one trip and seeing the large orchestra rise up on a floor lift before me. Seeing and hearing that orchestra was one of the most exciting experiences of my young life, almost too much to process. I couldn't imagine that I would eventually play in my high school and college orchestras and especially that I would one day conduct orchestras myself.

The first play I ever saw was *Julius Caesar* at the Shakespeare Theatre in Stratford, Connecticut as a freshman in high school. I wish I could say that in that very first experience I was bitten by the proverbial theatrical bug, but it wasn't so. I was, in fact, bored to tears at the time. I would see only one other play during my high school years.

This lack of theater-going experience didn't mean that I had no appreciation of entertainers, though. My parents were great music lovers and provided me with music lessons (saxophone and clarinet), and they fostered in me a love for the great film musicals from the Golden Age of Hollywood. As a family, we watched the likes of Fred Astaire, Judy Garland, Gene Kelly, and so many other film legends on a regular basis.

When I entered high school, I learned to play guitar and formed a rock band with three other friends, which we would call the Insight Out. The band was the best part of high school.

Along the way, despite having such little exposure to theater, my English teacher, Simon Rich (who would later become a colleague and friend), having heard that I was a good singer, invited me to try out for a production of *Once Upon a Mattress*. I had seen a version made for television starring the great Carol Burnett who originated the lead character on Broadway. That said, I still didn't have any sense of the entity we know as Broadway. For me, there were movie musicals and made-for-TV musicals – but I still had no sense of live Broadway musicals.

I auditioned because I believed it would please my mother if I appeared in a stage musical. I'm sure I had no idea how to audition for a play, and I don't doubt that I was too nervous and self-conscious to show what I could really do. I was cast, not in a role, but in the ensemble. Being a sports kid and someone who was far too concerned about what his friends might think, even though I had auditioned, I chose not to appear in the production. To participate in a play felt too threatening to me at the time, a behavior I would sometimes observe in male students when I became a teacher and director.

Meanwhile, the Insight Out thrived. We played at local school dances on a frequent basis, so my need to perform was addressed nicely.

When we hit our senior year, a female friend who played keyboard in our band would appear in a school play, Thornton Wilder's *The Skin of Our Teeth*. In support of my friend, to whom I was very close, I went to see the production. As it turned out, the play was intellectually over my head at the time. *If this is what live theater is*, I thought, *I want no part of it*.

A year later, as a freshman college commuter, I was dating a senior from a nearby high school who also appeared in a play that year. I don't recall the title of the play or much of the content for that matter, but my recollection is that it was a light comedy about hillbillies. Once again, I was underwhelmed by my third experience seeing live theater.

In the ensuing years, I had the opportunity to see a few more plays. During my junior year of college, a girlfriend, who had perhaps more of a cultural bent than I, convinced me to go to the theater with her. We visited a summer stock theater in Southbury, Connecticut. If memory serves me correctly, we saw Neil Simon's *Last of the Red Hot Lovers*. It was a more professional production than the high school plays I had seen, and certainly more entertaining, and I have no doubt that I enjoyed it. After all, I had seen Neil Simon's work on film, not knowing at the time that his work had its origin on the stage. Still, despite enjoying the play, I simply didn't picture myself in theatrical productions.

Finally, perhaps that same year, a group of my friends and I took dates to see *Jesus Christ Superstar* at the Oakdale Theatre in Wallingford, Connecticut. There might have been four or five couples, and my memory is hazy because it was so long ago, but I think we went somewhere – and by somewhere, I mean somewhere outside and woodsy – and had a few drinks before heading to the theater. Strange but true. I was hardly more ready to see *Superstar* and listen to Andrew Lloyd Webber's music than I was prepared for *The Skin of Our Teeth* a few years before. Although I would eventually direct *Evita* and *Joseph and the Amazing Technicolor Dreamcoat*, and even though I've seen various other musicals by Webber on the Broadway stage, to this day, I am not a huge fan of his work. At the same time, I understand that I can recognize an artist's greatness without being a fan. A case in point is I recognize the genius of a Goya or a Dalí without particularly loving their art.

The main point, though, is that *Superstar* no more drew me toward the theater than anything else I had seen. It might have helped if I had been completely sober when I saw it, but I doubt it.

In my world of friends, Duke wasn't the first to notice my flair for the dramatic. Not much more than a year before Duke urged me to audition for *The Boy Friend*, Los Angeles DJ Tom Clay, engineered a mash-up of two hit songs, "What the World Needs Now is Love" and "Abraham, Martin and John" replete with sound bites of newscasts from the infamous assassinations of the Kennedy brothers and Martin Luther King, Jr.

The recording also included Ted Kennedy's eulogy of his brother Bobby. The recording made it into the *Billboard* Top 10 in the summer of 1971. At the time, I literally memorized the entire narration and delivered it for coworkers. From the newscaster yelling, "Get the gun! Get the gun!" referring to Sirhan

Sirhan who shot Bobby Kennedy all the way to Ted Kennedy's eulogy, I could recite the entire recording word for word, complete with Ted's Boston accent and his voice shaking with emotion.

Again and again, my coworkers would ask me to do my version of the recording. I remember our restaurant manager, a guy only four or five years older than I, staring at me with eyes of admiration and commenting, "I don't get it. How do you know how to do that?"

I didn't have an answer for him. And never for a moment did I envision myself acting on stage or anywhere else.

And so it came to be. I took Duke's advice to heart, and on the audition date, I made my way to the theater building, one among dozens of candidates. The problem was, I didn't know the slightest thing about auditioning. My one experience hadn't prepared me for it.

ACT I, SCENE 2

LYMAN AUDITORIUM, 1973

I enter the cavernous auditorium at the Lyman Center. I've been in this space only a few times, at freshman orientation and also to see a concert – The Electric Elves (whom I hadn't previously heard of) and Livingston Taylor (brother of James). In those cases, every seat was filled.

Today, dozens of people are milling about, perhaps a hundred. Some are chatting, others are vocalizing, singing scales and making strange sounds ("ma-mae-mee-mo-moo"), something I have never heard anyone do before. I have my guitar in tow. The Southern newspaper had directed candidates to be prepared to sing, but I have no idea if there will be an accompanist. I would rather not sing a capella, so I'm playing it safe.

I am wearing a Dallas Cowboys t-shirt, bell-bottom jeans with an American flag belt, and two-toned shoes, red and black.

I notice that in the middle of the stage sits a grand piano, so my worries are somewhat assuaged. But now a new concern overtakes me. I can see other candidates looking over sheet music. I haven't brought music, so how will a pianist play for me?

A girl dressed in black, topped off with a baseball cap, yells out that everyone needs to fill out a form and return it to her.

Fifteen minutes later, the same girl who appears to be the director's assistant, calls out, "The first candidate is Gary Scarpa." I'm a little dizzy at the thought of going first.

I set my guitar down in front of the stage, approach the accompanist, and say in a hushed voice, "I didn't bring sheet music because I didn't know there was going to be a pianist. I can accompany myself on my guitar if I need to."

He is a distinguished looking middle aged man with a thick head of silver hair and metal-rimmed glasses.

"What song are you planning to sing?" he asks.

"The only song I know from a musical is 'Sunrise, Sunset,'" I reply. "Do you know that one?"

"I can probably plunk it out," he assures me, with at least a modicum of irony. And plunk it out he does. He begins with an eight measure introduction that ends in a haunting arpeggio, and we are off. Standing under bright stage lights, I can't see those watching in the audience, and I am more focused on what a great musician he is than on the song I am singing. I can only feel a harrowing sense of nervousness. It's as if I am having an out-of-body experience, seeing my trembling self from above and wondering if those in the audience can see me shaking.

Afterwards, I take a seat and watch others audition – two girls then a boy, all of them clearly more theatrical than I. The fifth candidate is tall and handsome and is wearing a sport jacket. He launches into "On the Street Where You Live" like it is opening night on Broadway, and now I know I've really blown it.

I am upset with myself because it isn't as if I don't know how to "sell" a song. I had grown up as quite a showman.

An hour later, we are given a short scene to read. I am assigned the role of Pierre, who has two short lines to deliver. The director, a balding Englishman, says to us boys that he would like us to deliver our lines with a French accent. Foolishly, I say to him, "I don't think I can do a French accent." He looks at me as if I have three heads, and before I know it, I am back on the stage, doing the scene with my group. On my first line, I try for the accent, but I feel foolish and abandon the idea on the second line.

We are told that a callback list will be posted outside the theater, but I have no idea what a callback list is. I check the next day, though, and there is a typed list on a bulletin board with about twenty names. Scanning, I see my name is not among them. There are unusual names, like Van der Shwag and Von Schleusingen, and I wonder if a person needs a fancy German sounding name to be cast in this play.

A day later, the final cast list is posted, and once again, my name is not on it. I am disappointed but not surprised.

I would learn that the audition I had taken part in is known as an open audition where all of the candidates watch each other try out. When I became a director, I would conduct only closed auditions, the more common practice, feeling that a candidate might feel less nervous or self-conscious with only the directing team and accompanist in the room.

I also would come to know several of the key players at that audition. The pianist, Dr. Jack Litten, was a music professor and a man I would come to love and admire. And that guy in the dapper sport jacket? His name is Paul Elkin, and he went on to win the leading role. Little did I know that he was a close friend of Fran's family, who had studied voice with her mother, and had even dated Fran when they were in high school.

I was very much bothered by not being cast. I would later learn that the nervousness I felt at that first audition is a universal feeling for the vast majority of people, including some professionals, and succeeding is a matter of a candidate controlling his nerves and making them work in his favor rather than against him as I had done.

But I wasn't about to give up. I may have been driven by my competitive spirit more than a genuine desire to make my way in the world of theater. I was willing to concede Paul Elkin was more talented than I was, but I had a burning desire to discover what was so special about the other candidates who had been cast. I was now on a mission.

I began by attending an evening of one act plays which the

theater department presented. These weren't musicals, but short plays. The program took place in what I would learn was called a "black box" theater instead of in the massive auditorium. The theater department referred to Southern's black box as the "Drama Lab." One of the plays was a little too much *The Skin of Our Teeth* for my liking, but the others were interesting and entertaining. I was impressed by a few of the actors, but for the most part, I didn't feel I was witnessing anything I wasn't capable of doing myself.

LESSON:
...the nervousness I felt at that first audition is a universal feeling for the vast majority of people, including some professionals, and succeeding is a matter of a candidate controlling his nerves and making them work in his favor...

The next step I took was to see the production of *The Boy Friend* itself. I thought my mother would enjoy it, so I took her. It was a beautifully produced show on the stage of Lyman Auditorium. Several of the actors impressed me – Paul Elkin and the Germans as well as the two leading ladies, all of whom I would come to know, but I felt that I could be as good or better than the others.

And I also felt I was a more capable dancer than any of the boys in smaller roles. As a child, my mother had taken me for dancing lessons for perhaps two or three years. I joke today that I was the daughter my mother never had. In truth, though, by the time I was ten, I felt a peer pressure that made me give up dance.

Possibly because of those early dance lessons, or perhaps just because of an inherent level of coordination which had served me well in sports, I knew in my heart I had what it takes to be cast in future musical productions.

My mother and I thoroughly enjoyed *The Boy Friend*, though, and we talked about the possibility of me appearing in a production at school. I didn't know how that would happen or when it would be, and I assumed it wouldn't be until the next academic year.

SHE HAUNTS ME

At the time, I was a great reader of bulletin boards, especially because I was looking for a summer adventure. As the spring semester was about to end, I happened upon a flyer with block letters: A PRACTICUM IN PLAY PRODUCTION. There it was, staring me in the face. Opportunity knocking at my door!

It was a summer course for credit, sponsored by the theater department, which would culminate in the major production of a musical. I called the phone number on the flyer, which turned out to be the personal number of the professor, Thom Peterson, who would teach the course and direct the show. He explained that, as a student in the course, I would have the opportunity to learn every aspect of play production from set construction to lighting, as well as audition for the production and perform in it. I realized I couldn't be cut this time. Except for the fact that it was local instead of out of state, it fit my criteria for a summer adventure.

The production would be a world premiere of a new musical called *She Haunts Me* based on a television series and film called *The Ghost and Mrs. Muir*. *She Haunts Me* would be a big, splashy production.

The course ran daily from 9:00 a.m. to 3:00 p.m. In the first few days of the summer semester, we auditioned, singing a song and presenting a monologue in another open audition situation. This time, I felt a little more confident. Still, I was impressed with the auditions of many of the other students, most of whom were theater majors.

I don't recall what I sang, but as an English major, I performed a soliloquy from *Richard III* – an odd choice for a musical, but what did I know? It is a very famous monologue that begins:

Now is the winter of our discontent,
Made glorious summer by this sun of York...

I had been impressed by a reading I had heard the professor of my Shakespeare class give of this and other monologues and soliloquies. Dr. Stewart was a blind man who dramatically delivered Shakespearean monologues from his Braille text. So inspired was I by Dr. Stewart that, before I knew it, I had memorized several monologues and would recite them alone in my car on my commute to school, trying to mimic my professor's tone, inflection, and histrionics. Again, there was that penchant for acting within me that I was unaware of.

As a college student, rather than choosing a minor, I decided to take electives that interested me. For all practical purposes, I had two minors (minus the requirements), in music and speech, earning eighteen credits in each department. Without knowing it, I was gravitating toward the world of theater. As a junior, I had taken a speech class, *The Oral Interpretation of Literature*, which I loved. We would pick passages from novels and short stories and give dramatic readings of them in class. My work in this class would lead me to perform in an entity known as Reader's Theater. Still, I somehow didn't envision myself on the stage, although it's easy to see that my venture into the theater department was, in its way, a natural next step.

After the audition period, Thom Peterson cast the play. I was cast in the ensemble, but I hadn't any expectation that I would play a role, and I was happy just to participate.

We began each morning with a cast meeting in the Drama Lab and then spent our days rehearsing and working on one crew or another, with the chance to try different things. One day we might be painting scenery and another hanging lighting instruments.

Thom Peterson was a strict taskmaster with high expectations. His goal, clearly, was to produce a highly professional show, from costuming to scenery to our performance. Besides directing the show, he designed the set and costumes. He was, to put it simply, a master of design. In rehearsal, Thom wouldn't accept anyone "dogging it," as we called it in the sports world, a methodology that I would adopt myself when I eventually became a director.

SOUTHERN CONNECTICUT CAMPUS, 1973

It is the third day of the course, and I am walking over to the student union to grab lunch. Even though I am enjoying being in the course, I still don't know a soul.

I hear my name called. "Hey, Gar! Who are you eating lunch with?"

It is a fellow cast member walking with two other girls. I am flattered that she remembers my name. In truth, we had all introduced ourselves and seen each other audition, but I wasn't expecting anyone to remember me. Strangely, I didn't recall seeing her audition, but I would later find out she was sick that day and auditioned privately for the director.

"I'm not eating with anyone," I reply, sheepishly.

"Well, come eat with us," she says. "My name is Francie, and this is Patty and Donna."

Francie has a nice ring to it, I think to myself.

After we get our food and sit down to eat, Francie appears to know everyone and introduces me to person after person. It is as if she is the sun and everyone else planets revolving around her. Clearly, she is socially gifted, and I am drawn to her magnetic personality, just like everyone else seems to be.

The next morning, in a music rehearsal, I hear a glorious soprano behind me as our music director Dr. Litten takes us through vocal exercises. Lo and behold, it is Francie, and if I hadn't already fallen in love with her at lunch the previous day, now I am a goner.

I would come to think of that moment in the music rehearsal as "love at first sound." Before we knew it, the cast of *She Haunts Me* began to refer to me and Fran (I would come to address her as Fran) as the "showmance" of the summer. It was true because we don't recall any other romances besides ours budding.

The performances of *She Haunts Me* were the most thrilling experiences I had ever had. We played to "standing room only" crowds for three or four nights in Lyman Auditorium's sprawling sixteen hundred seat auditorium.

Opening night was a new experience for me. I would learn what any theater person knows – there is nothing more exciting than an opening night. Because it was a world premiere, the creators (writers, composer, lyricist) of the musical came to the production in black tie, transported by limousines, only adding to the electricity. We met the creative team at a reception in the Drama Lab before the performance, which was quite an introduction to show business, I assure you.

As a member of the ensemble, I had eleven costume changes. There was simply no down time for me. When I wasn't on stage, I was making a quick costume change. To this day, I remember finishing one of my changes and standing in the wing, waiting to enter, feeling psyched up in a way I had never before experienced, not in the world of sports or anywhere else.

LESSON:

I would learn what any theater person knows – there is nothing more exciting than an opening night.

And in a sequence where the passage of time was shown with short acting vignettes, followed by ballroom dances – a waltz, a two-step, a jitterbug – Fran and I were dance partners. It was romantic and hectic and exciting and inspiring.

THE MAESTRO

One day, shortly before the production opened, a friend I had made asked me, "Have you met the maestro?"

I almost didn't know what he meant. I suppose I had a superficial understanding that a maestro conducted orchestras, but I couldn't imagine what maestro he might be asking about.

Seeing my puzzlement, the friend said, "Francie's dad. He's a very prominent opera conductor."

I had no idea. Fran hadn't mentioned it in the short time I

knew her. What I would come to learn was that Maestro Francesco Riggio had had a flourishing career in the world of opera although at this time he was retired. At seventy-eight, Maestro Riggio was old to have a daughter of nineteen. To put it in perspective, my father's birth year had been 1922; Fran's father was born in 1896!

I would learn that the maestro had grown up and been educated in Sicily and would go on to conduct throughout his native Italy. When he came to the U.S., he conducted in New York, Chicago, and Los Angeles to name a few cities, and for a period of time conducted the Metropolitan Opera's touring company. In New Haven, he conducted concerts at Woolsey Hall, Yale Bowl, and on the New Haven Green.

He met a pianist named Hilda Whitworth, a girl of English descent, on an Italian radio station where she had been hired to accompany live singers. He married her, and as a couple, their names became synonymous with music in New Haven.

During the golden age of New Haven's Shubert Theatre, Fran's father was the resident opera conductor/impresario, bringing in world famous singers from the Metropolitan to star in operas along with his local protégés. Even though Maestro Riggio was renowned for opera, in those years, the Shubert was often the last stop before Broadway for many legendary productions. Fran's sister Marian, fourteen years her senior, recalls accompanying their father to the Shubert when she was a little girl, and while he was in a meeting with the managing director of the theater, Marian would sit in the house while the likes of Ethel Merman or Mary Martin rehearsed for a big musical.

For years to come, I would find that Fran couldn't mention her name in a New Haven restaurant or store without a musically savvy waiter or store owner knowing who her parents were.

Fran tells a story of being taken to the Metropolitan Opera by one of her high school teachers who happened to know the world famous baritone, Robert Merrill, personally. Robert Merrill was so famous, in fact, that even I, who knew nothing about opera, knew who he was.

After the performance, Fran and her teacher visited Merrill in his dressing room. After meeting Fran, the world famous singer said, "Riggio? From New Haven? Wait! There's an opera conductor in New Haven by that name." Fran couldn't have been prouder to say that indeed she was the maestro's youngest daughter. Mr. Merrill went on to explain that he had never sung with Fran's father but had heard only the highest praise for him from his fellow Metropolitan stars.

Maestro and Hilda Riggio were two of the most revered people in the history of New Haven. Hilda's claim to fame was that she had trained a world famous diva by the name of June Anderson since she was thirteen. In the early 1970s, June became the youngest finalist ever of the Metropolitan Opera Auditions, and a few years after Fran and I married, June would make her Metropolitan Opera debut opposite Luciano Pavarotti!

I met the Riggios on opening night of *She Haunts Me*. Fran's mother was a silver-haired woman, elegant and refined; the maestro, a distinguished looking man who, while short in stature, was tall in presence. In his dark suit and bowtie and sporting a pencil thin mustache, Maestro Riggio commanded respect without saying a word.

The point is this. What I realized was that Fran came from a theatrical family. Music and opera were how her parents made their living. Opera was, in fact, the Riggio family's whole world. While I had many aunts and uncles and dozens of first cousins, Fran had very few blood relatives, and outside of her immediate family, none in Connecticut. Her family consisted of the community of opera singers who were the voice students of her parents.

It was a new world for me, and one, ironically, that I would end up fitting into beautifully, despite the fact that my father was a working class guy, a plumbing contractor, and my mother a housewife. Little did I know at the time that Fran and I would live a parallel life to that of her parents.

I sincerely doubt, in fact, that I would have had a life in the theater had I not married into the Riggio family. It was a natural! Ironically, it would be my drive, a little more than Fran's, that would propel us forward in the world of directing.

ACT I, SCENE 3

So here I was, in love with a maestro's daughter. While Fran herself sang opera and classical music beautifully, she was much more focused on musical theater, something else I knew very little about. We spent many a happy evening in the living room of the Riggio home where Fran played albums from musicals, explaining the plot of each and every one of them to me. I had blithely (or should I say *blindly*?) gone through my teen years having only listened to pop music hits, so this was a whole new education. In our first year together, she explained to me that the song "Till There Was You" was from *The Music Man*. I had seen the film years ago, but I had forgotten the song. Then, when the Beatles recorded it, I associated it with them, thinking the Fab Four had written it. I was surprised to hear that "Hello, Young Lovers" was from *The King and I* because it was a song on an eight-track tape I owned, *The Supremes and The Temptations Live in Vegas*, quite a different version, I would learn, than the Gertrude Lawrence recording on the original Broadway album. Those evenings were an education for me, one I delighted in.

When the fall semester began, Fran and I realized that, well before we had met, we had both elected to take a Vocal Performance class with none other than Dr. Jack Litten. She also told me she hadn't signed up for A Practicum in Play Production until the very last registration day because she had planned to attend a theater program at Yale that ended up falling through. But as students in Vocal Performance, we realized that we would have met even if neither of us had taken part in the summer program.

It was the fall of 1973, and a whole new world had opened up for me. Accompanied by Fran, I went to my first Broadway show, *Pippin*, starring the incomparable Ben Vereen. I don't remember why, but we ended up in the first row, and I was blown away by Ben Vereen's powerful stage presence, uncanny talent, and energy. He was a dynamo, the likes of which I had never seen before.

I liken seeing *Pippin* to my Cub Scout days of sitting in the first row at Radio City and experiencing a full orchestra so close to me that I could almost touch it. This time, though, I was more mature and could better process what was before me. *Pippin* touched me to my very core, unlike experiences I had had seeing plays as a younger guy. Maybe it was because I had now performed in a play or two myself. Maybe it was because I was seeing theater done at the highest level, Broadway. I would soon be using two of the title character's songs, "Corner of the Sky" and "Extraordinary," when I auditioned for musicals.

At that time, I couldn't have imagined that I would one day direct *Pippin* (1990), and I certainly couldn't have known that Fran and I would have two talented daughters, one of whom (Mia) would be accepted into the prestigious Broadway Theatre Project in Tampa, Florida, where one of her many famous teachers would be the legendary Ben Vereen. It was an experience she would carry into the future with her.

In those early years, Fran and I would buy standing room for Broadway shows and often see two productions on the same day. In the mid-70s, standing room could be purchased for less than ten dollars (I believe in the first years, only six dollars). We would stand at assigned places, right behind the last row of the orchestra. The people sitting in front of us had paid perhaps twenty-five dollars or more for their seats, while we saw the shows for a fraction of the cost. I had stood at many a football game, so I didn't mind at all. It was a way for the two of us to see play after play without breaking the bank.

During my senior year, I appeared in two more college productions: *Luther* by John Osborne, about a seminal leader of the Protestant Reformation, and a musical, *You're a Good Man, Charlie Brown*. In the first, I was cast in a non-speaking role, and in the second, I played Linus opposite Fran's Lucy.

I continued to perform in several Reader's Theater programs presented by the speech department and even performed at a Reader's Theater festival where a variety of New England colleges were represented. Fran also convinced me to join the Southern Connecticut State College Band, where somehow I ended up as drum major in the fall semester and played clarinet in the concert band in the spring.

It had been an amazing and fulfilling year of theater and music, making me sad to see my college years come to an end. At the time, it was hard to imagine how or when I would perform again in theatrical productions.

A CHANGE OF PLANS

Understanding that my relationship with Fran was rapidly growing more and more serious, I felt it would be expedient to pursue teaching jobs. With a new passion (theater), I no longer felt the urge to seek an adventure away from home, so I gave up on the idea of pursuing an MFA in Creative Writing in another state.

As a person with a degree in secondary education, I knew that teaching jobs were scarce. It was hard to even get an application, especially in my hometown of Shelton where I was told to just mail in a resume.

Then, that summer my fate took another turn. Having worked at a fast food restaurant, Duchess, I signed up to work the breakfast shift seven days a week, so I could be free to spend as much time with Fran as possible in the afternoons and evenings.

I soon noticed that Shelton's Assistant Superintendent of Schools, Mr. Edward Finn, came in for breakfast each and every morning. Mr. Finn had been a legendary football coach in Shelton, and he had also been one of my mother's high school teachers.

Mr. Finn drove a luxury car, a Cadillac or an Oldsmobile. Each day at the same time, he would pull into the parking lot, make his way to the counter, and order two bacon and egg sandwiches on hard rolls and a large coffee.

Soon enough I was looking for the nose of his car to pull into our lot at the appointed time. A group of retirees who hung out at Duchess assisted me by keeping an eye out for Mr. Finn. By the time Mr. Finn drove to the far side of the building, parked his car, and made his way to the dining room counter, I would have his sandwiches cooked, his coffee poured, and everything packaged to go.

When August arrived, I spoke up. "Mr. Finn," I said. "I know you don't know me, but my name is Gary Scarpa, and I'm a 1970 graduate of Shelton High School. Last spring I graduated from Southern with degrees in English and Secondary Education. I tried to get an application at your office, but the secretary told me to send a resume and I would be notified if any openings occurred, but I haven't heard anything."

Paying me for his breakfast, Mr. Finn said, "I'll see you tomorrow, Gary."

I wasn't altogether sure what he meant until the next day when he slid an envelope with an application enclosed across the counter. "Fill this out right away, Gary," he said. "And don't send it to the Superintendent. Send it directly to me."

I did as he directed, and a week later my mother called Duchess to tell me that the principal of Shelton High School called and wanted me to come in for an interview at 1:00.

It's a longer story, but that afternoon, the Shelton High School principal hired me, explaining that I was the only candidate he had thus far interviewed for the position. I have always believed that Mr. Finn had directed the principal to hire me. It was a lesson in putting your best foot forward. Consequently, I would come to tell young people who were in the midst of rehearsals for a show that one of our daughters was directing that, in the process of rehearsing, I was observing their energy, attitude, and body language – that, in a certain sense, they were auditioning for a future show yet to be determined. UCONN coach Geno Auriemma has often stated that in recruiting future players, he would observe their attitudes while they were in high school.

LESSON:
I learned a lesson about making a good impression on a person, which I feel is important in the audition process…

Ironically, that fall, my student teaching advisor from Southern was at the New Haven high school where my older brother taught and asked him what I was doing.

"He's teaching English at Shelton High School," my brother informed her.

"Wow! That's great," she said. "With jobs being so scarce, how did he find one?"

"He cooks a good egg," my brother replied.

It was true, though. I learned a lesson about making a good impression on a person, which I feel is important in the audition process, but I'll come back to that.

SOME LIKE IT HOT!

I managed to stay involved in the world of theater after college. That same summer before beginning my teaching career, Fran got recruited by a community theater group, the Orange Players, to appear in the chorus of *Bye Bye Birdie* even though she hadn't auditioned. Her older sister Marian was playing the lead female role, Rosie Alvarez, and the director needed someone in the cast who could hit high Cs. Marian volunteered Fran, a perfect choice, and Fran was all too happy to accommodate. I helped behind the scenes applying stage makeup to some of the actors before each dress rehearsal and performance.

During that first year of teaching, I appeared locally in a few productions. In one case, I took a graduate course at Southern so I could perform in another college musical there; in another, I auditioned for and was cast in a production of *Man of La Mancha* at Albertus Magnus College, also in New Haven.

But the most important theatrical experience I had that school year was as an audience member. The Shelton High School Drama Club presented the musical *Sugar*, based on the famous Marilyn Monroe film, *Some Like It Hot*. I remembered having seen the film and enjoying it.

LESSON:
Sometimes *crazy* things happen when you least expect them to...

During that year, Shelton opened a brand new high school building with a twelve hundred seat auditorium. I took Fran to see the show, which some of my English students were appearing in.

The enormous auditorium wasn't sold out, but it was at least three quarters sold. Nine hundred people isn't twelve hundred, but it's a huge crowd. My later observation was that most high school auditoriums seat only five to six hundred people.

I'm not really sure if, at the time, I knew what good theater was. What I *did* know was that I was overwhelmed by the electric current in the air. The sparks flying back and forth between the cast and the audience were intoxicating.

When I arrived home, Dad asked, "How was the show?"

"It was amazing," I replied. "Unbelievable!"

"Well," Mom interjected, "maybe one day you and Francie can direct the shows there."

"Yeah," Dad added. "That'd be great!"

"Mom...Dad, please," I replied. "That's wishful thinking. The teacher who directs is never going to give up the Drama Club. He'd be crazy if he did."

Sometimes *crazy* things happen when you least expect them to, though. At the beginning of the next school year, the director was gone. He had taken a sabbatical. I wasted no time in approaching our principal and volunteering for the position.

When I broached the subject, Fran looked at me like I wasn't quite right in the head and asked, "What do we know about directing?"

"I don't know," I replied. "I've been in a few college shows now, and you've been around the theater your whole life. I mean, let's not forget who your father is."

She tried to reason with me. "But that's my father. I've never directed anything. And you! You're still relatively new to the theater. Yes, you have a lot of talent...and yes, you've played some parts in the last few years since we met. But playing a few roles doesn't make you a director."

Despite her rational objections, I could see her begin to weaken. "What did you have in mind?"

"How about *The Music Man*?" I asked. "I remember that I liked the film."

It was true. I had probably been about eleven or twelve when I saw the film on television. I had grown up watching Ron Howard, who played Winthrop Paroo in the film, play Opie on *The Andy Griffith Show*. As a singer myself, I imagined playing Winthrop. I was also tickled that Winthrop sings a song called "Gary, Indiana," considering my own name.

Fran was skeptical to say the least. "*The Music Man*? Geez, Gar – are you crazy? That's a huge show with a gigantic cast, period costumes, elaborate scenery, a full orchestra. You and I have never directed before. What do we really know about mounting a major musical?"

Strange as it may seem, I had an inexplicable inner feeling we could do it. Fran, on the other hand, felt that even though she sang, acted, and danced, she wasn't equipped to direct or choreograph, having no prior experience doing either.

"Why don't we begin with something small?" she suggested. "Something we can handle."

"Like?" I asked.

"Well...like *You're a Good Man, Charlie Brown*. Or something with a small cast that doesn't ask too much of us in terms of costumes and sets."

Fran knew what she was talking about. It was she, after all, who had grown up in a theatrical family. Although her father had mostly retired from the world of grand opera some years before, he had brought shortened versions of operas to Southern Connecticut State College in his old age and even mounted and conducted a full scale production of *Madama Butterfly* as the inaugural event to christen Southern's newly constructed Lyman Center for the Performing Arts in 1968, which Fran appeared in as a young teen. So, given the world she grew up in, her many experiences performing, and her family lineage, Fran knew so much more than I did.

But my common sense broached another question: How does a drama club go from performing a show with a huge cast like *Sugar* to *You're a Good Man, Charlie Brown* with a cast of six actors?

I remained steadfast in my plan, and in the spring of 1976, Fran and I did indeed mount and present *The Music Man* on the stage at Shelton High School. And how did we manage all of the various moving parts germane to a major musical? As it would so often happen in the future, somehow things worked themselves out.

This first venture into the world of directing makes me think of a famous quote I would eventually discover that resonated for me in the years to come. The legendary choreographer Agnes de Mille said, "The artist never entirely knows. We guess. We may be wrong, but we take leap after leap in the dark."

In our case, when we took that first "leap," we would need a lot of help. Two college friends offered their services free of charge. Ron Lindberg, who had appeared with us in that fateful production of *She Haunts Me* and who asked me if I had met the maestro, offered to design and oversee the building and painting of scenery. Ron accomplished this feat with an all-student crew. Another friend, Maury Rosenberg, volunteered to oversee costuming the show. And the costumes Maury fitted were designed by Thom Peterson, our director from *She Haunts Me*, and constructed by Thom's friend and colleague, Richard Harding, a man who would become one of our most cherished lifelong friends and associates.

Our Shelton High School chorus teacher, Sheila Zito, who

had built a school chorus of over one hundred students, volunteered to teach the vocal music. Fellow teacher, Simon Rich, who had invited me to try out for *Once Upon a Mattress* some years before, took charge of designing, setting, and operating the lighting, something at that point I knew nothing about. Simon's and my paths were destined to intersect in the theater, apparently, and he turned out to be a great friend and ally to Fran and me in our early years of directing. All the pieces seemed to be fitting together beautifully.

I even remember being approached by a high school senior, a trombone player by the name of Peter Sanders, who stopped by my classroom.

"Mr. Scarpa," he began. "I heard you're going to be directing the musical. You'll need an orchestra, right?"

"Right," I said, not yet having the faintest idea of how that would possibly happen.

"Cool," Peter said. "Mr. McNamara conducted the pit band last year. I'll ask him if he'll do it again, and I'll gather the best players to be in the pit. You'll want Kathy Bizub. She's a gifted trumpet player and only a junior, so you'll have her again next year."

How fortunate I was that a high school student took the initiative to approach me about the orchestra and do all the leg work in getting it on its feet. Little did I know, at the time, that Pete and Kathy would go on to play in my orchestras for decades to come.

A new friend from the English department, Mary Ellen Sanford, volunteered to organize and oversee the sale of tickets. All of the details that I had, perhaps, not thought of myself were taking shape.

In mentioning this staff of teachers and college friends that had miraculously materialized, it's important to note that none of us were paid. My experience, then and now, is that teachers give of themselves freely because of their love of students. And our college friends were both thrilled to assist in mounting a major musical. Money wasn't important to any of us at the time. And, in that sense, the mounting of *The Music Man* had a purity of heart that few endeavors in life have.

This may sound strange, but in the theater I learned that, with the right vision and intention, the universe provides. What's the tagline from the film *Field of Dreams*? "Build it and they will come." It's true! Time and time again I would see that if we needed to have a plan in place for each and every detail, to have every *i* dotted and every *t* crossed, we might never have begun. It was often a process of jumping in the water and then figuring out how to stay afloat.

Not that having a plan is a bad thing. As we grew as directors, through the years, we got better and better at planning.

LESSON:
…in the theater I learned that, with the right vision and intention, the universe provides.

ACT I, SCENE 4

While Fran and I had auditioned for productions, we had never organized and run an audition. At least one hundred and twenty students tried out for *The Music Man*. Many people who would come to enjoy our work thought we were the ones who had sparked the interest in theater that existed in 1976 when we took over. But Shelton High School had had a drama club for as long as I could remember – and I had seen that student interest in action when Fran and I enjoyed *Sugar* a year before.

I also feel the mid to late seventies were incredibly vibrant years in the school. It was a new high school, which opened the day I began teaching in September of 1974. The building sparkled in its pristine newness; on Thanksgiving of '74, for the first time in years, Shelton had beaten their archrival, Derby, in football on our new football field, the Edward C. Finn Stadium (named for the man who hired me); and that production of *Sugar* I had seen a year before had been the first in the new twelve hundred seat auditorium. *The Music Man* would be the second.

It was a time when all kinds of kids wanted to be in the play. I had a student in my junior homeroom, a football player (and captain as a senior), who approached theater with the same winning attitude he had on the gridiron. Blond-haired and blue-eyed, he was the quintessential All-American boy, and a born leader. He was one of a few boys, at that time or any other, whose utter lack of self-consciousness rubbed off on others. Quite a few major athletes joined him in our early productions – football, baseball, basketball, and hockey players.

Many years later, I started to hear other adults on the periphery of our work in theater call the kids something I never liked – "theater kids," or in some cases "theater geeks." There were no theater kids or theater geeks when Fran and I began directing. Rather, our casts were an eclectic blend of the student body.

I like to think of high school as a time when a student finds more than one positive activity to occupy his time. After all, when a football player is in the school play, is he a sports kid or a theater kid?

I am reminded of a conversation I had with a track coach years ago.

Stopping me in the hallway, he asked, "How come you have to rehearse your play in the middle of my track season?"

Annoyed, I replied, "How come you have to have your track season in the middle of my rehearsal period?"

"But you have so many of my kids in the play," he whined, to which I parried, "And you have so many of *my* kids on the track team."

My knee-jerk instinct was to reply sarcastically. The point is that there is neither any such thing as a "theater kid" nor a "track kid," unless the person has strictly dedicated himself to that activity with the probable plan of going professional, which is realistic for so few people.

In any case, I don't think the track coach and I liked each other after that exchange. Actually, I don't think we liked each other before the exchange.

Even today, I think of a recent high school graduate, a boy who got rolling with us at Center Stage when he was in elementary school. During his high school career, he not only played leads in drama club productions, but he was also president of his class, captain of the swim team, a member of Student Council, the National Honor Society, the school magazine, and the Italian

Club. So, with so many interests, how can we pigeonhole this student? To whom does he belong? The drama director? The swim coach? The journalism teacher? Let me make it easy. He belongs to himself – and his parents. Personally, it was never my style to refer to students as "theater kids" or as "my kids" outside of the context of a rehearsal. In the vast majority of cases, students who appeared in our productions were all-around kids in the school and community, and it is, no doubt, as true today as ever. It's my very strong opinion that pigeon-holing them into one activity seems to miss the mark.

AUDITION MAYHEM

It was with plenty of anticipation and excitement that Fran and I ran our first audition. Certainly, we had both been candidates at auditions, Fran more often than I because she was more experienced. Some of those auditions were well run and others – not so much. I would have to classify our audition for *The Music Man* in the latter category. First of all, as mentioned, there were well over one hundred candidates, numbers we weren't prepared for. We allowed all candidates to sing their entire song and to read from the script. For the reading, we somehow paired them up and allowed them a few minutes (or more than a few depending on how backed up we were) to practice the scene. Let's just say, the two days of initial auditions were long ones, going well into the evening.

We also called back way too many candidates. The intention of a callback audition is to determine major roles. Because we didn't know the kids or their abilities – and also because we somehow wanted to reward kids who did a good job – we called back an army of candidates.

That afternoon, we had dozens of kids gathered in the auditorium without much of a plan, except to have them sing again for the various roles they were called back for and read a scene or two from the script. To make matters worse, dozens of other kids hung around that afternoon to support their friends who had been called back. As I moved in and out of the chorus room where we were seeing candidates, I found the general mayhem overwhelming. Somehow, we saw everyone and got the play cast, and in retrospect, I think we miraculously chose the right people for the right roles.

Many of the candidates at that callback audition would become lifetime friends. One in particular, a sophomore at the time, has teased me about that callback audition ever since. Upon entering the auditorium to fetch candidates to come into the chorus room to audition, I looked at her and asked, "Are you here for the callback?" We had seen so many people over the course of a few days that I was unsure if she was a candidate or just a passerby. "You didn't even know who I was!" she would joke years later.

That student would go on to play a secondary role in *The Music Man* and win major roles in her junior and senior years.

In order to give the maximum number of students the opportunity to participate, we cast eighty students. Fran and I had the challenge of placing them and moving them about the stage, which though larger than any other we had ever encountered, was hardly large enough for the multitudes we cast.

Over the years to come, we would refine the audition process, fine-tuning it and organizing it with scheduled times and an efficient plan.

But in the late winter of 1976, we were underway. It was the most exciting of times, and for Fran and me and our cast, it was a love affair from the first rehearsal. With the departure of their former director, the students were grateful to still have a drama club and the opportunity to perform in a big musical. Together, we learned and we felt our way from the darkness to the light. We must remember that Fran was a senior in college, only four years older than the twelfth graders in the cast. To them, we became "Mr. Scarpa and Fran," and as they got to know us better, some called me "Scarps."

One of my most vivid memories of that first endeavor into directing was the day, weeks into the rehearsal process, when we had our first full run-through once all scenes had been staged and the music and choreography had been learned. At the end of the rehearsal, the cast sat in the front rows of the theater, looking at us with eyes of hope. The rehearsal had been rough, for sure, but we had made it through the whole play. I took a deep breath and said, "Well, guys, I think we have a show here," and the cast erupted into a euphoric ovation.

LESSON:

I have always considered what we do in amateur theater, no matter how well or not-so-well we do it, an experience in accomplishing the impossible.

In years to come, we would hone and refine the rehearsal process into such an efficient system that after a first run-through, it was a foregone conclusion that we had a show. That first time was different in the most exciting kind of way. That first cast, knowing that Fran and I were novice directors, were in our corner and pulling for us in the biggest of big ways.

Another memory is the excitement after each performance. After enthusiastic responses from our near capacity audiences, Fran and I would slip out of the exit doors and make our way down a long hallway alongside the auditorium, leading to the stage door. There we would meet our cast, embracing each and every one for a job well done. Together, we shared a "we did it" attitude. And it was true.

Oh, and let's not forget Mom and Dad. Lovers of music and entertainment, they attended all three performances of *The Music Man* and sat on house right, in row D seats 2 and 4 as they would for the remainder of their lives.

Another lesson learned from that first experience – and then learned over and over again – is that Broadway plays are not written for amateurs. When Meredith Willson sat at a piano to write the music and lyrics for *The Music Man* and collaborate on the book with Franklin Lacey, I sincerely doubt that Willson was remotely concerned with whether it was practical or doable for high schools to produce the play. What he and every creator of professional theater were undoubtedly concerned with was getting their work produced on Broadway. In this sense, I have always considered what we do in amateur theater, no matter how well or not-so-well we do it, an experience in accomplishing the impossible.

LESSON:
Broadway plays are not written for amateurs.

Our courtship, Fran's and mine, spanned three years, which in retrospect seems like a perfect length of time to get to know another person, especially if you're not living together, which was certainly not a possibility for the two of us, given who our fathers were. We had probably begun talking about marriage, though, within a year or so of dating. The only question was when it would happen. We did feel a certain urgency, though. Not that either of us realized it at the time, but we both know today that deep inside us was a need for freedom. Both of us had been commuters to Southern. Neither of our fathers was amenable to us living away from home. For me, personally, my father had built a beautiful new home when I was seventeen, and I think he just couldn't imagine why I would want to live anywhere else. He also thought it a foolish waste of money to live on or off campus when it was such a convenient commute. I have little doubt that Fran's father felt the same way. After all, she lived in New Haven, not more than ten minutes from campus.

For our two-year dating anniversary, I decided to give Fran an engagement ring. It was a year before we would direct *The Music Man*, so the idea of directing plays wasn't yet something we saw in our future.

I had gone to Las Vegas with a friend a few months before, during my spring break from school. I wasn't lying when I told her I lost money in the casinos, but I was essentially trying to throw her off, lest she have any suspicions about a ring. I went to Schpero's Jewelers in Ansonia, my father's favorite jeweler. My dad had always dealt with the owner, Art Schpero, purchasing lots of expensive jewelry through the years, but I met with Art's son. We went into an office in the back of the store where he had cases and cases of engagement rings. For quite a while, he showed me rings, and I nixed one after another. I apparently knew what I didn't want. Finally, he showed me a ring with a sparkling, medium-sized diamond and roses on a vine delicately carved in pink and green gold. It was the most unique ring I had ever seen, and I knew it was the ring for Fran.

On the night of our anniversary, we planned to go out to dinner at a favorite restaurant, The Millpond Tavern, just outside of New Haven. Fran lived near an attraction in New Haven known as East Rock, a high elevation overlooking the city where people would hike, picnic, and, quite frankly, go "parking." Fran and I may have spent a few dark evenings there during our courtship!

I drove up there before heading for the restaurant because I told her I had a gift I wanted to give her in private. Upon arriving at East Rock, I pulled the car over and asked her to close her eyes and hold out her hands. I popped in an eight-track tape – our favorite song, "Time in a Bottle" by Jim Croce, and then I placed the open ring box in her palms. My plan appeared to have worked because her tears of surprise and happiness indicated that she really wasn't expecting it.

At the restaurant, the two of us barely touched our food, so caught up were we in the moment and so apparently dazed by the prospect of marriage. After dinner, we visited Fran's older sister and brother-in-law, who were the first to hear the good news.

Fran decided that she would tell her mother later that night, but it was best not to tell her father yet because I hadn't asked him for his permission to marry his daughter. The maestro was old-school and had certain expectations. I would tell him the next morning.

COTTAGE STREET, NEW HAVEN, 1975

I haven't slept very well. The excitement and anticipation are overwhelming. I had never imagined myself asking a girl's father for her hand in marriage. It was, after all, 1975, and it seemed like an antiquated custom. But Fran had told me that her brother-in-law, years before, was required to do so and that I would have to as well. "But don't worry," she had said, "you won't have to say anything. My dad will do all the talking."

I receive the call that I am to report to Fran's Cottage Street home at 10:00 a.m. On the drive to New Haven, I am a bundle of nerves. I am not certain how to broach the question. "Mr. Riggio, may I request your permission to marry your daughter?"... or shall I go with something less formal, "Mr. Riggio, is it okay with you if Fran and I get hitched?"

Fran answers the door and says, "He's been ready since 8:00."

"What?" I ask in a panic.

"Yes...as he was having breakfast, I sat down and told him you wanted to stop by this morning and talk to him, and he said, 'Why-a today? I don't-a feel like-a talking today!' And I got all emotional because he was resisting, so I ran into the bathroom crying, and my mother told him why you wanted to come. He was so cute. He knocked on the door and said, 'Francie, why-a you cry? You tell-a the boyfriend to-a come over. I talk-a to him.'"

"Oh geez," I say, "then what happened?"

"Then he sat in his chair, and I said, 'Daddy, it's only 8:00, Gary's not coming for two hours.' 'That's-a fine. I wait,' he said. And he's been sitting there ever since."

"You're not doing anything to calm my nerves," I tell her.

It feels like I'm in a Fellini movie when I enter the Riggio living room. Light is streaming through the windows that surround the white baby grand piano, and the maestro is sitting in his chair, dressed in a maroon sport jacket, a white Arrow Dectolene shirt, and a bow tie.

I approach him and greet him with an affable, "Hi, Mr. Riggio."

The maestro puts his hands on the arms of his chair and slowly rises to his feet. He looks into my eyes, penetrating them with his own, and he says in the most dramatic fashion, "I know!" Then he kisses me on the cheek.

I shoot Fran a panicked look, as if to say, "Is that the kiss of death?"

But keeping my wits about me, I'm thinking: If he knows, then I don't need to formulate the words to ask, so, feeling relieved, I say, "Oh gee, that's great...I'm glad that...that you know."

Mr. Riggio then leads us into the dining room where he reads me a passage from a letter he was in the midst of writing to his sister in Sicily. "Francie," he began, "ought-a to marry a very nice-a boy. Clean-a cut. No beard."

He then invites us to resume our meeting back in the living room. He takes the center chair, I sit on the nearby couch, and Fran sits in an upholstered chair opposite me. (I had learned that in the Riggio home Fran and I were never to sit too close together. There is a story that once her father saw her sister and brother-in-law holding hands when they were dating and the maestro said, "If this is what-a you do in the house, imagine what-a you do outside!")

Sitting together now, Fran's father looks at me and says, "So, you want-a to talk. Then talk!"

I shoot Fran another distressed glance: You said, I wasn't going to have to say anything!

It's my moment of truth. "Well," I begin tentatively, "we were just, uh, wondering...uhm, you know, well, if it's...uhm...alright with...with, ah, uhm, with you...if we get married."

Then, mercifully, he completely takes over – going through the Ten Commandments, starting with "Thou shalt not bear false witness"... and explaining why they're important to a married couple. His explanation is a combination of English and Italian... although whenever he lapses into Italian, he asks me, "You know what-a this means?" When I reply that I don't, he says, "Ah..." and explains.

Somewhere around "Thou shalt not kill" Fran's mother tries to save us. "Frank," she says, "the kids have to go. And besides, Gary doesn't understand Italian."

"Hey, go away!" he shouts. "I tell-a them about-a the Ten-a Commandments! He's a smart-a boy. He went-a to the university."

And so our meeting goes until the maestro decides it's over.

I tell this story, not only because it's entertaining and a great memory, but because, as I've said, I am certain that had I not married into this family, I wouldn't have had a life in the theater. Much as I loved the theater, I needed this particular partner to create the life that we would have.

I often think about a girlfriend I had a serious relationship with during my first two years of college. She was a wonderful person, and to this day I'm grateful for her place in my life. On the emotional night that we broke up, she tearfully asked me why, and I felt lost and confused because I simply didn't have an answer. I would one day realize the reason was that it wasn't our destiny to build a life together. She and I were meant to have other spouses and bring our own, respective children into the world.

It would be my fate to have a Vietnam veteran point me in the direction of the theater where I would meet the girl I was meant to spend the rest of my life with.

ACT I, SCENE 5

A word about Fran as a bride-to-be. In the six weeks leading to our wedding day, Fran co-directed a major musical with me at Shelton High School; she prepared and performed a full scale concert in twentieth century American vocal music at Southern, singing songs by composers only the most cultured have heard of like Samuel Barber and Gian Carlo Menotti to more well-known composers like Cole Porter and George Gershwin; and she did one other little thing – she finished her final semester of college and graduated.

Fran remembers her mother saying to her at the time, "The last thing on your mind right now is this wedding."

It was true! Fran was much too busy to worry about a silly matter like our wedding, and she was as far away from being a bridezilla as a young woman could ever be. Consequently, our wedding, though a lovely one, was a stress-free event.

What's important to note is that, when Fran and I married on June 26th, 1976, the cast of *The Music Man* attended our wedding ceremony at the historic Trinity Episcopal Church on the Green in New Haven. We couldn't afford to invite the eighty kids to our reception (although we would have loved to), but we toasted with pewter goblets with the inscription, "*The Music Man,* 1976," engraved on the polished silver, a gift from the cast.

In a way, those goblets and the cast attending our wedding defined who we were and who we would become, setting in motion the course of the rest of our lives, an inextricable link between our married life and our theatrical life.

THE EARLY YEARS

I mention that link because there were countless examples of it manifesting itself. In those early years, we opened the small apartment we lived in to cast members. We often visited with anywhere from two to a half dozen cast members, and during the Christmas season, we'd invite dozens of them to go caroling with us in our neighborhood.

With each passing show, our small apartment was decorated with theatrical memorabilia: our pewter goblets; a handmade coffee table, the bottom of which was engraved with the name of every cast member of *Mame* (1977); a beautifully mounted and framed violin after *Fiddler on the Roof* (1978); and more. A few years into our directing career, our good friend Ron Lindberg who had designed our first set even painted the logos of the various shows we had directed on our shower doors for goodness sake. We couldn't even get away from our life in the theater while taking a morning shower!

I will certainly not mention all of the shows we directed over the course of forty-three years. After all, there were over two hundred. But those directed during the first eight years were, perhaps, the most important. We followed *The Music Man* with *Mame*, *Fiddler on the Roof*, *Hello, Dolly!*, *Anything Goes*, *Oklahoma!*, *The King and I*, and *The Mikado*. There were also a few non-musicals mixed in, *A Christmas Carol*, *The Man Who Came to Dinner*, and a creative hodgepodge of songs, scenes, and poetry we called *Mélange*. These eleven productions were the nutritional building blocks, packed with artistic vitamins and minerals, that prepared us for a lifetime in the theater. Each of these shows was a learning experience, our hands-on laboratory for becoming accomplished directors who would one day open our own full-time theater. But more on that later.

When you direct high school theater, you need to learn many skills and wear many hats. A teacher friend recently told me that, even though his job is to musical direct productions at his middle school, he often finds himself reviewing choreography with the cast. I can certainly relate.

LESSON:

Each of these shows was a learning experience, our hands-on laboratory for becoming accomplished directors who would one day open our own full-time theater.

By my second show, I found myself conducting the orchestra. While our band director had been doing it for a few years, I felt his plate was too full to ask him back. With his many band responsibilities (and believe me, the Shelton band was first rate in those years, marching with well over one hundred participants, including seven tuba players, the word S-H-E-L-T-O-N spelled out on the bells of their instruments), I felt that, realistically, he didn't have the time to give our orchestra members the number of rehearsals they needed.

Consequently, I began our rehearsal period for *Mame* in 1977 with the intention of finding a new conductor. After asking several people if they'd take on the job, I realized I was going to have to do it myself. Ironically, a close friend who is a gifted composer and pianist, declined, saying, "Gary, I don't have the confidence to conduct a full orchestra." Apparently I did.

The only experience I had conducting was as the drum major of our college band, which hardly prepared me for this experience. Somehow, though, when it came to theater, I was fearless. In the process, our first trumpet player, Kathy Bizub, who was now a high school senior, guided me with unusual time signatures and helped me to succeed, something she would do in the years to come, long after graduation. In the process, I discovered I had a gift for conducting – an inherent ability for rhythm and tempo and setting a musical mood – something I could never have predicted before I found myself with a baton in my hand.

In fact, it is with some measure of pride that I recall Fran's father saying to me after a performance of *Mame*, "You can-a be good at this, Gary!" That's just one little success that I enjoyed during those early years of directing. There were many for both of us.

Fran and I look back on this era with tremendous fondness, as a person might remember his college experience with a happiness, a warmth, and a nostalgia that fills the heart.

In the midst of these years, even during our summers, Fran and I couldn't extricate ourselves from the theater. We found ourselves performing in plays (*Flower Drum Song* and *Guys and Dolls*) and also directing and choreographing (repeats of) *Mame* and *Fiddler* with the Orange Players, the closest community theater group to us. It was a different experience, directing adults instead of kids, but the Orange Players were dedicated to quality, and we have wonderful memories of those summers.

We also performed in a professional setting. Our mentor, Thom Peterson, had taken on a professional endeavor, Theater in the Park, an open air theater in Edgewood Park in New Haven, where equity actors performed alongside local actors. Fran and I were dying to get involved there, and we soon spent a summer there in *The King and I* (Lady Thiang and Sir Edward Ramsay). We were also slated to perform in *Little Me*, a hilarious but seldom produced musical, the same summer with Fran playing the female lead and me cast in a nice supporting role. Unfortunately, the weather gods didn't cooperate, showering "The Park" with torrential rain all summer, forcing Thom and his board of directors to cancel the remainder of their season. Still, for at least two more summers, Fran and I appeared as featured performers in cabarets in the pavilion at Edgewood Park. It was all valuable experience.

Our second venture directing a major musical came in 1977 when we tackled *Mame*, a bear of a show. Very few amateur groups produce *Mame* and for good reason. It was during *Mame* that I had a revelation, but not necessarily a good one. It may be a common experience for amateur directors or artists of any kind to wonder if their work is any good. Particularly in the performing arts, until you have an audience to react to what you've created, you don't know exactly what you have. I was, perhaps, too overwhelmed with *The Music Man* to have had such worries, but I distinctly remember having them during our rehearsal period for *Mame*. Sitting down after a dress rehearsal, utterly drained and exhausted, I thought to myself, *Is it possible that I have worked this hard on something, given all of myself to it, and it's not any good?* My fears were dispelled, thankfully, when *Mame* was well received as the cast, now in their second year under our direction, did a stellar job. To this day *Mame* remains one of our most cherished memories.

I was learning that directing high school theater was a different kind of teaching. When you teach English or history or biology, not every student is a willing learner. It's possible that not even the highest achieving students *like* the course work. In their case, the only thing you can be sure of is that high achievers want an A in your class.

LESSON:
Think of it – teachers and students working together in harmony with one common goal – the success of the other.

But in theater, despite any lack of experience, students are there because they *want to be*. It's very special to have a cast of highly motivated learners before you. Consequently, great strides are made quickly.

In fact, I can't think of any other endeavor I've ever personally been involved with where, at the end of a short time span, let's say eight weeks, the result is a marvelous product that hundreds of people want to see, enjoy, and applaud for.

Let me add a point I've already made but can't emphasize enough. The students in our casts wanted us, as young directors, to succeed just as we wanted them to. We were both pulling for each other. Think of it – teachers and students working together in harmony with one common goal – the success of the other. What a dynamic!

INSPIRED BY A FILM

In the spring of 1978, our third musical would be *Fiddler on the Roof*. I recall a close friend in our world of theater questioning why we would choose a play with such a complex and dramatic story – a story that she felt high school students might not be able to grasp. Instead, she suggested we consider something lighter like *Bye Bye Birdie*, where most of the kids would play their own age.

Being who I am, I welcomed the challenge presented by a show like *Fiddler*. First of all, before getting involved in live theater, I had had a profound experience with the film version. During my college years, a date with a girl often consisted of going to see a movie and then out for a snack. Perhaps a year before Duke urged me to audition for a play, one fateful Saturday night I took a girl to see the film version of *Fiddler*. I hadn't chosen it for any particular reason. It was very much serendipitous.

I was completely blown away by a brilliant performance by an actor I had never heard of named Topol as Tevye, a poor Jewish dairy man in the early years of the nineteenth century, and the story of family and persecution of an entire people. I was especially struck by the custom of arranged marriages portrayed in the film. A related story my mother had told me about my maternal grandmother would become the material for a scene in my recent novel, *What are the Chances?*

The two sisters come home from a dance and the older teases the younger by tattling on her.

"Mama, I don't know about you, but I don't think it's very seemly for Cecelia to be kissing boys she hardly even knows." Not that Mama knew the word seemly, but she got the gist of it.

"Stop it, you!" Cecelia warned. "Mama, I did not kiss anyone.

A boy I danced with walked me to the bridge. He was a perfect gentleman the entire time."

"Don't believe her, Mama!"

"You stop it, you b-i-t-c-h! That's my final warning," Cecelia vehemently whispered, as if she could, in fact, do anything about it, considering Connie had beaten up just about every boy in the neighborhood while they were growing up. Cecelia knew she was no match for her sister, and Connie knew it better.

Finally, their friend came to the rescue through her laughter and tears. "No, Cecelia is telling the truth, Mrs. Alberino. She didn't kiss anyone tonight. At least I didn't see her kiss anyone."

Persisting, Cecelia's sister said, "Just because you didn't see her kiss anyone doesn't mean that she didn't. Cecelia is often hiding behind a column kissing one boy or another."

"C-o-o-o-nnie-e-e!" Cecelia shouted.

Of course, her dismay caused the two girls to nearly fall out of their chairs.

Mama just kept nodding her head before muttering, "Ridi? Ma queste sono cose che dovrebbero farti piangere."

"Wait...wait," their friend said. "What did she say? What did she say?"

Through tears, Connie translated. "She said, 'Laugh? These are things you should cry about!'"

To Cecelia's horror, the two girls exploded into an even greater clap of thunderous hysterics.

Then Mama waved a threatening hand at Cecelia. "You-a better not-a kiss-a the boys, or I gawna give-a you a good-a schiaffo!"

Knowing Mama had never hit her, even Cecelia couldn't resist laughing now.

"Hmph...Smetti di ridere!"

"Okay, Mama, I'll stop!"

"But Mama, didn't you kiss Papa before you married him?" Cecelia asked.

Mama just smirked and shook her head in the negative.

"But how did you know if you loved him if you didn't kiss him?"

"Baciarlo? Nemmeno l'ho conosciuto," she said with another smirk.

"What do you mean you didn't even know him?" Connie asked in stunned surprise. "How could you marry someone you didn't even know?"

"Becawz-a...becawz-a...my papa tell-a me to."

Sitting in a dark movie theater and watching Tevye's powerful story and the challenges that went with it reminded me that only two generations before me, arranged marriages were commonplace, even in my own Italian family.

My heart broke for Tevye and for his daughter Chava, who chose to elope with a man unacceptable to her father. It was heartbreaking to watch a parent, struggling with the conflict between tradition and change, disown a child.

The story touched me so deeply, in fact, that the next day I went to see it again. This time I took my mother. I wanted her to see and experience the story as I had.

So, directing *Fiddler* in 1978 was more than a mere choice. It was a mission, a calling. *Bye Bye Birdie* would come later, but in this time and place...and with these young people...*Fiddler* was meant to be.

THE TURNING POINT

That *Fiddler* cast embodied, as much or more than ever, how "in our corner" our cast members were. I told them about the challenge I felt had been presented to me. I told them there were people who wouldn't be optimistic about their chances of succeeding with such a serious story. From our Tevye, an extremely mature senior with serious acting ability (audience members would ask if he was a teacher) to our other leads, to each and every member of the ensemble, the cast approached the rehearsal process with a seriousness of purpose that you don't see in high school students every day. And it wasn't that our previous casts or future casts wouldn't have that same seriousness of purpose. They did and would! It's just that, as we journey through life, we can only take in and digest so much. I feel this was the first time Fran and I became completely cognizant of the commitment and passion kids brought to the process of mounting a play. After all, we were on a mission, and by proxy, so were they.

At the time, it was common for a high school production to hold three performances, Thursday through Saturday. On opening night, our large auditorium was about half full – typical on a weeknight with work the next day. The audience seemed to really enjoy the production, but they didn't stand during the curtain call.

At the time, there was no technology, so selling tickets occurred in only two ways: by giving the students tickets and asking them to sell to family and friends and by selling them at the door. So it was a little hard to keep track of how many tickets were sold for a given performance in advance.

At our Wednesday night final dress rehearsal, I had urged the kids to turn in any unsold tickets the next morning. Going back to my predecessor's production of *Sugar*, a typical Friday or Saturday night sold nine hundred to a thousand tickets, a great "house" but still a few hundred shy of a sellout.

On Friday morning before school, my ticket chairperson, Mary Ellen, had news for me.

"Guess what," she said.

I was too tired to guess.

"We're sold out for tonight, and we have fewer than fifty tickets for Saturday!"

I was stunned. After three years and five productions, I was convinced our auditorium was too large and would never sell out.

They say that "word of mouth" is the best kind of advertising, and I have a hunch that our Thursday night audience called everyone they knew and told them not to miss *Fiddler*. Friday night, there was bedlam in the high school lobby and in the auditorium. Hundreds of people had shown up to buy tickets at the door, only to be turned away. In a flash, the handful of tickets for the Saturday night performance sold out.

Inside the auditorium, preshow, it was a different issue. At the time, we sold only general admission seating. Many people left one or two seats between themselves and other parties. With the house sold out, this would never work. Groups of three, four, and five were finding it impossible to find seats together. I had to make several announcements from the stage, asking audience members to move over to eliminate vacant single seats.

Once everyone was seated and settled, I took my place in the orchestra pit. From the first downbeat and the melodic strains of the solo violin, it was a magical night. The audience was totally immersed in the play in a way that I had never before witnessed. The ovations for exciting moments like the "To Life" number and the bottle dance in the wedding scene were epic. The audience was quite literally cheering. Fran had taught boys who had no prior dance experience to succeed in a way that is almost impossible to comprehend. I would equate it to taking a group of boys who had never played football in their lives and turning them into a state championship team.

Speaking of athletes who gravitated to the stage, among those that appeared in our 1978 edition of *Fiddler* was the starting backfield of the football team, two of the three of them playing major roles, Perchik and the Constable. I remember, in fact, that the boy who played the Constable, our quarterback, had played baseball in Little League with our Tevye, a guy who was a high achieving student. Here were two boys who traveled in different social groups while in high school. The former would grow up to be a deep sea scuba diver and the latter, a lawyer. These were two seniors who would have had very little contact with each other had it not been for the spring musical, which reunited them once more on the same team. I will always remember their rehearsals together and the mutual respect they showed for one another.

We would have athletes in our plays, both male and female, for years to come, but never so many as in the 1970s. It seems to me that, in the modern era, many athletes (especially football, baseball, and basketball players) have become specialists – football players lifting weights year around and baseball and basketball players participating in AAU in the off-season. I loved those days when so many of them spent the springtime on the stage.

During that first *Fiddler*, I remember Fran tapping into the natural athletic ability of these athletes in staging "To Life" with boys leaping from tables and platforms, soaring through the air like eagles in flight.

The bottle dancers were given hats and bottles from day one and told there would be no gimmick – the only thing to keep the bottle on their heads, *balance*, all while dancing at the same time. It is worth noting that gimmicks are often used in both amateur and professional productions: magnets, Velcro, and even plastic bottles. In our case, we used none of those. Ours were real glass bottles, and the only aid we used was sand in the bottom of the bottles to weigh them down. I suspect, in real life, wine gave the bottles weight, but in case of a bottle falling, we couldn't take the chance of liquid spilling on the stage. Fran told our boys if the bottle fell off their heads, they would have to drop out of the dance, which put a lot of pressure on them to succeed, and succeed they did. Not a single boy dropped a bottle over the course of four performances.

Those boys demonstrated a tenacious commitment that spring, and Fran and I have very fond memories of them sitting in the audience with their bottles on their heads when they weren't rehearsing.

But, speaking of balancing bottles on dancers' heads, a bit of *Fiddler* trivia: Fran and I would go on to direct eight productions of *Fiddler* during our career. That means we did at least forty performances of the bottle dance over the course of those productions with dozens of amateur performers. During those many performances, only two bottles were dropped (ever!), and, ironically, they were dropped by arguably the two best dancers who ever appeared in any of our productions of *Fiddler,* one of whom would go on to dance with the Joffrey Ballet in New York. In neither case, luckily, did the bottle break.

To get back to that 1978 production – each night, a pervasive anxiety filled the auditorium as the boys dramatically performed the bottle dance, accompanied by a solo clarinet, and each night when the dance reached its conclusion and the boys let the bottles fall from their heads into their hands, the audience went crazy. Talk about doing the impossible!

At the same time, the audiences demonstrated they were completely immersed in the other scenes and songs. Our cast had been taught to tell the truth, and tell the truth they did. Many audience members shed tears at those performances.

A COMMAND PERFORMANCE

That night, our principal was in the audience, and after the show, he urged me to add a "command performance" the next weekend.

Also in the audience that weekend was the editor of the daily newspaper for the region, who made his Saturday editorial about our production, calling it more than a play, but "a happening," and lauding the performance he had witnessed. He urged people to try to get tickets if they could, but none were available. The editor did not yet know we'd be doing a command performance.

On Saturday night, I asked the cast, orchestra, and crew if they could be available the next weekend. As it turned out, our first violinist, a high school junior who would, in years to come, attend and teach at the renowned Juilliard School of Music, had another commitment. Thankfully, we had a good second violinist as well, so we were able to commit to the command performance.

On Monday morning I called the newspaper editor to tell him we were planning an extra performance. The best he could do at that point was to print a one-column article on page two of Tuesday's paper. Then, the craziest thing of all happened. On Wednesday morning, I had cast members who had study halls man the phone in one of the offices and take ticket orders. By noon, the command performance was completely sold out. And remember, ours is the largest high school auditorium I've ever seen — twelve hundred seats.

For years to come, I would meet people for the first time, and they would say to me, "Wait, aren't you the guy that directed that *Fiddler on the Roof*?"

I would get that reaction many times, even twenty or more years later. It was only natural that, through the years, Fran and I would get better and better at mounting productions, and it only makes sense that many future productions would be of an even higher all-around quality than *Fiddler*. But it was the 1978 production of *Fiddler* that put us on the map and somehow set us apart. Now people were really paying attention!

COLUMBIA, MY COLUMBIA!

During that incredible 1977-1978 school year, besides directing *Fiddler on the Roof* in the spring and *The Man Who Came to Dinner*, a Kaufman and Hart comedy, the previous fall, I did a little something else. I pursued a graduate degree program in theater at none other than Columbia University in New York. Since a teacher needs to earn a master's degree within ten years of being hired, I thought I'd do it in the discipline I loved: theater. But Columbia University's Teacher's College was the only place I could find anywhere near Shelton where I could do it at night. I was happy to be accepted.

Somehow, I commuted to New York City several times per week while still directing my fall production. Looking back, I don't know how I did some of the things I used to do.

In my directing class, I needed two actors to present my final project, a scene from the famous Tennessee Williams play, *The Glass Menagerie*. Columbia provided me with an acting major for the role of Laura, but I would need to find my own actor for the male role, the Gentleman Caller.

The only option I could think of was to use one of my Drama Club students. I felt I needed someone who wasn't in my production of *The Man Who Came to Dinner*. Since football season had ended by the time I needed to begin rehearsing the scene, I asked the quarterback of the football team, whom I've mentioned would play the Constable in *Fiddler* that spring.

He traveled to New York with me four or five times to

rehearse with the actress and to perform the scene for the class, and there are no words to express how proud of him I was, such a young guy in a grown-up environment.

It was one of the many wonderful bonding experiences that theater afforded us to have with students. I recall that on the Sunday after our first weekend of *Fiddler* (but a week before the famous command performance), the student called me at home.

He was trying to process what it had meant to him to be so involved in theater. Overflowing with emotion, he told me how important the Drama Club and especially the *Fiddler* experience had been to him, explaining that it was better than having beaten nearby rival Derby in football on Thanksgiving Day – no small thing for a player to say in a town like Shelton where football was (and still is) king. And he also thanked me, profusely, for taking him to Columbia, explaining how much that bonding time together, commuting back and forth to New York, meant to him. Recalling that phone conversation fills my heart even today, almost fifty years later.

Sadly, I received a letter from Columbia that spring, informing me that they were phasing out the Master's in theater and that I would need to finish it in the next eighteen months. I realized that it would be impossible for me to teach and direct while earning so many college credits in such a short time. I would have to abandon the program. A degree in theater was not to be, especially considering the other twists and turns my life was about to take.

ACT I, SCENE 6

Our wedding wasn't the only family milestone interwoven with our work in theater. To this day, I think of major life events, not in terms of what year they occurred but in terms of what show. *Fiddler*, a show about the importance of family, became another in what would be a series of inextricable links between our family life and our theatrical life.

Indelibly burned in my heart and mind to this day is the afternoon that Fran and I visited her gynecologist in New Haven to find out that she was pregnant with our first child. I recall there was a small mirror in the waiting room, and being only twenty-six, I stared into the mirror thinking: *Is this the face of a father?*

When Fran came out and told me the doctor confirmed the test was positive, we both knew our lives were about to change in a profound way. Since we were in New Haven, Fran's hometown, she wanted to swing by her parents' house and tell them about the upcoming blessed event. Then, we went to dinner at a great little New Haven eatery that no longer exists, Annie's Firehouse Soup Kitchen, where they made the best soups I've ever tasted. Fran and I looked across the table at each other, both feeling excited disbelief about the prospect of becoming parents.

We had rehearsal for *Fiddler* that night, and I'm going to be honest and say that, after a glass of wine or two at Annie's, I felt a little tipsy. Hopefully the cast didn't notice. After running the rehearsal, we sat the cast down and shared our good news. I will forever remember the loving and supportive faces of those kids as they listened to our announcement. They knew that, as cast members, they were part of our family.

Gina was born in November of 1978, and when we began rehearsals for *Hello, Dolly!* in the winter of 1979, Gina was at just about every rehearsal, sleeping in a portable crib in the middle of the auditorium as the sounds of Jerry Herman's great show tunes permeated her little infant body.

By the time we got to *Oklahoma!* two years later, Gina, not even yet three, loved to play a game with us. When we put her to bed at night, we would sing a song from the show, "Many a New Day" or "Out of my Dreams" or the title song. We would sing half of a line from the song, and Gina would complete the line.

Us: Many a new day will...
Gina: ...please my eye...
Us: Many a new love will...
Gina: ...find me...

There wasn't a song in the score she couldn't successfully respond to.

And so our story would go. If someone were to ask me when our second daughter Mia was born, the answer would be *The King and I* rather than 1982. Even years later when I think of our grandson Michael being born, rather than the year coming up in my mind, the show does, *Godspell*.

Consequently, our children, particularly our daughters, grew up in the theater. Gina appeared as the smallest child of the King in that first production of *The King and I*. She was only three. Mia appeared as Molly in a summer production of *Annie* we directed in 1986 when she was four. As young as she was, Mia did every step of the choreography with the older orphans.

And if in a court of law we were accused of picking shows that had children in the cast, we would have to plead "guilty as charged." It was easier than finding babysitters, and besides, both girls were gifted singers and outstanding performers, given their heritage and circumstances.

When we did shows that didn't feature children, which was the case more often than not, the girls were regularly at rehearsal – particularly on Saturdays – sitting in the auditorium, coloring, playing with dolls, and even roller skating up and down the aisles of the auditorium when they could do so without it being a distraction...and maybe sometimes when it was a distraction!

As our children grew, Fran and I had to modify our rehearsal plan. In the first few shows, she and I would often double up, Fran working on a production number in the same hour that I was working with major characters. It was a highly efficient method to rehearse a show. But as the girls got older and started school, it became less and less practical to have them at rehearsal. I would schedule either Fran or myself on a given night, so the other one of us could be home with our children. It was truly a juggling act.

Directing teens meant that we had a cast of eager babysitters, but only when they weren't scheduled for rehearsals.

If it sounds like a crazy life, I suppose it was. But in another sense, it was kind of a built-in gifted program for Gina and Mia. Show after show, they witnessed or participated in a major musical, learning different styles of performance, and in the process, knowing at a very early age the difference between choreographers, from Jerome Robbins to Michael Bennett. Plays are also set in different time periods, so there was the historical aspect as well. The girls observed talented teenagers and they saw what does and doesn't work on the stage. It would prepare them to be better performers themselves and eventually skilled directors/choreographers in their own right.

PARENTHOOD AND MONEY WOES

Parenthood brought with it new concerns, though. As any parent knows, raising children is expensive. With the birth of our first child, I began to worry about money. As I looked into the future of our family, I felt a responsibility to increase our meager income. Here we were, spending hundreds of hours in the theater without pay. My father felt that a person should be compensated for his services. He was fond of saying, "A man who works for nothing is worth nothing," a message that in one sense stung a little, but in another sense, his point was well taken.

It's no secret that, historically, teachers have been underpaid, but in those years, it was far worse than it is today. When I was hired in 1974, my first year's salary was $8660, a number I have never forgotten.

When Fran and I took over the Drama Club a year later, it was not a stipended position. All athletic coaches received a stipend, but theater was not yet recognized as being worthy of pay. Many teachers of that era and before – I daresay most – supplemented their teaching salary by moonlighting at night and/or on weekends. My own older brother Edmund certainly did, and he advised me to do the same. Although Edmund's recommendation was well-intentioned, directing high school productions didn't allow much time to moonlight. During the school year after *Fiddler*, with a newborn baby at home, I found it hard to justify spending so much after school time without compensation.

Despite how celebrated we had become as high school directors, I felt compelled to take action. I sent a letter to Mr. Finn, now superintendent, explaining that, to continue, I would need to be compensated.

Strangely, several months passed without a response. I was really at a loss as to what to do. I announced to the Drama Club that the superintendent and the board of education didn't feel my request was worthy of a response, so I wouldn't be continuing as their director.

To say that our students and their parents were outraged would be an understatement. I did not attend, but our Drama Club families attended the next board of education meeting en masse, making their plea that a stipend be created for the Drama Club.

A few days later, Mr. Finn called me to his office. He was not pleased. He told me that there were ways to go about these things, that there was a teachers' union with whom I might have addressed this matter. In truth, I knew very little about unions or how they operated. Certainly, I was unaware that the union negotiated stipends for coaches and advisors. In the fall of my second year teaching, the year I started directing, Shelton teachers along with teachers across the state and the country went on strike. While I felt a lot of pressure to participate in the strike, I couldn't completely relate to the situation, not yet being a married man with a family. At the time, my eight thousand dollar teaching salary made me feel like a rich man. Now my circumstances had changed dramatically, pun intended!

In my meeting with Mr. Finn, I simply explained that I had written him a letter that had gone unanswered. It wasn't that I didn't appreciate the fact that Mr. Finn had been instrumental in my being hired. Somehow when it came to theater, though, I was willful. I say that without apology because I observed that, too often, theater wasn't afforded the same respect other activities were, particularly sports.

To cite an example, after our second musical, *Mame*, the principal called me to his office and questioned a few show expenditures, particularly costume rentals. I don't remember the figure, but in years to come we would spend much more on costumes as well as all other aspects of a production. Let me add that the Drama Club was, and I believe is today, a self-sustaining organization, funded by ticket sales and other club fundraising. Still, the principal didn't like what some line items cost.

LESSON:
…theater wasn't afforded the same respect other activities were, particularly sports.

"Why can't the kids come up with costumes from their own closets?" the principal asked. "A suit? An old prom dress?"

I looked him in the eye, young as I was and not yet tenured, and asked, "Why can't the varsity football team play their games in practice uniforms?"

An avid sports fan myself, I had observed the football team

periodically getting brand new uniforms. And from what I gathered, seniors were allowed to keep their jerseys as souvenirs.

Our principal didn't have an answer for that one, nor did Mr. Finn have an answer for allowing my written request to go unanswered.

What happened is the Board of Education created a stipend for me, but it wouldn't go into effect until the next school year. In the meantime, the parents of our cast members created a souvenir program with pictures and bios of each cast member which they sold at performances of our 1979 production of *Hello, Dolly!* In the process, I believe they raised over a thousand dollars to pay us.

Ultimately, the stipend was modest, only five hundred dollars, but it somehow helped me to justify spending hundreds of hours, usually directing two plays a year. In the musical *Annie* which we would direct five times, Daddy Warbucks talks about making his first million. "And in those days," he says, "that was a lot of money!" Well, in 1979, five hundred dollars was a lot of money – at least for us it was.

Not surprisingly, my advisor's stipend would never be close to an athletic coach's stipend, particularly to that of the coach of a major sport like football or basketball, nor to an assistant coach of those sports. But also not equal to a minor sport either. Many years later, well into the 2000s when Shelton established its first wrestling team, I perused our contract and saw that the new wrestling coach, not even a member of our teaching staff, was awarded a stipend higher than mine, after approximately twenty-five years of directing. It certainly didn't feel right. Here was a coach with perhaps ten boys on the team, while our plays allowed more than a hundred students to participate. We can assume that the crowds for wrestling matches were small, while we regularly sold out our productions, selling thousands of tickets and giving the school a very positive level of notoriety in the process.

At the time, I decided to approach our union president in his classroom.

"I just stopped by to tell you I figured out how you guys work out stipends," I said.

"Oh. How's that?"

"Well, obviously, when you have a new position, you need to make the stipend as low as possible, so you say, 'Let's look at what Scarpa makes and add five hundred dollars to it.'"

Our union guy didn't like my sarcasm, but I felt a little better.

Obviously, though, I wasn't in it for the money. But it would be money that would cause me to temporarily walk away from not only theater but also teaching.

THE DRAMA OF CAREER CHANGE

After Mia was born in 1982, we really felt the squeeze. Fran was a stay-at-home mom, and making ends meet was a challenge to say the least. To illustrate how poor we were at the time, my low teaching salary qualified us for WIC (Women, Infants, and Children), a welfare program that allowed us to receive certain food staples like milk, eggs, and cheese for free. It's hard to believe that a public school teacher was even eligible for this program, but it's true.

Given the arrival of our children, about six years into my career in education, I began to feel an overpowering responsibility to change careers. It wasn't that I didn't love teaching, but just about everyone I knew was making twenty thousand a year. At thirty, my salary would be eleven thousand, and believe it or not, it was impossible at the time for me to imagine ever making twenty.

The question was, what else would I do? Then one summer, an acquaintance who knew I was looking offered me a job at a "headhunting" firm. He didn't use that term but instead called it a recruiting agency. He explained that it was a "no pressure" situation because I could try it out for the summer. If I didn't like it or was no good at it, I could simply go back to teaching in September. It made sense.

What I learned was that the business searched for engineers, contacted them, and tried to convince them to leave their current job and go to a new company.

It was all phone work. I was trained to call an engineering

department and lie about who I was, so a typical call went something like this:

Secretary: Good morning, Sikorsky Aircraft.

Me: Hello, my name is Tom Smith from Design Products in Chicago (no such company). Yesterday, one of your design engineers called me, and I couldn't speak at the moment but told him I'd call him back. Wouldn't you know it? I can't seem to find the slip of paper I wrote his name and number on.

Secretary: How can I help you, sir, if you don't even know his name?

Me: You know, his name is right on the tip of my tongue. If you throw out a few names of engineers in your department, I know I'll recognize it when I hear it.

Secretary: Well, was it Walter Johnson?

Me: No, ma'am. That's not it.

Secretary: How about Edgar Williams?

Me: Uhm...that doesn't seem to ring a bell.

Secretary: Let's see. Was it Michael Davidson?

Me: No, ma'am, I don't think it was him.

Eventually she'd get fed up and end our call, but my call had been a success. I had just been given the name of a handful of engineers. Then, over the course of the next few days, I would call the company and ask to speak to the specific engineers, with the intention of trying to convince them to consider leaving their current position for a job at another company. When they asked how I got their names, I would say that I couldn't reveal my source. Although I was something of an actor, this was work I couldn't do. Lying for a living didn't work for me. Actors, I would argue, are not lying, but they're telling the truth. But that's a subject for another chapter.

In September, I was happily back in the classroom. Happy, but still poor.

I continued to search. I even took a career course that met once a week at an agency in New Haven. The instructor worked with a text called *What Color is Your Parachute?*, an excellent career book that is still popular today.

I remember an aspect of the course required us to identify words in the work world that helped us crystalize what career categories we felt passionate about.

One of the words I came up with was *entertainer*. What good that would do me in trying to change careers was anyone's guess. I might have chosen *artist*, a label that I would certainly choose today, but a) it was another descriptor that didn't feel practical, given that my endgame was to make more money than I was making, and b) at the time, it somehow felt too pretentious to call myself an artist.

In my ongoing quest to find a new career, I ended up going on an interview with a company who sold fundraising paraphernalia to schools – products like mugs and towels and pillows with the school mascot emblazoned on them. But a colleague at school suggested I pursue a job with a company who sold products that every school was sure to purchase each year, specifically yearbooks, rings, caps and gowns, or diplomas. I liked the idea.

I found the idea of working for a yearbook company especially appealing. It turned out that there were three or four national companies who did yearbooks across the continent. I would spend the next months researching and contacting yearbook companies. Instead of responding to job listings or want ads, my plan was to contact the companies and tell them I was interested in going to work for them.

ACT I, SCENE 7

GETTYSBURG PA, 1982

It's a hot July morning, and I'm driving to Southern Pennsylvania, a five-hour trip. I have a lot to think about on the long drive. What will it be like to leave teaching? To not direct shows anymore? Will I miss the kids?

I have been offered a job with Herff Jones Yearbooks, whose regional office is in Gettysburg, at a salary of eighteen thousand, which is seven more than I'm making as a teacher. Plus, there is the opportunity to earn much more – even a mind-boggling six figure income – if I can convince new schools to print their yearbooks with Herff Jones. For the time being, my territory will be all of Connecticut, and I am inheriting fifteen schools, including Trinity College and Fairfield University.

It doesn't feel like too much of a stretch as I'll be assisting yearbook staffs with designing and preparing yearbooks for printing – a position closely akin to teaching. It kind of feels like a good fit.

My day will start with a tour of the printing plant. I already have a fascination with factories, and will in the future love visiting factories that manufacture Martin guitars, Louisville Sluggers, and Bigelow Tea, to name a few. Seeing how yearbooks are printed, collated, covered, and packaged is impressive to say the least.

The tour is given by a regional sales manager, Tom James, but Tom isn't the man with whom I've been in contact over the last few months. I have been speaking to C. Kilburn Roulette, more familiarly known as "Kib," but due to a recent car accident, he is convalescing from a whiplash injury at home. I will meet Kib later.

After the tour, Tom takes me to lunch. As a teacher, I am not used to being wined and dined, but it is something I will experience again and again in the next few years, whenever I'm in the presence of a sales manager.

Dressed in a tailored suit, Tom is charming and witty and, in all respects, appears to possess all of the outward signs of success. I laugh all through lunch. Kib will one day tell me that Tom has a gift for zeroing in on a particular person's sense of humor, a skill I hope I will acquire as well.

After lunch, I visit Kib Roulette at his home, a sprawling and tastefully decorated ranch not far from the plant. Kib is a wonderful, grandfatherly man with white hair, a mustache, and a bow tie, which doesn't surprise me. His appearance goes along with the kindly man I have had a half dozen phone conversations with.

Sitting in his living room, he explains to me that they want to hire me but that they won't need me until January 1st.

"What do I do between now and then?" I ask, a tad befuddled.

"What you do," Kib explains with an air of wisdom and experience, "is you go back to teaching, and on December 1st, you give thirty days' notice, which is standard in business and industry."

His recommendation sounds logical, although it gives me pause. I am disappointed, but I feel like there is no turning back now.

I can't quite pinpoint where Kib might have grown up, given his folksy speech regionalism. "I think you're gonna really like sales, Gary. I've been in sales mah whole life, and, I don't know, it's just... how shall I put it? Sales is just in mah blood."

That expression haunts me on the long drive back to Connecticut. What is in my blood? It's a question I've never before asked myself. And the more I think about it, the more I realize: Theater *is in my blood. But what am I to do about that, I wonder.*

What I *was* going to do was direct one last show (or so I thought). It's so long ago that I don't remember how I pulled this off, but I somehow came up with an alibi about how, in this particular year, Fran and I would need to do the musical in early December instead of in the spring. Kib had advised me to keep my plan to leave on the first of the year a secret until a month before starting my new job with Herff Jones.

We chose a Gilbert and Sullivan operetta, *The Mikado*. Fran had played the role of Yum-Yum in college. Aside from enjoying Fran's performance, I had never had any direct experiences with Gilbert and Sullivan, though. Created and originally performed in 1885, *The Mikado* was different from anything we had previously presented, and I was more than ready for a new challenge.

THE WINDS OF CHANGE

At the time, Shelton High School was enjoying a vibrant era in music and theater. Thinking of the famous Rodgers and Hammerstein song, the hallways were "alive with the sound of music." I am of the strong opinion that the music department and the Drama Club fed on the success of each other. From our very first show, many members of the cast were chorus students, used to learning and singing harmonies daily, and the members of our orchestras were band students.

In the 1980s, besides their annual concerts, for a few years the band and chorus mounted a pops concert in the gym during the early spring. And what a wonderful event it was! The students decorated the gym with themes like "New York, New York" and "April in Paris," and the kids performed not only with the band and chorus but also in smaller ensembles, organized and directed by the students themselves. Patrons were seated at tables of ten, cabaret style, and the gym was packed to the gills.

With the spring musical only weeks away, as people left a pops concert, even if they had never previously seen a Drama Club musical, they were knocked out by the talent of Shelton students and primed to see our kids perform once again.

Consequently, coupled with being connected to the music

program and our previous directing successes, selling out our auditorium became a given – and would remain so for years to come. I could almost predict sales in advance. Our opening performance on Thursday, being a weeknight, usually sold about six hundred, half the house. Friday would typically be a sellout or a very near sellout and Saturday an absolute sellout, show after show.

Sheila Zito, our chorus teacher, was simply a human dynamo and a brilliant teacher.

In the midst of this success, students, teachers, and parents were stunned when the Board of Education cut the chorus program. Sheila, a tenured teacher with seniority, would be reassigned to an elementary school. However, she argued, "I'm a high school chorus teacher, not an elementary music teacher," and, ultimately, she resigned and took a position at another high school. The new high school's gain was Shelton's loss, and our chorus program would never come close to accommodating the number of students and presenting concerts of such high quality again.

And now, Fran and I would be leaving Shelton High School, further adding to the disappointment of our students.

The fall of 1982 was a surreal time for me. It was almost as if I was dying and had the good fortune to see my life before me. Each school experience seemed like my last. I remember the pep rally before the Thanksgiving Day football game. *This is the last time I will ever attend a pep rally,* I thought. (Spoiler alert: it wasn't!)

The Monday before we opened *The Mikado,* we sat the cast down and informed them that the day before Christmas vacation would be my last at Shelton High School, explaining our reasons as truthfully and sensitively as we could. The cast was simply rocked.

The next day in school, I delivered the news to my five classes. It wasn't that I hadn't had a great rapport with my students through the years, but somehow this year, each class was a love fest. My students seemed just as upset as our cast was. A few were even angry with me because they couldn't understand how I could walk away from teaching and leave them.

I didn't fully know it at the time, but going back to my first meeting with Kib Roulette, I could have also concluded that, not only *theater*, but also *teaching* was in my blood. It was a lesson that would take me a little longer to learn, but learn it I would.

Added to the emotional strain was the fact that *The Mikado* was an amazing experience for me, Fran, and the cast. We were exposing them to an historic operetta – a style based in classical music. With Sheila Zito's departure, I had taken on the responsibility a year before of teaching the vocal music, and along with staging the actors and conducting our orchestra, I experienced great artistic satisfaction and empowerment working on the production.

Besides her talent directing and choreographing, Fran was demonstrating with each passing show that she had a serious gift for makeup and costuming. She created a confluence of Kabuki style costumes, makeup, and wigs, and along with a minimalist set that I designed, consisting of clean, pagoda-like rooftops, the total look and quality of the production was artistically satisfying to say the least.

A few days before opening night, *The Evening Sentinel* even did a front page article on my departure, which included a photo of me. "**Scarpa Retires**," the bold headline read. At each performance of *The Mikado*, I received an ovation when I entered to conduct the orchestra from audiences who had heard of my impending departure. In all respects, it felt like an ending, and I really believed it was.

When I came home from school on that fateful day before Christmas vacation, I collapsed on my bed and wept. Everything felt wrong. What had I done? Had I made a terrible mistake?

I was certain that my theatrical and teaching careers had both come to an abrupt end, something I wasn't emotionally prepared for. At the same time, I was acting for the greater good of my family.

Ironically, based on the newspaper headline, people would ask me in the near future if I had truly retired – a ridiculous question, considering I was thirty and could barely pay my bills.

We didn't leave the Drama Club in the lurch, though. Not

feeling there were any teachers on staff interested in or capable of being our successors, we asked a friend with experience directing musicals, Brad Blake, if he would be interested in the position. He agreed, and he would direct for the next three years, continuing the culture of excellence.

We had another concern as well. After years of sellout performances, *The Mikado* hadn't done as well at the box office as any of our previous musicals. Perhaps it was because the production was in December instead of the spring. Perhaps it was because our local audiences weren't familiar with Gilbert and Sullivan operettas, considering they had been originally produced almost a century before.

MR. STUDENT BODY SAVES THE DAY

In any case, since the productions were strictly funded by ticket sales, *The Mikado* left the Drama Club in the red, and we wanted to rectify the situation. Fran and I, at the time, had had the pleasure of seeing her nephew perform in a show at his high school. It was called The Mr. Trident Pageant, a fundraiser for the school newspaper, *The Trident*, and it was a spoof of the Miss America Pageant, but with male contestants. The contestants competed in evening wear (tuxedos), gym shorts (instead of swimsuit), and talent (all comical in some way). The show was a ball, and I decided to contact the teacher hired to replace me, Jeff Moriarty. Jeff was a theater guy, but not a musical theater director, so he would serve as advisor and our friend Brad would direct the spring musicals.

We told Jeff about the Mr. Trident Pageant and suggested a similar fundraiser at Shelton High School, to be named the Mr. Student Body Pageant. Fran and I would help him organize it (he had plenty on his plate), and I would serve as Master of Ceremonies. The pageant turned out to be a wonderful success, and it would come to be a fundraiser for the Drama Club for many years to come. Even when the Drama Club eventually relinquished the show, the Student Council picked it up and it became a lucrative fundraiser for them for decades.

In the meantime, I was now a yearbook sales and service representative. In my position, I assisted schools in preparing their yearbooks for printing, and I visited schools in hopes that they would sign a contract to have my company print their yearbooks. Although I was still in school buildings, this work was a far cry from teaching in the classroom. There was a lot of pressure when yearbooks arrived in the spring at each school. Because a yearbook is such an individualized product, mistakes are bound to occur, and figuring out whether they are school mistakes or plant mistakes is a challenge. The representative is the middleman, absorbing the heat. At the end of my first months, I wasn't sure what to think about it.

THE YOUTH CONNECTION IS BORN

As the summer of 1983 was approaching, I realized that, in a certain way, a yearbook representative's schedule wasn't very different from a teacher's. Since teachers and students were off during the summer, so was I for the most part. A few meetings and business trips were on my calendar, but there wasn't much I could do except meet with the few yearbook staffs who wanted to get a jump start on their books during the summer, and there weren't many of those.

So, Fran and I set the wheels in motion to start a summer theater group. With no funds, we were afraid to use the high school auditorium as the custodial and air-conditioning costs could be significant. We approached Shelton's mayor, Eugene Hope, whose daughters had been in our shows, and without reservation, he gave us the keys to a closed down elementary school, Huntington School, which would in years to come undergo renovations and become what is today the Shelton Community Center.

We called our group the Shelton Youth Musical Theatre, open to high school and college students, and mounted our first summer production, *West Side Story*. Huntington School had a small stage, too tiny for what we had in mind, so we built out, creating a suggestive set with a second story bedroom and balcony.

We gathered a great group of musicians and housed them on the stage behind a scrim. We placed a camera at the back of the audience, and I conducted the orchestra looking at the action on a small television screen.

Our cast was comprised of not only Shelton High School students and alumni but also talented kids from other Connecticut communities. Our Maria, a resident of Branford and a voice student of Fran's parents, would go on to a career in the professional world of opera; our Tony was a great singer from Orange; our Bernardo from Trumbull; our Riff was an Amity High School graduate; and our Anita an SHS grad now majoring in theater at Carnegie Mellon University. It was an outstanding cast from top to bottom.

LESSON:

From the very beginning, Fran and I had approached the directing process with a one-pointed focus – to mount the very best production possible, given our means.

Most of the leads were college students and recent college grads, a natural trend that would repeat for years to come.

With the seating capacity in the small gymnasium of about two hundred people, we planned nine performances, and *West Side Story* played to nine sellout crowds and nine standing ovations with only large fans to help patrons beat the heat during that sweltering summer of 1983.

It's ironic to think that on that last day of school, only months before, I had truly believed that I would never direct again. But the founding of our summer theater group was only the beginning of a passion that I would jokingly come to refer to as an illness.

I say I "jokingly" referred to my passion as an illness, but I was gradually learning that many artists are obsessive, a quality that certainly described me. From the very beginning, Fran and I had approached the directing process with a one-pointed focus – to mount the very best production possible, given our means.

We have a memory of Fran coming home to our small apartment and turning on the light switch only to find that the pendant Tiffany lamp over the kitchen table was gone. In another instance, Fran discovered that our living room furniture was missing. Where were these items? Dressing the set of our latest production. At least twice, through the years, we used our own dining room furniture to decorate a set. Those are good examples of the extent of our obsession – or at least mine! Fran had, after all, not given me permission to use our furniture.

West Side Story was the inaugural production for a theater group which we would direct for thirty-five years and which is still alive today.

The next year, Fran and I would move our show to Shelton High School and change the name of the group to the Youth CONNection. The name change came as the result of a number of factors. First, participation wasn't in any way limited to Shelton residents. Also, though Mayor Hope had been kind in allowing us to use a vacant school building, the town of Shelton was in no way funding our group.

Fran and I liked the Youth CONNection better. It was a name that invited kids interested in theater from around the state to audition, it better captured the identity of the group, connecting talented kids with each other and with an audience we had built over time, and it was uniquely our own. I even had a former student who was a graphic artist create a logo which illustrated the first four letters of CONNection in the shape of the state. It was perfect!

In a matter of a few short years, the Youth CONNection became an institution in Shelton. We would sell out the Shelton High School auditorium for multiple performances of our summer shows for the next few decades. Some patrons even explained that they planned their summer vacations around the dates of our shows.

The Youth CONNection would become a family affair for us

Scarpas. That first summer, my older brother dusted off his saxophone and played in our orchestra, something he would do for the remainder of his life. A few summers later, my brother's wife sold tickets and oversaw "will call" at the door, my parents and my father's brother and sister-in-law sold refreshments, and along with my children, my brother's children appeared in Youth CONNection shows throughout their high school and college years.

The further we got into our theatrical career, the more Fran and I realized that theater was an activity that permeated every aspect of our lives.

ACT I, SCENE 8

In the fall after we founded the Youth CONNection, we were contacted by Sacred Heart Academy, an all-girls high school in Hamden looking for new directors for their musical. We had appeared in several college shows with their former director who was relocating, and she told the principal, Sister Rita Mary, that she heard we were no longer directing at Shelton High School.

Before I knew it, I found myself on a phone call with Sister Rita Mary, thanking her for considering us, but explaining that during the school year I needed to devote myself to my business.

"Don't say no yet, Gary," she said. "Please pay us a visit, you and your wife, and just meet the sisters."

Just meet the sisters! I reluctantly agreed even though I wasn't quite sure why I was meeting the nuns. The night of the meeting, I personally felt like Bing Crosby in *The Bells of St. Mary's*, an all-time favorite movie of mine. Sitting before me were at least a dozen nuns, clad in their black veils and habits.

Sister Rita Mary introduced each of her fellow sisters. "Sister Annabelle is the vocal director, and Sister Edith is in charge of sound," she explained. "Sisters Cordelia and Serafina are in charge of costumes, and Sister Edna organizes fathers of the girls to build the scenery, and Sister Mary David sees to it that the scenery is painted, and Sister Gertrude oversees the lighting."

I was dumbfounded. We had had so little adult help in Shelton, and now I was being presented with an entire adult staff, a crew of nuns of all things, to do the work that mainly kids had been doing for us at Shelton High School from the beginning. In our eight years with the Shelton High School Drama Club, scenery, for instance, had been built by students. That may have worked for awhile but I would eventually find that skilled student carpenters wouldn't be available to us every year.

In our first year or two, a crew of boys helped build scenery. In the next six or seven years before we left Shelton High School, a pair of brothers, Jim and Rob Hawley, had taken on the task, and the good news was that, due to their age difference, one succeeded the other. Not only did each of the Hawleys appear in supporting roles in our productions, but they expertly built our sets. Not surprisingly, Jim would go on to become a building contractor. Rob could certainly have done the same but chose another career path. In the early summers of the Youth CONNection, Rob Hawley single-handedly built our scenery, which was too much to ask of any one person. After he was gone, it would be a very long time before we would have a student with the building skills of the Hawley brothers.

As Sister Rita Mary and her staff looked at us with hopeful eyes, it was hard to resist their offer. And besides, how do you say "no" to the veil?

Fran and I would go on to direct productions at Sacred Heart for the next decade.

It was different from Shelton High School in many ways. On the negative side, there wasn't an auditorium, so the shows were presented in their gymnasium, the audience sitting on hard folding chairs. The stage was fairly small and the school had a no-cut policy, so we had to cast every girl who auditioned.

Quickly realizing that the stage couldn't accommodate eighty cast members, we learned to "platoon" as we would come to call it. Each production number would have only a portion of the chorus. That said, we tried to pick shows, always, that had plenty of production numbers, something we had been doing in Shelton as well, and we tried to organize ourselves so each cast member could perform in at least three production numbers.

Interestingly, it would come to our attention that we hadn't invented platooning. It's a practice that we would, in the future, sometimes even observe in Broadway shows.

Since Sacred Heart is an all-girls' school, we had to recruit boys from elsewhere, but still, we always had a significant imbalance of boys and girls, causing us to dress some girls in the chorus as males. Not what we would have liked in terms of realism, but necessary given the circumstances. We still tease a Sacred Heart grad who went on to win the Miss Connecticut Pageant that, when she was a freshman, we had her dressed up as a man, complete with a fake mustache!

There had been a time at Sacred Heart, not a great many years before we came on board, where girls played all of the male roles. Fran recalls seeing a girl play the King in *The King and I* very effectively. Similarly, in years to come, we would rent costumes from Choate Rosemary Hall in Wallingford, and adorning the walls of their theater (the Paul Mellon Arts Center) are wonderful photographs of a time when the school was all boys. The photos show boys in female roles, a la Shakespearean times, and with beautiful costumes and wigs, the illusion was masterfully successful.

There were many plusses at Sacred Heart as well. With our staff of sisters, all Fran and I had to do was direct and choreograph the show. Sacred Heart had a conductor who gathered and hired an ensemble of very good musicians. And the nuns took care of everything else. Furthermore, the musical at Sacred Heart was considered by the administration as a major event in the school year. They compiled an ad program, with homerooms competing to sell the most ads, that seemed as thick as an encyclopedia. At the time, I was told it raised over forty thousand dollars.

The Sacred Heart community, which included not only current students and alumni but often rows and rows of nuns from the order, came out in great numbers to see the performances, and hardly ever were there any empty seats, despite those folding chairs. It warmed our hearts to see the Sacred Heart community support the productions so enthusiastically and genuinely.

THE ROAD BACK TO TEACHING

As I moved into my second year with Herff Jones, I continued to be haunted by Kib Roulette's words about selling, "It's just in my blood."

It was becoming more and more evident, now directing two productions a year at Sacred Heart and with the Youth CONNection, that *theater* was in my blood. What was also evident to me was that, unlike Kib, selling was *not* in my blood. I simply wasn't any good at it, and I knew I had to figure something else out.

Ironically, in the spring of 1984, I was contacted by a distant relative who was the English department chair and yearbook advisor at Weston High School.

"Gary," he began in a phone call, "I'm not calling to change yearbook companies. I'm calling to see if I can convince you to come teach at Weston High School. We have a teacher who is moving, and I need to replace her right away. I'd love to have you on board here and do the kind of theater with our kids that you did in Shelton."

I told him I hadn't considered going back to teaching, but, like Sister Rita Mary, he asked me to come to Weston and meet everyone. He introduced me to each member of the department and to the principal, saying to each and every one, "Gary is taking a look at us today to see if he'd like to come teach here." It was a very different approach than anything I'd seen before. Our former Shelton High School vocal director Sheila Zito was at Weston High School now, so in many ways, the offer was tempting. But springtime is when high schools receive their yearbook orders, and to leave Herff Jones at that time would have left the company and Kib Roulette in the lurch. Reluctantly, I declined the offer.

During the summer, though, my visit to Weston High School weighed on me. *Come on, Gary,* I said to myself. *You know what you were meant to do and where you're meant to be. In the classroom.* I called the principal of Shelton High School, told him I was considering coming back to teaching, and asked him if he had any openings.

"Yes, we do," he said. "Come in today, and we'll hire you."

It felt good that, based on my past performance as a teacher, he thought so highly of me that he would immediately hire me. My excitement would be short-lived, though. I would soon find out that my teaching certification wasn't up to date because I needed more graduate credits. I mistakenly thought that a teacher had to earn a master's degree within ten years of teaching time, but the fact is that the clock began ticking from the time I was hired in 1974 and the degree needed to be earned within ten years of that date, whether I was teaching or not. It made me sad that the Columbia program hadn't worked out. Going back to Shelton High School wouldn't be in the cards for September.

LESSON:
Sometimes, a person needs to walk away from something to realize what he has.

Depressed I was still a yearbook representative come fall, I spent the next months vacillating about what to do. At the mid-year point, I enrolled in a college program to earn the correct number of credits to renew my certification, this time in School Counseling, and as the next school year approached, there was unbelievably another opening at Shelton High School, and once again, the principal was happy to hire me.

I couldn't have been happier when school began. My time away from teaching had given me a look at the world of business and a greater appreciation for education. Sometimes, a person needs to walk away from something to realize what he has.

NO TUNE LIKE A SHOW TUNE

During this era, we were still heavily involved in directing at Sacred Heart Academy during the school year and with the Youth CONNection during the summer. In 1985, our third summer with the Youth CONNection, we decided to create our own show, which was a first for us.

A friend who is a theater trivia buff (I am not) told me that the song "It's Today," one of my all-time favorite showtunes from one of my all-time favorite musicals, *Mame*, had been written by Tony Award winning composer Jerry Herman for other shows and recycled for *Mame*.

Legend has it that the song was first written for a musical revue called *Parade* in 1960 (not to be confused with the 1998 Broadway musical by Jason Robert Brown) and called "Show Tune." Herman then recycled the tune and called it "Only Love" and inserted it in an Off-Broadway musical called *Madame Aphrodite* which only ran for thirteen performances in 1961.

My guess is that, while Herman had to give up on the show, he knew he had a great song and wasn't about to give up on it. Enter *Mame* in 1966, and the song now became a show-stopping number with the title, "It's Today."

Jerry Herman's original lyrics to "Show Tune" went something like this:

There's just no tune
As exciting
As a show tune
In two-four

I had loved directing *Mame* with the SHS Drama Club in 1977 and loved the song so much that hearing its interesting history inspired me to create a show around it. Now I was not doing an established musical but, rather, my own creation.

We would call our show, *No Tune Like a Show Tune*, and I wrote a simple but effective script which centered around a Broadway rehearsal for *A Chorus Line*. A young mother in the cast brings her pre-adolescent son to the rehearsal who strikes up a conversation with the building custodian, who incidentally was played by Lee Coffin, who wrote the foreword to this book. The kid doesn't think very much of Broadway musicals, but the custodian tells him about one and another, which magically come to life before his eyes. At one moment, the custodian is telling the boy about a musical like *Hello, Dolly!*, and in the next moment the show comes to life in the boy's imagination, with our cast regaled in full costumes.

The nature of the show, given that we mainly drew splashy production numbers from various musicals, allowed us to amass a cast of over one hundred kids – from talented children to recent college grads. It was quite a summer with the hustle of arranging rehearsals for different segments of the show and especially with Fran choreographing several dozen major dance numbers from different musicals while simultaneously organizing and fitting literally several hundred costumes. On top of everything, I had the task of finding and working with an orchestrator from New York since orchestrations for the musicals were not available to us.

The play ended with the boy saying a heartfelt goodbye to his new elderly friend, and the custodian alone in an empty theater, singing the first lines of "Show Tune," which segued into the entire cast taking their curtain call in costumes representing a cavalcade of Broadway hits. Undoubtedly, it was one of our most exciting all-time curtain calls.

Add to all of the excitement, after rehearsal every night, which took place in an elementary school gymnasium, the college students and I created a basketball league, with games played between 9:30 and 10:30 p.m. I was, after all, only thirty-three years old, so why not combine two of my favorite activities?

No Tune Like a Show Tune remains one of so many happy times that we had in the theater. It's no wonder we would go on to spend more than four decades directing productions.

FUNNY GIRL

Back at Shelton High School Jeff Moriarty, as drama club advisor, suggested, since I was back in the saddle, that I take over the reins for the spring musical once more. "Why hire someone else when you're right here in the building?" was his reasoning, and I couldn't disagree. In the spring of 1987, never one to shy away from a challenging production, I chose *Funny Girl*, a huge show, and we were back on the job. Why not come back to the Drama Club with a bang?

Despite the excitement of mounting a production, it was never without stress. I don't want to paint a picture indicating that our life in the theater was always happy. Far from it. I have never forgotten a moment related to the pressure and stress I sometimes felt. As it was our lifestyle, both of our daughters were often in attendance at rehearsals and certainly at performances. I can't recall why, but after a performance of *Funny Girl* in 1987, I couldn't face mingling with audience members, who would have undoubtedly only offered their praise as had always been the case. I just needed to be alone.

Taking eight-year-old Gina and five-year-old Mia with me, after a performance, I hid away in the band room at the high school. I needed to catch my breath. I simply sat in a chair while Gina and Mia gravitated to the blackboard and began doodling with chalk. They had learned to amuse themselves in the theater. I suddenly began to feel very emotional. Who knows why? Maybe because I knew I was back where I belonged – teaching and directing at Shelton High School. Maybe, while watching our two little girls draw on the blackboard, I found myself questioning what kind of life this theatrical world was for them. Here it was, after 11:00 p.m., and they were awake and out of the house.

Before I knew it, involuntary tears were streaming down my cheeks. Mia was so absorbed in what she was doing, I don't think she noticed. But Gina, upon observing my tears, crossed the room, climbed into my lap, and without a word, wiped the tears from my cheeks with her small fingers. Then Gina rejoined her sister at the blackboard. I'm not sure I ever felt as understood, accepted, or loved more in my entire life. There are moments in life that don't need any words, and this was one.

MEMORY: A RANDOM ACT OF KINDNESS

Speaking of Gina and Mia when they were children, besides the many experiences they had of being in plays and watching rehearsals at an early age, as our children they were often exposed to all kinds of performance genres. I remember being home alone with the girls when Fran was out once and turning on PBS, which was airing a production of *Pagliacci*, an opera in Italian by Ruggero Leoncavallo. My recollection was that they were not more than six and three years old. Remarkably, both girls sat and watched the entire opera.

Mia's attention span was so good, in fact, that we took her to see a production of a straight play, *The Man Who Came to Dinner*, which her cousin was appearing in at Amity High School, and, sitting in the first row, Mia sat through this full-length sophisticated play, paying complete attention the entire time. I'm not sure exactly how old she was at the time, but I recall that she had a pacifier in her mouth, which gives us a clue.

With such attention spans, we felt comfortable taking the girls to see Broadway plays like *Cats* when they were very little girls.

A favorite memory took place at a restaurant across the street from the Shubert Theatre in New Haven. I had made a reservation because, for her birthday, we were planning to surprise Mia with tickets to a production of *Peter Pan* starring Cathy Rigby who, after her Olympic days as a gymnast, made a career of playing the role. Mia had been obsessed with a video tape of a made-for-TV version starring Mary Martin, from way back in 1955, watching it repeatedly until she practically wore out the tape.

In booking the restaurant reservation, something seemed ever so slightly odd, though. When I called, I asked for a 7:00 reservation since the performance began at 8:00. An hour before seemed sufficient. In the process, I shared that we were bringing our little girl to see *Peter Pan*. The person I spoke to strongly recommended a 6:15 time, which seemed earlier than necessary, but I agreed.

Even as we ate dinner, Mia didn't know what her gift was. Being who we are, we often enjoyed playing "Name that Tune" to keep the girls engaged when out and about, and this night was no different. But Fran, Gina, and I had a method to our madness. Each of us repeatedly hummed a song from *Peter Pan* until Mia finally asked why we kept doing that. Brandishing the tickets, I replied, "We're singing songs from *Peter Pan*, Mia, because the Shubert Theatre is across the street, and we're going to the show right after dinner. And it stars Cathy Rigby!"

Suddenly and unexpectedly, a woman at the next table leaned in and said, "And I heard she's terrific in the part!" She had apparently been eavesdropping on our conversation and our game, but we didn't mind because it turned out the woman was Cathy Rigby herself. We were all stunned. I said, "Oh my God, Mia, this is Cathy Rigby!" I will forever remember the look of surprise and delight on Mia's face that night.

I could only infer that the restaurant employee who took our reservation knew that Ms. Rigby would be having dinner before the show and purposely seated us next to each other in hopes of orchestrating this not-so-chance meeting.

It wasn't always *Peter Pan*, though. Today, Mia muses that when she and Gina were kids, we wouldn't let them watch *The Simpsons* on TV, but they were allowed to watch *All that Jazz,* a film directed by and based on the real life of choreographer Bob Fosse and which contains profanity, sex, nudity, drug and alcohol use, and various surrealistic scenes related to Fosse's heart surgery.

Such was the life of Mia and Gina when they were children.

MAGIC TO DO

Getting back to me – going forward, I planned to stick even more tenaciously to the idea that *theater is in my blood*. I made a decision. After my foray into the yearbook business, nothing would deter me, going forward, from devoting myself to the world of theater.

I remember a former student calling me at that time, which was a time of landlines and phone directories.

"Mr. Scarpa," he began. "My name is Steve Jones, and you were my English teacher in 1981."

When I asked Steve Jones what I could do for him, he continued, "Mr. Scarpa. I have a business opportunity I'd like to talk to you about. I'm working on something very lucrative, and we're looking for a few sharp people. I immediately thought of you. It's a great opportunity."

"I'm very flattered, Steve," I said, "but let me ask you this. Is this business venture in the world of theater?"

Steve paused briefly on the other end of the line, before saying, "What do you mean?"

"I mean that I would only be interested in meeting with you if this is a theatrical opportunity."

Steve was baffled, but I stood firm in my resolve. My mission was, in fact, even more specific than that. At this stage of my life, I was very clear that my highest priority was to work with high school and college students in the theater.

In another instance, I was approached by a local businessman whose wife was a talented performing artist. His plan was to begin a professional theater group in a nearby town, and he wanted me to direct their first production. Not that I wasn't interested, but I explained to him that I was already directing three major musicals a year and I didn't feel I could find a place to fit in a fourth. The businessman had trouble grasping why I wouldn't want to direct "professionals."

In yet another instance, a musically gifted cousin of mine wanted me to become the fourth singer in his doo-wop group. The same conversation took place. How could I make a commitment to him with my yearly schedule? While my relative couldn't understand why I would pass up such an opportunity, I understood why – and that's what was most important.

At Sacred Heart Academy, Fran and I became close with one of the nuns, Sister Barbara Thomas. One day, in a conversation with Sister Barbara, Fran explained that she was looking for a volunteer service opportunity – a ministry if you will. Sister Barbara, a bit wiser than we were, said, "Fran, you and Gary are already being of service to people through your work in theater. This *is* your ministry."

It was true. We were in our mid-thirties and finally understanding our calling: teaching and directing. We would see again and again how kids benefited from being involved in productions, not only on the stage but behind the scenes.

Fast forward to 1990 and a production of *Pippin* and it was shades of *The Mikado* for me. Once again, I felt like there was nothing in the musical theater canon that we couldn't do. I feel that my friend, colleague, and fellow Drama Club advisor Jeff Moriarty was skeptical. He seemed to have the attitude, *You guys are great with classic musical theater – Rodgers and Hammerstein and the like – but let's see how you do with something more contemporary.*

Fran and I had a great fondness and affinity for *Pippin* since it had been the first Broadway show I had seen and it was, after all, a Fosse musical, so my motivation to bring our own production to life was sky high.

LESSON:
With each passing production, students found that performing in a show choreographed by Fran was an enriching educational experience in dance styles.

I also feel it was synchronistic that we would be directing a play where the central character is searching for purpose and meaning in life at a time when it had become so very crystal clear to us what our purpose and meaning in life was.

Fran, with her formidable dance vocabulary, was amped to choreograph a Bob Fosse-inspired production. With each passing production, students found that performing in a show choreographed by Fran was an enriching educational experience in dance styles.

At the time, we had a superhuman set builder/designer, a recent grad named Marc DiJon, who single-handedly built our sets as the Hawley brothers had done some years before. Marc had appeared in SHS productions while I was in the yearbook business, and as a postgraduate, he was invested in helping Jeff Moriarty and me mount our productions. This was a young man of enormous skill and creativity, a quality that he brought to the design and construction of our scenery. With a little input from me and Jeff, Marc created a set for *Pippin* that any professional theater would be proud to have. If it seems that I attribute an enormous amount of credit to those who built our scenery, whether an individual or a crew, I do so with good reason. Talented actors were always, on some level, abundant; carpenters, not so much. I have always felt that divine providence was at work in providing Fran and me with special people, though small in number, who created high level scenery for our productions. Marc was such a guy.

And while Google tells us that Patina Miller, in the 2013 Broadway revival of *Pippin*, was the first woman ever to play the Leading Player (the role originated by Ben Vereen), Fran and I had cast a female in the role more than twenty years before. It so happened that, considering our most talented student was a girl, we decided to go with a female as the Leading Player back in 1990.

LESSON:
I have always felt that divine providence was at work in providing Fran and me with special people...

I believe that our production of *Pippin* gave us confidence that we could mount a more contemporary off-beat musical as well as we could a classic, conventional musical.

And what ever happened to Marc DiJon? Sadly, after building another great set for our production of *Anything Goes* in 1991, he died in an accident at the Connecticut Post Mall where he was creating scenery for an enormous Christmas display, leaving all of us who knew him heartbroken. It would be the first time death touched us in the theater. In the future we would experience other deaths in our theatrical family.

It was a hectic life, to be certain. Fran and I both liked rehearsing on Saturdays for all shows. I would work scenes in the morning, and then Fran would arrive in the early afternoon, girls in tow, to work on choreography. In the process, Fran and I flip-flopped, juggling our directing and parenting responsibilities. Similarly, I would typically rehearse two evenings a week and Fran would rehearse the other two evenings.

Our activities extended beyond our productions of musical plays, especially where the Youth CONNection was concerned. We added events like Christmas shows and New Year's Eve parties (complete with DJ, dancing, and catering) to our plate in order to raise money. Looking back, I can't believe the pace we kept.

Throughout the later 1980s and into the 1990s, we organized a group of six or eight performers, known as the Youth CONNection Singers, who performed at these events and others, including Independence Day celebrations in our hometown.

And by the time our daughter Mia was five or six, we Scarpas, as a family, often performed at these events and others – a local version of the von Trapp Family Singers if you will. Fran and I had duplicated her parents' life in a manner of speaking. Here we were, like her father before us, mounting multiple major productions replete with large orchestras and elaborate scenery and costumes. When we had met, her father was retired from the opera world, but her mother was active, taking talented voice students, both young and old (including us), to perform for clubs and civic organizations. Now, here we were, presenting our own musical programs in the community just as Fran's mother had for so many years, most often without compensation. *Yes, Sister Barbara, a ministry to be sure!*

And sometimes, we would repeat shows for the sake of keeping our sanity or, more importantly, because a set had been built at Sacred Heart Academy, which we could reuse with the Shelton High School Drama Club or the Youth CONNection. In fact, we repeated shows for a number of other reasons as well – because we felt a show would do well at the box office, because a show allowed many to participate, or simply because we loved a show. In our forty-three year career, we would direct *Mame*, *Guys and Dolls*, *Les Misérables*, *Footloose,* and *Joseph and the Amazing Tech-*

nicolor Dreamcoat twice each; *The King and I*, *Oklahoma!*, *Bye Bye Birdie*, *The Music Man,* and *The Boy Friend* three times each; *Anything Goes* four times; *Annie* five times; and *Fiddler on the Roof* an unbelievable eight times.

LESSON:
For me, theater was the ultimate experience of living in the present moment.

Often, through the years, a reporter, a patron, or a parent would ask me which, among the countless shows we had directed, was my favorite. The answer was simple. "The one I'm currently working on."

For me, theater was the ultimate experience of living in the present moment. It generally wasn't my nature to look back on a show like the 1978 *Fiddler*, for instance, and think, "That was the best show ever," but rather to keep striving to be better at what we were producing and finding ways to make the show we were working on the best ever – something that wasn't always possible, but a worthy goal to strive for.

ACT I, SCENE 9

During those years, whenever I attended a production, I watched not as an audience member but as a director. Whether at another school production or at a Broadway show, I watched it to see what worked and didn't work. In a way, it had been this way for me from the very beginning. In my second production on stage in college, *Luther*, I had a lot of down time during rehearsals since I wasn't in a speaking role. While other ensemble members socialized in the green room when they weren't needed on stage, I found an inconspicuous corner of the wing and watched the leading players rehearse, soaking up what they were doing to develop their characters.

Similarly, at Broadway shows, I studied the lighting, the scenery, and the movement of the scenery, trying to determine, within our more humble means, how we could achieve the same effects. Many set pieces for Broadway shows, for instance, move by tracks in the floor or "fly" in. I sought ways that we could fly in set components on our stage, despite not having full fly space, or how we could have scenery appear to move on or off without stagehands being visible. I remember the first time we accomplished this feat. It was our production of *The King and I* in 1982, and the units were built so stage crew members could move them from behind without being seen. It was magical!

WEARING MANY HATS

As we progressed, Fran and I learned more and more about all aspects of theater in part because we never knew how much help we would have. Fran and I are only two people. Looking back, I can't even wrap my brain around how many things we did and what we asked of ourselves.

I not only directed actors, taught the vocal music, and conducted the orchestra, but I was also quite involved with the design of the scenery as well as being sure the scenery was built and painted on schedule.

While we had students building scenery in the early years, we would learn that we wouldn't always have capable student builders available to us. I realized at Sacred Heart that the parents of kids were a good resource to assist with tasks like building or painting scenery. That said, some years we had more parental help than others. Mounting a musical is a gargantuan task. I recall watching a documentary on a Broadway revival of *Guys and Dolls* that we had taken our own cast to see when we were doing the show. The documentary mentioned that the Broadway production had a costume crew of eight people who were responsible for laundering, pressing, and mending costumes. At the time, I thought to myself, *Fran and I don't even have eight adults assisting us with the entire production.*

While a team of dads may have built our sets, they didn't know how to design or what the needs of the show were. It was typically my concept for a set design that our parents brought to life for us. The same was true with lighting. The lighting of a show is a collaboration between the director and the lighting professional. Along the way, I had to learn what the capabilities of our lighting equipment were, like washing the stage in a particular color or isolating an actor, and meet with our lighting guy for long hours to decide on and set the lighting cues for each and every scene. What the layperson might not understand is that there might be well over one hundred different lighting cues even in an amateur production – especially a good one.

Another example of the many hats I wore is that I trained the stage crew in how to move the scenery for each show. In this case, I was faced with a crew of a dozen or more brand new kids a week and a half before opening night. I immediately committed their names to memory and assigned them units of scenery. Mia would remark in years to come that it was impressive that in the middle of a dress rehearsal, I would stop and say, "Sarah and Tom, your set piece is off its mark!" And, in truth, I'm not usually good at remembering names.

Fran worked with actors too, although not quite as extensively as I did, since her main responsibilities were choreographing as well as overseeing costuming, hair, and makeup. Still, I needed her valuable input on the scenes I was working on. As directors of amateur theater, as a pair, we were responsible for each and every aspect of the production.

Speaking of costumes, it was our great good fortune to develop a close working relationship and a deep friendship with a master creator of costumes, Richard Harding, whom I've mentioned. We rented Richard's spectacular costumes for our entire career. At his business, *Bustles and Breeches*, Fran had Richard's permission to go into his storage and "pull" the costumes according to her own judgment. She had a real knack for taking something off its hanger, holding it up in front of her, and being able to determine if it would fit one actor or another based on the person's height and shape. One of her many superpowers! She used measurements, of course, but a costume store isn't a department store. It isn't as if every costume comes in multiple sizes.

And Fran's mastery of hairstyles? Well, let's just say that whether using an actor's real hair or styling a wig, she became so good at it, she probably could have sought a career doing that kind of work on Broadway, although I believe a person needs a hairdressing license to do so. The reality is, though, that if Fran were to have had a career on Broadway, it would (and should) have been as a performer rather than a hairstylist, even though it wasn't the path she chose. Quite simply, Fran's overall theater IQ was formidable to say the least.

Enjoying our shows as they did, people would often ask me if

I would have liked to direct on the professional level. I'd receive such questions from theater patrons, newspaper reporters, and parents of our cast members. It was an easy question to answer: never did I spend even a moment wishing I were doing something else. I would often share my feelings on the subject with our casts, telling them, "You have before you a person who is doing exactly what he was meant to do and what he loves to do." In saying it, I was being totally transparent. Fran and I, both teachers, really embraced working with students and considered ourselves "teaching directors."

There was another matter that was a bit of a mystery. Besides having an inexplicable gift to direct, I also had a gift to conduct – not so much because of my knowledge of music but because of an innate understanding of how the orchestrations enhanced the production in relation to tempo, mood, and dramatic effect.

I loved conducting as much as anything I'd ever done. In the orchestra pit, I felt totally connected to the entire production: the actors on stage, the stage crew, and the musicians before me. I felt like I was the conduit through which the entire performance happened, and I relished that role. In some cases, while conducting the orchestra, using a headset, I called the lighting cues and communicated with my stage manager in the wing. Some people might have described me as a "control freak!" My reaction to such a criticism? Hey, baby – I am what I am!

LESSON:
You have before you a person who is doing exactly what he was meant to do and what he loves to do.

In preparation for conducting, I would listen to the Broadway cast recording many dozens of times, making the music a part of me. I remember an experience with dress rehearsals of a production of *Fiddler* we directed elsewhere. The group had its own conductor, a very sweet man, who assembled a fine group of musicians. But at the dress rehearsal, I had to repeatedly stop the pit band because the tempos weren't right. In fact, in saying they "weren't right," I'm being nice about it. The tempos were *way* off!

By this time, I had not only directed *Fiddler* three or four times but had conducted it as well, so I knew the score inside out. Some of the band members shot daggers at me for stopping them again and again, or at least that was my perception.

On opening night, the conductor addressed our cast, wishing them well.

"I love conducting for you," he said, "and every year in preparing for the musical, all I do is listen to musical soundtracks. Why, just today, I listened to *Les Mis* all day!"

You should have listened to Fiddler, *buddy,* I thought to myself.

There are very few things I would change about my life as a play director or, for that matter, my life in general. I have to confess, though, that I loved conducting so much, I occasionally imagined myself being a professional conductor.

FRAN, THE OPERA SINGER

As for Fran, she certainly could have sought a professional career as a performer. I wouldn't say the same about me, but given her lineage, she was clearly a gifted performer – a versatile singer who could sing anything from Sondheim to Gershwin to Puccini.

Despite her parents' background, Fran never considered herself an opera singer. Early in our marriage, though, she told me she was going to enter a Connecticut opera competition, named for Gianna D'Angelo (1929-2013), a celebrated professional opera singer born in Hartford.

"Yeah," she said. "I talked to my mother about it. I have no chance of winning because obviously I'm not an opera singer. (It wasn't obvious to me!) But it'll be fun! It'll be a hoot!"

And it certainly was a *hoot* when professional opera hopefuls from a number of prominent university music programs were finished singing and the judges announced that among the three winners was Francesca Riggio Scarpa. I shouldn't have been surprised.

Through the years, despite the many shows we were directing, Fran managed to remain active as a performer.

My mother would become fond of saying, "Every time Fran sings, you fall in love all over again." She was kind of teasing me, but it was true!

NEW YORK CITY, DON'T TELL MAMA – 1990-SOMETHING

It's slightly after 11:00 p.m. right after a show, and we stop for a drink at a piano bar on 46th Street, Don't Tell Mama. We've been wanting to check the place out for a long time, and here we are.

It's open mic night and the place is packed. After squeezing into a small table against the far wall, we quickly learn how it works: if you want to sing a song, you write the title on a cocktail napkin and give it to your server. She, in turn, delivers it to the pianist who can apparently play just about any show tune or standard.

The crowded room is long and narrow with the piano at the far end away from the entrance. As we sip our drinks we listen to different singers take their turn in the spotlight. Like a night at a karaoke bar, some singers have decent voices while others do not. The best are waiters and waitresses, no doubt Broadway hopefuls, who occasionally take their turn at the microphone. What I notice, though, is that no matter how good (or bad) a singer is, the audience seems to quickly lose interest (if they had any in the first place), and chat at their tables, rudely ignoring the singers except to give them a cursory round of light applause at the end of a song.

I have faith in my wife, though. "Fran," I say. "Sing a song."

Always modest to a fault, she replies, "No! Get out. I'm not going to sing."

I keep after her, though, until she asks me what she would sing. I suggest the title song from Cabaret.

"I don't know," she says. "That's a cheesy song, don't you think?"

"Maybe," I say, "but, then again, this is a cheesy place."

"I don't know."

A guy sitting in close proximity to us pipes in. "C'mon, Fran, sing a song." It cracks us both up.

When Fran hands the waitress her napkin, the same guy says, "Wait! Lemme see that!" He inserts a twenty dollar bill, a tip for the pianist.

"What are you doing?" a puzzled Fran asks.

"I want to make sure he calls you up there," the guy offers. His girlfriend seems amused.

"But you don't even know if I have any talent," Fran argues. "What if I'm terrible?"

"It'll be worth twenty bucks either way." The guy, very pleased with himself, holds his glass up in a toast to Fran.

When Fran is called up, she begins the song. The chatter in the room is at a high level, and I am concerned. Maybe this isn't such a good idea.

But then a strange thing happens. A minute into the song, the room quiets and Fran miraculously has everyone's full attention. And I mean everyone! She shifts into full performance mode, and when she gets to the high point of the song: "When I gooooo, I'm goin' like Elsie," the room cheers. When Fran hits her last note, she receives a rousing standing ovation with chants of "Encore! Encore!"

I watch her confer with the pianist, and they decide to follow with Duke Ellington's "I Got it Bad and that Ain't Good."

Personally, I'm thinking, No! This is a bad choice! As great as Fran sings it, I feel certain by choosing a ballad she will lose the audience. The room grows silent and attentive once more and stays quiet throughout the entire song – and when Fran reaches its dramatic conclusion, hitting high notes that seem humanly impossible, the audience responds with another standing ovation.

As we traverse the long room to the exit, person after person stops Fran to compliment her and to ask who she is and what Broadway show she is appearing in.

Moments later, walking down 46th Street, I complain: "Geez! I'm married to Barbra Streisand! I'm married to Liza Minnelli! So why am I so poor?"

It's one of my favorite memories of Fran, and I tell it to illustrate that this was my partner in the theater. This is the woman with whom I was creating magic back at home.

THE SHUBERT SUMMER ACADEMY FOR THE PERFORMING ARTS

Moving into the late '80s and '90s, we were immersed in a major performance project with each season: Sacred Heart Academy in the fall; a Christmas show or New Year's Eve fundraiser (or both) in the winter; the Shelton High School show in the spring; and the Youth CONNection musical in the summer.

Add to this crazy pace the fact that in the late '80s we were contacted by an acquaintance, Dr. Louis Negri, a Connecticut educator and highly esteemed voice teacher. Lou had approached the managing director of New Haven's acclaimed Shubert Theatre with a plan to institute a summer theater program for kids. We hardly knew each other, but when he called me, he said, "I've seen your shows. You and Fran are the best, and I want you on our team at the Shubert!" He asked Fran and me to teach acting and direct a culminating production. He already had an accomplished dance person on board, Lee Lund, who had danced professionally on Broadway and in television variety shows like *The Sonny and Cher Comedy Hour*.

It was especially apropos for Fran to work at the Shubert. After all, her father had presented grand opera there decades before. It was just another example of following in the footsteps of her celebrated parents.

The program would be called the Shubert Summer Academy for the Performing Arts and would be open to high school and junior high school students. It would culminate in a performance: the first year, a musical revue, and the second and third a full-scale production of *Godspell* – which Fran and I would direct.

We were honored to be invited by Dr. Negri, and for the next three summers, we spent our days at the Shubert and our nights at Shelton High School rehearsing our Youth CONNection productions. It was an exciting but a grueling schedule – theater morning, noon, and night. Our daughters spent the day with a babysitter, and in the evenings, they were in the casts of shows like *Hello, Dolly!*, *The Music Man*, and *The King and I.*

We were fortunate, during those Shubert days, to have a great babysitter all three summers whose family had a swimming pool and had Nickelodeon on cable, who took our girls out for ice cream, and who taught them how to roll their jeans and slouch their socks '80s style. And, let's not forget that our daughters loved performing in big shows, so Mia and Gina look back on those years fondly.

Something occurred to us, though. After three years at the Shubert, Fran and I realized that we didn't need to travel to New Haven to run an educational summer program, and in the early '90s, we started our own theater camp at Shelton High School.

The first year, our enrollment included high school students. It soon became evident, though, that the parents of high school students, especially juniors and seniors, wanted them to work in the summers. We realized that we'd be better off gearing the program strictly toward kids in grades three through eight. And now our daughters could attend our theater camp. It was the beginning of us bringing theater education to our region for years to come. Our programs continue to live on today.

During those years, students at our theater camp took acting, singing, and dance classes each day, very much modeled after our program at the Shubert. However, while the Shubert program purported to be a pre-professional program, we wanted our camp to be fun and non-stressful for everyone. Our philosophy was focused on enrichment and appreciation for the performing arts. Beyond the daily class schedule, we filled in with other creative activities – everything from mask making to "dress up" days.

The last hour of each day was spent rehearsing for a culminating "share" performance, free to family and friends. Our philosophy was not to have any stars, not even soloists. All musical numbers were ensemble in nature. The program was so successful that for several years in the '90s, we had so many students enrolled that we had to run simultaneous sessions at Shelton High School and nearby Derby High School. After a few years, we began to hold double sessions – from 9:00 to 12:00 and then from 1:00 to 4:00. It's important to note that, in years to come, our staff was comprised of our two daughters along with college students, with teen assistants, all Youth CONNection cast members, so after a full day at theater camp, it was rehearsal all night.

Summer theater camp continued to thrive for years and would become the foundation for the theater we would found in 2005. As we moved into the early 2000s, one or the other of our daughters would run the summer program, depending on who was available.

Another phenomenon that occurred during the late '80s through the late '90s was that Sacred Heart Academy students started coming out to Shelton to audition for our Youth CONNection summer productions, very often winning major roles in the process. Sacred Heart girls from the Greater New Haven area played major roles in nine of eleven of our summer productions between 1987 and 1997.

These Sacred Heart actresses who appeared in major roles or the ensemble continued a trend where our casts were composed of students from a broader geographic range, extending the scope of our audiences in the process.

Theater wasn't the only thing in our lives at the time. I was working on a master's degree in school counseling, driving to Southern Connecticut State University several times a week. I'd go home after school, take a short catnap, and then stop by Wendy's on my way to New Haven, wolfing down a dinner of a chicken sandwich and fries in the car. It took me a number of years (six, I think) to finish the degree, trying to fit in two classes a semester between rehearsals.

FRAN JOINS THE CONVENT

Meanwhile, Fran was cast in the premiere production of *Nunsense II* at the Seven Angels Theatre in Waterbury run by a friend and former voice student of Fran's mother, Semina De Laurentis. Semina had worked with the writer/composer, Dan

Goggin, in developing the first *Nunsense* musical, having appeared in the original cast, and was also featured in a television version starring Rue McClanahan.

Dan Goggin wanted Semina to test out his sequel in Waterbury before bringing it to New York. The production was a gigantic success in Waterbury and ran for several months. The way I would come to describe this production is this: when we mounted a show, it was "a" production of, say, *Annie*, but this was "the" production of *Nunsense II*. It was directed and choreographed by Dan Goggin's personnel with the express purpose of testing it before bringing it into New York.

From the start, it seemed like way too much of a commitment given our life. But, as the ever modest Fran first explained, "Semina wants me to read for the part, but I won't get it."

More realistic, I argued, "Fran, she seems particularly interested in you for the cast. She knows your talent."

"Yeah, maybe you're right," Fran replied. "It would have been fun to audition, but I'll just tell Semina, with our kids and our shows, I have too much on my plate."

A week later, we took an old family friend of the Riggios whom we called "Auntie Katie" to dinner and to the movies. Auntie Katie was well into her eighties, so when we brought her home, I saw her to the door.

After saying goodnight to Fran and the girls, Auntie Katie called out as we were walking to her door, "Oh, and good luck at the audition, Fran!"

When I got back to the car, I glared at Fran, "Anything you want to tell me?"

Fran would go on to play two different roles at Seven Angels over the course of several months, and it came as no surprise to me that, upon the conclusion of the Waterbury production, Semina told Fran that there was a contract available for the New York show and asked if she would be interested in pursuing it further.

As good as that may sound, it truly wasn't realistic. *Nunsense II* would be in an Off Broadway venue, which means a smaller theater and not a very high paying one. If memory serves, she would have gotten a one year contract for eighteen thousand dollars. We had to ask ourselves how far that money would stretch with daily train fare to New York and meals. We also had to ask ourselves who would replace Fran as my co-director/choreographer and, more importantly, what we would do with our children, because we were partners as both parents and directors. As much fun as it might have been (and Fran had a blast in Waterbury!), Fran turned down the offer.

Even Dan Goggin, upon hearing the news said to Fran, "So, Fran, I hear you're hanging up your nun shoes. I'm sorry to hear that!"

Nunsense productions were running in major cities around the country. Several of the Waterbury cast members had played roles in major U.S. cities. You might call it, in effect, the *Nunsense* circuit. It's entirely possible that Dan felt Fran might be a good candidate to join that circuit. But it wasn't Fran's destiny to join the convent, long term...not just yet!

Even without the offer of a professional contract to appear in *Nunsense II* in New York, with such a staggering pace, something had to give. It was hard to let anything go, but a decision had to be made. After ten years at Sacred Heart Academy, we decided to resign as directors there – not an easy decision. They had been great years where we had formed wonderful friendships with students, sisters, and parents alike. But the commute alone to Hamden for evening and weekend rehearsals would save us valuable hours each week.

Fran did end up in the convent, though. Instead of going to New York with *Nunsense II*, she became the Director of Religious Education at our church in Shelton, St. Joseph's. Since there were very few nuns in the modern era, Fran's office was located literally in the old convent. I would tease her that she had finally become a nun.

ACT I, SCENE 10

Those nights of traveling back and forth to Southern for graduate classes paid off because in the '95-'96 school year, I was promoted to guidance counselor. Around that same time, we decided to let go of the Mr. Student Body Pageant. We felt it had lost its original intention and charm. It was becoming increasingly harder to convince the contestants that it was supposed to be a spoof, and that winning shouldn't be the object. The National Honor Society, seeing how lucrative Mr. Student Body was, had adopted a corresponding girls' pageant, called The Miss Sweetheart Pageant, and like the girls, the boys in Mr. Student Body very much wanted to win...to be crowned Mr. Student Body.

In the first few years of the event, the talent portion was all satirical – a non-piano player who "played" a duet with an experienced musician, but only playing the very last single note of the piece – or a contestant with a chef's hat teaching the audience how to make pizza and making quite a mess in the process. Now the contestants were showing up with more serious acts, often without the talent to make them work. When we let it go, the Student Council, as mentioned, picked up the event and it continued to be a fruitful fundraiser for them as it had always been for us.

THE BIRTH OF *ADAPTATIONS*

It's important to note that producing a major musical is a costly venture for any theater group. Securing the royalties alone, the mere permission to produce the show, costs thousands of dollars. The greater the seating capacity in an auditorium, the greater the royalty cost. Add to that, money was spent to buy lumber and paint, rent costumes, pay musicians, custodial and air-conditioning fees in the Shelton High School auditorium, and more. In those years, it was commonplace for us to spend in excess of forty thousand dollars on a show. The Mr. Student Body Pageant had served an important purpose because even with some sellout performances, we couldn't be sure we were going to meet all expenses.

At the time, a student who assisted me as stage manager planted a seed. She told me about a book she had read and a corresponding movie entitled *Sing* that she had seen and loved. The story was about an event that took place for many years at public high schools in New York City centered around a drama competition where four one-act musicals were presented, one by each grade. Each production was created and performed by students. The film's production notes indicate that Paul Simon, Neil Diamond, Barbra Streisand, Carole King, and Neil Sedaka, all of whom at various times attended Brooklyn and Queens high schools, participated in *Sing*.

I read the book and watched the film, and I really liked the idea, but my inner wisdom told me that some things needed to be modified. First, the name. I would call it *Adaptations* and each show would have a faculty member who would create the script and direct the production. A number of teachers were amped to direct a short production.

It could be an adaptation of anything from Shakespeare to a television comedy (one director created a musical adaptation of *Friends*) to a thirty minute adaptation of a Broadway musical.

It also wouldn't be a competition, another smart move on my part. I would find out some years later that the *Sing* competitions had some shady goings-on. A friend and gifted musician who would eventually conduct several shows for me had gone to school in New York and participated in *Sing* competitions, serving as student musical director. He explained to me that all kinds of shenanigans went on during intermission where one class would try to sabotage the performance of another. A drumstick might find its way into a piano or the lighting instruments in the catwalk might get "readjusted" to miss their mark.

Not being a competition and having faculty leadership, *Adaptations* didn't have any of those problems. Typically, one class was pulling for another. A tradition began where the sophomore class would wait at the stage door after the freshman class took their bow and high five each cast member as they exited the wing. Each older group would greet the previous class after their curtain call.

Adaptations was better for the Drama Club than Mr. Student Body on several levels. First of all, it was a theatrical performance. Second, each cast was comprised of thirty to forty kids, giving well over one hundred students an opportunity to perform on stage. With so many participants, each performance selling out was a given. For the less experienced students, it was a chance to perform on stage and possibly gain the skills and confidence for the spring musical auditions a few months later.

Adaptations worked best when each class appeared better than the previous one – the freshmen adorable in their inexperience, the sophomores better than the freshman, the juniors more polished than the sophomores, the seniors on another level altogether. That said, because the most talented kids in a given year could be underclassmen, that's not how it always worked out.

Adaptations is still alive and well at Shelton High School almost thirty years after its inception. It was a terrific idea, and I'm grateful to the student who suggested I read and watch *Sing*.

FROM SHELTON HIGH SCHOOL TO BROADWAY

During the mid '90s, it was also my good fortune to have an extraordinary student take an interest in the technical side of theater. As a rising sophomore, Erik Hansen had been on our stage crew for our 1994 summer production, and in the next school year, he asked to be stage manager for our spring musical. Because he was young, I was dubious. I preferred my stage managers to be seniors or, at the very least, juniors. I often had a senior as stage manager and a junior as assistant stage manager.

I'm glad I said yes to Erik, though, because he would turn out to be one in a million. He quickly took an interest in set construction and lighting design. By his senior year, Erik was doing internships at New Haven's Long Wharf Theatre and Bridgeport's Downtown Cabaret Theatre through a career program at school known as CASH (Careers at Shelton High School).

I remember an English teacher friend complained to me about the class time Erik was missing. I explained that this was the work he would be doing for the rest of his life, and I was correct. After earning a degree in technical theater from Boston University, Erik toured for a few years with a Broadway show called *Blast!* which was a theatricalized drum and bugle corps event, and ever since, he has only worked on Broadway. Today, as I understand it, he is responsible for overseeing the building of scenery, making sure it is built to spec, and determining how that scenery will move on the stage (whether it will move on and off via tracks in the floor or whether it will "fly" in or rise up on an elevator). I have no doubt that is an oversimplification of Erik's work, but sufficeth to say he is a main facilitator of bringing scenery to the Broadway stage.

During his last two years of high school and over the summers while he was in college, Erik oversaw the building of all of our scenery, leading a small group of parents and building much of it himself. In his senior year of high school, we mounted *Carousel*, a production I feel was a technical gem, mainly because of Erik's skill behind the scenes. The set and lighting designs were his magnificent creation.

In theater, things are sometimes inclined to go wrong, though, and the fathers on our crew had motorized the carousel as requested by me. They used a lawnmower engine somehow connected to a wheel beneath the platform of the carousel. It worked, but the motor was inordinately loud, competing with our live orchestra in volume during the musical prologue.

Erik and I decided to scrap the motor on opening night. We gathered Fran and the cast together a few hours before curtain and held an emergency rehearsal. Erik taught the crew to move the carousel around from the upstage (back) side of the action. Holding on to the unit from one side to the other, three or four boys rotated in a half circle, pulling the unit from right to left before letting go and then moving back to the far side. This way, the crew was hardly visible.

Fran and I adjusted the staging of the cast, creating movement that would camouflage the possibility of the stage crew members being seen.

When the carousel moved during the overture, it was a magical moment of technical theater and, for me, perhaps the most exciting technical element in any show I would ever direct. And, coupled with Richard Rodgers' magnificent overture, our audiences greeted the carousel revolve on our stage with explosive applause.

When Erik was a college sophomore, we did a production of *Evita* with the Shelton High School Drama Club in 1999, and Erik convinced a fellow Boston University student to come to Shelton with him whenever they could slip away. The two tech theater students built a raked (slanted) stage floor complete with panels that lit up in different configurations throughout each performance. An accomplished artist friend of mine created wood block prints which would become giant murals on our set, depicting the poverty and anguish that the people of Argentina faced in the time period. From a technical perspective, *Evita* was a cutting edge production for a high school or perhaps any theater outside of Broadway, in part because of the participation of Erik Hansen. As I witnessed Erik's growing skill set during high school and college, it didn't surprise me at all when he transitioned to a Broadway career in technical theater right out of school.

At the time, we had an auspicious circumstance occur. *The Connecticut Post* was in our building meeting with a colleague who was the director of guidance, and the reporter asked him if we had a drama club. "A great one," my colleague told him. The reporter contacted me and said he had been assigned to do a series, three front page articles, on a local drama club production. It was our good fortune because even getting a single article inside a major daily newspaper had always been a challenge. The attitude was and probably still is, if we write about your high school production, we have to write about everyone's. But for some reason, this reporter had been given this assignment.

Evita played to three sellout audiences. The second and third performances of *Evita* would have likely sold out anyway, given the epic nature of the production and our track record, but it was the only time a Thursday night performance ever sold out at Shelton High School. With the exception of our 1978 *Fiddler on the Roof*, already recounted in this book, no other Shelton High School Drama Club production, before or since, ever sold out three performances. And, like our first *Fiddler* back in 1978, the cast of *Evita* was honored to be given the responsibility of bringing such a serious piece of theater to our high school stage and approached the rehearsal period with an inspirational determination to succeed on the highest level.

I don't recall why we didn't do a command performance as we had with *Fiddler* years before, but I assume it was because the school calendar wouldn't allow it.

That spring, Mia and I visited the Boston Conservatory where a young admissions officer gave us a campus tour.

"What musical did you do this year?" he asked Mia.

"*Evita*," she said, not revealing that she herself had played Eva Perón.

"That's an interesting choice for a high school," he replied, his tone tainted with skepticism and irony.

I managed to hold my tongue, but I wanted to say, "Our *Evita* was like no high school play you've ever seen, my man!"

FACING CHALLENGES

Moving into the early two thousands, our many theater activities were taking their toll on us, and especially on me. There is a hectic pace to prepare a show for performance, and on some productions, we didn't have a lot of behind-the-scenes help.

During production week, I was at school from morning until midnight. In the afternoons, I could be found in the theater doing any one of a multitude of things – going over lighting cues, hanging backdrops, or putting final touches on scenery with a paintbrush. I think most directors of high school theater can relate to what I'm saying.

At least once or twice on opening night, I greeted the audience in my work clothes, covered in paint, apologizing and explaining that the set was still wet, and then I made my way to the orchestra pit to begin conducting the overture.

In the spring of 2000 before the final dress rehearsal of the musical, *Good News*, I was alone in the theater in the late afternoon attending to some of these last minute details. The cast and crew would be arriving at 5:30, and I felt I needed to rest, so I made my way to the aisle along the side of the auditorium and I lay down on the carpet. I dozed off for a short while and was awakened by the sounds of the cast arriving. I heard them near the stage, greeting each other and talking about the rehearsal in their excitement.

Okay, I better get up now, I thought to myself, but my body wasn't cooperating. I remained on the carpet in my prone position, only half awake, as my ears were met by the sounds of more and more cast members arriving. Then I thought to myself, *I can't get up*. I really began to worry, and I felt I should call out to the kids to come help me. I felt so exhausted and utterly incapable of running a full dress/tech rehearsal that I thought I should tell them to call 911 for me. As I started to feel a little more alert, I decided instead to make one final attempt to get up and carry on. I rolled onto my side and grabbed the arm of the chair near me and dragged myself up onto my feet – and then, somehow or other, I miraculously pushed myself through the rehearsal. As a high school and college student I had been a distance runner, and I well knew about having a "second wind." There hadn't been anything wrong with me except sheer exhaustion. Adrenaline can take a person a long way.

In sharp contrast, a year later, we chose *Chess*, a musical I had seen in New York and loved. I would rate *Chess* as the most challenging musical we ever directed, but I thrived on challenges. The score was a bear for the kids to sing and for the orchestra to play with all kinds of irregular time signatures. Our set consisted of periaktoi (tall triangular towers) that moved about the stage like giant chess pieces, creating different interior-like configurations. The units were moved from the inside by students who navigated with only peep holes to look out of.

With only three dress/tech rehearsals before opening night, we had, after a number of years of very late nights, decided to run Act I on Monday, Act II on Tuesday, and both acts on Wednesday. That way, if necessary, we could iron out problems during the first two techs. In our earlier days of directing, we had run dress rehearsals without stopping, but I had changed my philosophy on the subject. If there was an important problem to work out, I now felt it was expedient to stop and do so. Doing only one act on the first two nights made it feasible, time-wise, to do this.

Typically, the cast had, at best, one rehearsal with the orchestra prior to production week. With *Chess*, between the difficult score and the challenging scene changes, Monday night didn't go well, and Tuesday night was worse. At the end of the night on Tuesday, I announced to the cast, crew, and orchestra that we wouldn't be having a dress/tech on Wednesday – that Fran would rehearse with the stage crew and that I would run a music-only rehearsal with just the cast and orchestra in the band room.

Those adults assisting us as musicians, as lighting and sound technicians, and as costume crew didn't feel it was a good idea. It would mean that we would never run the play in its entirety before opening night. But I had experienced sloppy dress rehearsals through the years, dress rehearsals that ran past 11:00 p.m., dress rehearsals where adult musicians walked out because they had to go to work the next morning. At a given point, I made a decision that the absolute latest that I would release a cast would be 11:00, no matter what the circumstances. In the case of *Chess,* my final non-dress/tech was a smart choice, and our production ran that weekend without issue – musical or technical.

A director must be prepared to make difficult, sometimes

unpopular, decisions. Over the years, we had occasionally restaged things early on opening night to correct a problem as was the case with *Carousel*.

Carousel wasn't the only time we did some rethinking and restaging only hours before an opening night performance. Back in a 1989 Youth CONNection production of *Hello, Dolly!*, we called a 5:30 rehearsal on opening night because we felt the song "Put On Your Sunday Clothes" had been sloppy in our dress rehearsals and we wanted to make a few adjustments. And, in 1993, we dealt with what seemed like an insurmountable problem with our set for a Youth CONNection production of *Meet Me in St. Louis*, which will be discussed in the second half of this book.

LESSON:

A director must be prepared to make difficult, sometimes unpopular, decisions.

I would learn, years later, reading a book about a musical we would eventually direct, *Making It Big: The Diary of a Broadway Musical*, that on opening night of *Big* on Broadway, they stopped the show eleven times because of technical problems with the set.

The very challenges we faced from one show to another helped us to grow as directors. While set problems were typically my responsibility, Fran herself was constantly solving other issues, often of the costuming variety.

Mounting a major production, we would learn, required us to be problem solvers especially because theater has an inflexible deadline known as *opening night*. What became increasingly clear to me with each passing show was that I possessed the inner strength to make those crucial decisions again and again.

ACT I, SCENE 11

Clearly, whether a high school or a Broadway show, preparing a production for an audience is a pressure packed endeavor. After my encounter on the carpet during *Good News* and, a year later, wrestling with the challenges presented by *Chess*, I was feeling burnt out. Even before those two productions, I had realized I needed a break and had suggested to Fran that we take a year off from the Youth CONNection summer production. Fran didn't think it was such a good idea, though. The reader shouldn't think that we always agreed on everything.

We made a plan where she would mount a production of *The Sound of Music* without me, except that I would conduct the orchestra. It was a show that required very little choreography and which wasn't extremely challenging musically. But the truth is – neither of us had ever directed without the other.

Two or three weeks into the rehearsal period, she invited me to visit and give some input. I don't remember what I saw exactly, but watching the rehearsal, I realized that she needed me. Fran directing without me wasn't going to work. I was the yang to her yin, so I felt I needed to climb back on board.

So that very much needed rest wasn't to be. Then came the stressful *Chess* the next spring, and in the summer of 2001, we brought *Children of Eden* to the stage.

RETIREMENT NUMBER TWO?

So – as the spring of 2002 approached, I was fifty years old and seriously contemplating retiring from directing. Added to the utter exhaustion and the feeling of burnout I was experiencing, I simply felt it would be in our best interest to slow down to a stop, which would give us more time to spend with each other in the most non-theatrical sense of the phrase, and more importantly, with our family and friends.

After discussing the matter at length with Fran, we decided, at the very least, to take a sabbatical from the theater. We would direct *Footloose* with the Drama Club, and we chose *Peter Pan* for our summer production. After that, we would take a break for a few years from the world of directing.

Early in the rehearsal process, we sat our 2002 *Footloose* cast down and told them our plan. The kids, like our 1982 cast of *The Mikado*, were similarly rocked upon hearing the news, but I think they understood. I would spend the rehearsal period writing reflections about our experiences with the Drama Club and sending them to the cast via email. It was a cathartic process for me, and once again, I felt that my directing days might possibly be over.

A few Drama Club alumni engineered a reunion at a performance of *Footloose*. Over one hundred alumni, most of whom were from our first eight years of directing, attended the reunion, coming from as far away as Mexico City. After the curtain call that night, the alumni announced that they were giving us a trip to London where our daughter Mia would be doing a semester abroad in the fall. It was an exciting and emotion filled night, and we felt grateful and blessed to have lived the theatrical life.

As the summer approached I received an interesting and enticing flier in the mail. A major licensor of musicals, Music Theatre International, was releasing what they called *Les Misérables School Edition*. *Les Mis* was still playing on Broadway, and usually a production was restricted while still running in New York. This appeared to be a special program for high schoolers.

That spring, a friend and a lover of theater told us that his alma mater on Long Island had been selected by Music Theatre International as the first school in the country to produce *Les Mis*, and asked us if we were interested in seeing it with him.

From what I understood, our friend's high school had a lot of assistance from Music Theatre International. That said, I had to admit that they did a fine job with a very challenging piece. Let me add that it was almost indecipherable how the "high school" version differed from the Broadway show. I would later learn that the only difference was, here and there, a few verses were deleted from songs. Otherwise, in all respects, from orchestration to the libretto, it was *Les Mis*.

As we drove home from Long Island, I was preoccupied with an overwhelming desire to direct *Les Mis*. *That was a great high school show,* I thought, *but we can do better*. It was shades of competitive little Gary Scarpa in the early 1960s wanting to be better than all the boys in the Scout shows!

GOODBYE PETER PAN, HELLO JEAN VALJEAN

With our summer production of *Peter Pan* approaching, I made a radical decision. I announced that I was switching gears – that I was scrapping *Peter Pan* and planning to direct *Les Mis*. In my mind, feeling that our summer production could potentially be my last ever, I wanted to go out with a bang!

I had to also announce some bad news for our college age performers. In the contract, Music Theatre International stipulated that no performer could be older than a recent high school graduate. Since founding the Youth CONNection, it had been open to college students and even recent college graduates. Our age limit, at the time, was twenty-five.

Our college students weren't happy. I couldn't help myself, though; the pull to do *Les Mis* was too great. Our college students would have to sit out that summer. That population of post-high school performers, by the way, included both of my daughters. In those years, though, our daughters had begun moving over to the directing side of the table. In fact, in 1999, as a rising high school senior, Mia had been accepted into the renowned and competitive

Broadway Theatre Project at the University of South Florida, founded and run by Broadway's Ann Reinking, so Mia couldn't appear in the production. Instead, both Mia and Gina helped choreograph *Joseph and the Amazing Technicolor Dreamcoat* that summer.

Now in 2002, Mia joined us as an assistant director and choreographer for *Les Mis*. Wanting to make sure we didn't leave the Youth CONNection or the Shelton High School Drama Club in the lurch, we asked Fran's niece and her husband, Andrea and Rob Kennedy, to assist as well. They would take over the Drama Club, and we would utilize *Les Mis* to mentor them into the world of directing. Andrea and Rob were both alums of the Youth CONNection, had studied theater in college, and both had some experience performing professionally.

The stars were aligned for our production of *Les Mis*. At the time, we had a group of boys at Shelton High School who were excellent singers and actors. Typically, amateur productions are heavier in female talent than male, something I have found to be true in both educational and community theater. At the time, though, it seemed the talent of the boys was equal to the girls.

I believe ours was the first amateur production of *Les Mis* in Connecticut, and it brought lots of candidates from nearby communities. Our Valjean, a sixteen-year-old whose voice rivaled Colm Wilkinson, was from Weston and our Cosette was from Stratford. Besides our Shelton boys, lots of newcomers came out of the woodwork from other communities to fill out what was a great ensemble.

Normally, I spent hours on the phone, filling in our orchestra beyond our core group, especially searching for strings and double reed players. In this case, I found myself being contacted by superb musicians who explained, "I'd give anything to play *Les Mis*!"

A number of our college students, ineligible because of age, still chose to be a part of the excitement by volunteering to be on our stage crew, the reverse of what was usual. Typically, stage crew had been comprised of younger teens who had either been cut or weren't interested in performing. In this case, it was gratifying to see so many of our college students come forth to support our cast, and their level of efficiency moving our scenery was superlative.

Those very same college students had wondered how a cast of high school students could possibly succeed with such challenging material, but as they assisted on stage crew, they supportively watched their younger counterparts bring *Les Mis* to life with passion and skill, transcending what they had ever seen high schoolers do on the stage.

The rehearsal process was intensely creative on the part of all involved. We found out, as we had in '78 with *Fiddler* and in '99 with *Evita*, that our students thrived on the challenge of serious material. Once more, we had a cast that was totally invested emotionally in the story. I even found myself allowing the boys in the cast to help create the staging, something that happened in a completely organic manner.

The excitement surrounding our production was an awesome thing to behold. We took a cast trip to New York to see the Broadway show in preparation, and throughout the summer, the Shelton High School stage was a bees' nest of activity. One night I counted over forty parent volunteers working on the set.

Fran and I had always been detail oriented, and in this case, more than ever. In costuming the show, for instance, we went beyond our Connecticut costumer, renting a few items from Eaves Costumes in New York in order to get the exact pieces we wanted.

I even remember spontaneously taking my daughter Mia to see *Les Mis* on Broadway again, only weeks after our cast trip because I was bothered by something. Although we had a top hat of excellent quality for our Valjean, it looked silly on his head for some reason, and it was driving me crazy. I didn't remember what it looked like on the Broadway actor's head and needed to see it for myself. Remember, this was before YouTube, so it was the only way to check. I don't know if it was a coincidence, but we learned that night that Valjean carried the hat the entire time, never once putting it on his head. This is just one example of how fanatical we could be about directing a show.

Normally, our summer productions could count on having a good crowd on opening night, a larger crowd for performance number two, and two sellouts on our second weekend. Not surprisingly, *Les Mis* sold out all four performances in advance.

The following May, the Broadway *Les Mis* would close after a run of sixteen years. On closing night, the finale of the Broadway show would include high school students from across the country on stage with the Broadway cast to convey that the production was being turned over from the Broadway world to the high school world. Auditions were held in New York, and two of our cast members were selected to participate, appearing in the finale and then joining the professional cast for a closing night party at Tavern on the Green. Quite an experience.

And that friend who had taken us to see *Les Mis* on Long Island? I will always remember his reaction after seeing our production. He was stunned, I think, considering his alma mater had done such a nice job with the same material, and he just looked at me and shook his head as if to say, *I can't believe what I just saw!*

After closing our production of *Les Mis*, I had some soul searching to do. Could I really give up directing? I had, after all, almost twenty years before come to the conclusion that directing was in my blood. Can one give up something that is in his blood? I realized I could not. I decided to hold on to one show a year. The Kennedys would take over the Drama Club as planned, but we Scarpas would remain at the helm for the Youth CONNection. In its way, as far as retiring from the theater goes, it was another false alarm.

While it may seem odd to have said we were going to give up directing and then not do so, theater had been such an integral part of our lives for so long that walking away from it was easier said than done.

I remember in those years when Fran was working in religious education, a priest asked her, "Why doesn't Gary ever help you at religious education considering that you help him on all of his productions?" But what the priest didn't realize was that they weren't *my* productions but rather *our* productions. Fran and I had met in the theater, and now having been married for more than twenty-five years, we realized we had never had a year in our courtship or marriage where we hadn't participated in at least one production as either actors or directors. Fran and I would joke for the remainder of our directing career that we didn't know what it was like to be a couple without theater.

LESSON:
Can one give up something that is in his blood? I realized I could not.

Something else we began to notice after that 2002 production of *Les Mis* was a new trend as we had seen with Sacred Heart Academy students some years earlier. Now super talented students from Bunnell High School in nearby Stratford began to win roles in our summer productions. Starting with the role of Cosette in *Les Mis*, Bunnell students would win major roles in all but one show between 2002 and 2014. In the case of Sacred Heart Academy, at least we had directed the girls who came to Shelton and won roles. But in this case, Bunnell students were completely unknown to us. They simply told each other about the Youth CONNection in the ensuing years. This casting trend became so evident that Shelton cast members eventually began referring to their Stratford castmates as "the Bunnells," and it was almost as if there was something in the drinking water of the two nearby towns that produced talented teenagers.

During those next few years, life slowed down a tad for us, but that slower pace would be short-lived. In March of 2004, Fran turned fifty. For her birthday, our good friend, Michael Pereira, who had once appeared in our productions, treated Fran to a motivational lecture at the Philadelphia Convention Hall and Civic Center given by Oprah Winfrey, who coincidentally had also turned fifty just a few months before Fran. The theme of the program was "Live Your Best Life," and Fran returned from the day feeling motivated and excited to begin some kind of new venture. But what would it be?

JAMAICA, 2004

It is a hot day on the beach, but it's a good heat. Every day in Jamaica is a good heat day. We seem to have made it our practice, in recent years, to vacation on an island. A few years ago it had been Aruba; last year, Puerto Rico.

Considering the staggering pace of our lives during the year, we need relaxing vacation destinations where there is nothing to do. The island life is just what the doctor ordered.

We enjoy the pristine white sand and the crystal blue water of the ocean. Every now and then a ganja boat passes by, the hustlers doing their business, but we ignore them. Well, to be fair, Fran buys a beaded necklace from one!

Right now, though, we are resting. I am semi-comatose. More than anything, I need to rest and recharge.

Sitting in the Sandals Resort beach chair next to me, Fran says, "I can't stop thinking about Oprah."

"Oh?" I reply, my eyes closed and my book resting on my chest.

"Yeah," she continues. "I really want to start living my best life."

I flip over on my side to look at her. The sun is blinding. "I've been thinking about it too because, you know, if you're going to live your best life, we'll be living it together."

"True," Fran laughs. "But what do we do?"

"Well, I've got a crazy idea."

"What's that?"

I've clearly captured Fran's interest.

"Well, you know that idea my nephew Steve has about opening a theater?"

"Yeah..."

I can see that Fran's wondering where I'm going with this. Since he was a college student, my brother's son had an idea about opening a small theater that would also double as a bookstore.

"Yeah...well, first of all, if he ever does it, it won't be anytime soon – and he won't be doing it in Shelton. I picture Steve wanting to open such a business in New Haven. And second, he doesn't have the capital to open such a business, anyway. Maybe ten or twenty years from now."

"And do we have the capital?" Fran asks.

I sigh. "Maybe. We could look into getting a small business loan, couldn't we?"

The seed was planted, and the wheels were in motion. Fran and I left Jamaica energized. It was hard to believe that after almost retiring from the theater a second time, we were now going to open up our own theater. In the process, we acted fast. A force we had no control over propelled us forward. We located a business space on Center Street in downtown Shelton that was vacant. It had once been a bank, and it seemed like a great place to open an intimate theater. Our plan was that it would be a multi-faceted business – not only a theater and bookstore, as my nephew had envisioned it, but also a coffee shop, replete with lattes, cappuccinos, espressos, and pastry.

THE FOUNDING OF CENTER STAGE

Having no real prior experience operating a full-time business, getting a business loan wasn't in the cards, so we opened a $150,000 home equity loan on our home. Why not? If I could use furniture from our home for productions, why not bankroll our home equity to make our dream come true? At least that was my thinking. If I could go back in time, I'm not sure I would risk such a loan again.

A few years after opening the home equity line of credit, I would joke about making risky money decisions. "If you want sound money advice," I would say to friends, "let me tell you what I did with mine, and if you do just the opposite you'll be good!"

I had already made one major money blunder when I left teaching. Being young and feeling brash and bold, I had withdrawn the money I had contributed to teachers' retirement to purchase a new car, thinking I wasn't going back to teaching. The eight thousand dollars I withdrew at the time would cost me *eighty* thousand to buy back almost thirty years later. In both the case of my teachers' retirement plan and eventually paying back the balance of the home equity loan, I needed to mainly use the income from my parents' estate. These decisions meant that my children will receive a smaller inheritance when Fran and I are gone than they otherwise would have.

What I was also learning about myself during my theatrical odyssey is that I am a risk taker, something I hadn't previously realized. Even while I was taking risks, I didn't realize I was. Certainly, leaving teaching with a wife and two small children at thirty was risky, and opening our own theater was riskier still.

I recall standing outside our parents' house with my older brother Edmund after one of our weekly visits, telling him about our plans. He just looked at me, and said, "You've got brass balls, man. I could never do what you're doing."

It was true. I think being a risk taker goes hand in hand with being a creator. There were smaller risks leading up to the opening of a theater. To choose a large scale musical like *The Music Man* as our first directing endeavor was certainly a risk. To walk away from the security of a tenured teaching position was yet another. To choose to begin a summer theater group with no capital was, undoubtedly, a risk. To open our own theater camp was another. To direct and produce challenging plays like *Les Mis*, *Evita*, and *Chess* were still others, for sure. The list goes on and on.

That said, it was a very exciting time, converting the Center Street building into a full-time theater. Fran flew to Denver to attend a seminar on how to open and run a bookstore business, and a building contractor friend got busy renovating the interior of our place.

The wheels were turning. A small stage was built. Our contacts from the world of theater got on board. Fred Santore from Horizon Sound set us up with a sound system to be paid for when we were able. Hugh Hallinan, who ran Bridgeport's Downtown Cabaret Theatre, sold us and installed an appropriate lighting system to suit the needs of our small space. Bookshelves and books were ordered; coffee and cheesecake decided upon; the small space was being furnished and outfitted from floor to ceiling. Fran and I and our daughters, who would become such a vital part of our successful team, all felt invigorated.

I remember meeting with the landlord to sign the lease. "You'll be an LLC, correct?" he asked.

"Oh, definitely," I replied, not having the slightest idea what an LLC was. But we made another call, and a lawyer friend created our LLC. We decided to call the business *Center Stage on Center Street* (or just *Center Stage* for short), but we had difficulty thinking of a tagline. Fran's hair stylist solved that problem. While doing Fran's hair, she said, "That's easy. Your tagline should be: 'Book, Beans, and Broadway'!" Fran and I both loved it.

We would also need a logo. I contacted Marianne Feroce, a parent of two of our performers who was a gifted artist, and she created the logo that would go on a lighted sign on the front of the building – the words "Center Stage" set in a theatrical font with small white lights around the perimeter, the words "on Center Street" below the box in the same font, and "Books, Beans, and Broadway" in an elegant script topped off with line art of a coffee cup and a book. Marianne added a star here and there for good measure, and the various elements of the design blended in a symbiotic manner, perfectly expressing the nature of our business. When the sign was created and installed, it was one of the most exciting moments of our storied life in the theater.

Our daughters, now in their twenties, who had run our theater camp for years were key in the building of Center Stage. From rolling up their sleeves and painting to planning a theater education program to be delivered year round to directing children, teens, and adults, their impact was critical to the growth and success of the organization, as the reader will see in future chapters.

I'll always remember the planning and zoning meeting at which we received approval to open our theater. The P & Z members couldn't have been happier to give us their seal of approval. I also remember that, at work, our school principal had told a fellow colleague that we were going to die downtown. His perspective didn't bother me in the least. I can be quite a cynic myself, and downtown Shelton wasn't thriving at the time. My colleague and friend replied, "I wouldn't be so sure. Gary and Fran have a great track record." Hearing about the exchange ignited in me an even greater desire to succeed.

At the time, my father, sadly, was sick with cancer. One of my most bittersweet memories was when I swung by to show him the place weeks before we opened. He couldn't get out of the car, but we looked through the windows and he could see the tradesman, busy at work, renovating the walls and floors through the large windows.

"Now don't charge an arm and a leg for a cup of coffee," Dad said. "This isn't Starbucks!"

"Yeah, okay, Dad, we won't," I replied.

"But don't give the goddamn stuff away either," he continued. "I know your wife, and she'll give it away if you let her."

That was Dad. He never met a thought he didn't want to express, and you could never win with him. But I knew that he was excited for us and proud of what we were about to do.

Sadly, Dad died on January 25, 2005, the day the bookshelves were delivered a few weeks before we opened. He would never get to see Center Stage in action.

On Valentine's Day, we had our Grand Opening, attended by a great many friends and supporters who enjoyed light refreshments while browsing our bookshelves and marveling at our kitschy theater space. We were a welcome addition to the business community in downtown Shelton. A former Drama Club member who had been doing film work as an extra stopped by that day. He was knocked out, saying, "It's like someone took an Off Broadway theater and plopped it down on Center Street in Shelton." I couldn't have felt prouder of our space and the adventure we were about to undertake.

ACT I, SCENE 12

Shortly after we opened, we were approached by a local businessman whose four children had all appeared in our productions while they were in high school or college. Don Opatrny suggested to us that while we knew a lot about theater, he suspected that we knew very little about running a business. He offered his services as business manager, gratis, until we could afford to start paying him. Fran and I agreed that he was right – we didn't know much about business – so Don came on board.

I had known Don, not only through his kids, but also from working together a few times on a retreat program for teens. He reminded me of self-help gurus I had read when I was that young thirty-year-old who left teaching to seek a greater income – Norman Vincent Peale (*You Can if You Think You Can*) and Zig Ziglar (*See You at the Top*). He was successful and impeccable in dress and manner, a wonderful family man. A devout Catholic, Don wore a cross around his neck, prompting a local merchant to ask me, "Is that guy working for you some kind of minister?"

Don asked us how many productions we were planning to offer. We explained that we hadn't thought a lot about it. Talk about having no business plan! We figured we'd offer regular evenings of acoustic music most weekends and perhaps two or three small cast productions per year.

Don had other ideas. At an early meeting, he strongly recommended that we put together a full season of plays and start canvassing for subscribers. It sounded a little grandiose to us. A full season of plays? Subscribers? Little us?

"How many plays per season?" I asked.

Don squinted and pursed his lips. "I'm going to say seven."

"Seven? Are you trying to kill us?" I moaned.

Fran shared my reservation. "That's asking a lot, Don. I don't know how we'll pull that off considering the bookstore and all we have on our plates with that."

Don replied with candor: "I know it'll be challenging. But trust me – Gary and Fran Scarpa are known for directing plays, not for selling books."

He had a point.

Still, we were also directing the Youth CONNection summer production, so that would make eight.

But Don's logic was essentially on the mark, and moving forward, we planned seven productions and started asking our patrons to become season subscribers. Everything happened the way Don had suggested. Audiences flocked to Center Stage, and our subscriber list began to grow.

THERE'S NO BUSINESS LIKE SHOW BUSINESS

This work was different from what we had done in the past. Through the years, we had mainly directed high school and college students. But now we'd be directing adults as we would be producing plays with age-appropriate casts. We had directed two productions with adults, *Fiddler on the Roof* and *Mame*, both years ago with the Orange Players, but otherwise our work had been limited to kids.

Casting seven productions would become a challenge. In my mind, I felt we knew a good many people who had acting experience. There were the alumni of the Shelton High School Drama Club and the Youth CONNection, and we had friends from college and community theater. But finding actors who are the right age and type for seven plays per year would be a challenge.

After all, Shelton is not New York, where a director has his pick from thousands of actors. I often found myself recruiting people to audition.

In our haste to get a first production up and running, we chose to produce *Steel Magnolias*, and, too overwhelmed to hold auditions, we simply asked five women we knew, including our daughter Mia, to appear in the production.

Those first experiences mounting plays with the Shelton High School Drama Club and the Youth CONNection were very special to us, and our first production at Center Stage was no less special. We even have a photo of our first rehearsal where all of us are wearing coats because the building didn't yet have heat. What memories!

We would quickly transition to holding auditions, but the right people for some roles were not among the audition candidates. Besides the fact that we sometimes needed to recruit actors, we also found that, as often as not, we would need to cast and direct adults who had little or no experience.

LESSON:

I have a theory, you see, that there is an actor inside of all of us...

I would learn that, in the world of amateur theater, there are seasoned actors who audition for and perform in plays throughout the region – something that didn't surprise me at all. I'm sure that's true in every part of the country. These are people who may have worked professionally when they were younger or who may not have chosen to pursue professional careers but could have. We had quite a few such skilled actors at Center Stage through the years. But I personally loved introducing adults to the stage who had no prior experience – or reintroducing them after a long absence. Often, their experiences on the stage at forty, fifty, sixty and beyond gave them a new lease on life.

I have a theory, you see, that there is an actor inside of all of us, and it was especially gratifying to me to bring that actor out... to take on the challenge of, say, having someone new to the stage be cast opposite a seasoned performer, and to help that person reach a level of excellence where the audience couldn't tell the difference between the two.

In the casting process, Fran would often say to me, "Do you really have that much confidence in this new person to succeed?" to which I would reply, "I have that much confidence in *myself* to help them succeed."

In mentioning this, I think of a young woman who had somehow heard something that prejudiced her against me. Not having ever worked under my direction before, she told a fellow candidate that she heard I treated everyone like a teenager. That simply wasn't true. I like how one of the most talented actors who worked under me put it. "You meet actors where they are," he said.

I would no more direct a novice actor in the same way that I would direct a skilled actor than I would, if I were a music teacher, teach a student who never touched the clarinet the same way I would teach an experienced clarinetist. It is basic math to say a novice needs more guidance than a veteran. I certainly wouldn't hand a clarinet to a new student and say, "Here, figure out how to play this thing since I don't want to risk offending you by showing you how to play it." He needs to be shown which keys and holes in the instrument correspond to which notes on the musical scale. How would he otherwise learn? To suggest that someone new to the stage should "find his way" without lots of guidance is foolhardy in my opinion.

LESSON:

...our work in theater had an energy of its own...an energy that was capable of overcoming and solving each and every challenge we met.

In amateur theater, we deal with varying levels of ability and experience in the same productions, and each one needs to be directed accordingly for optimum success. In education, it's known as "individualized instruction." All actors are not created equal. They have different levels of ability and experience.

Casting was just one of many challenges we hadn't fully anticipated. The reality of the matter is, if we had anticipated every challenge and every bump in the road, we would never have opened Center Stage; in fact, we would have never begun directing in the first place. The lesson is that our work in theater had an energy of its own...an energy that was capable of overcoming and solving each and every challenge we met.

Running a full-time theater is a marriage in and of itself, not very different, I don't feel, from running a restaurant. Center Stage consumed us. It wouldn't, in fact, be hyperbole to say it swallowed us whole. What seemed like a great idea on the pristine white sand of a beach in Jamaica, in reality, turned out to be more than we expected.

And let's not forget that, besides the bookstore/coffee shop and educational aspects of the business, I was still working full-time as a guidance counselor at Shelton High School. So my workday began at seven-thirty in the morning and often lasted until ten or later at night. Additionally, with my father gone, I visited my mother every night after rehearsal, spending an hour or more with her. I would get to her at 10 p.m. and stay until 11:30. In the process, I would bring her a Tupperware container of whatever our family had eaten for dinner that night. On Fridays and Saturdays, she typically attended our performances, seeing each and every play as many as eight times. She was a regular fixture in the front row at a performance, and our subscribers, actors, and crew made a fuss over her. She loved it.

That said, it was a grueling, albeit exhilarating, pace. As in the case of Don Opatrny, the universe kept providing for us. Another detail we hadn't planned for was set construction. Fran had convinced her good friend, JoEllen Lisi, to climb aboard and run our box office and coffee counter. JoEllen had a young adult son who was a sheetrocker. She recruited her son, along with a friend of his, to build the scenery for our first few productions, *Steel Magnolias* and *Nunsense*. After a long day of work, I'm sure Chris Lisi and his buddy weren't overly excited about building scenery, but they did it.

THE WIZARD OF CENTER STAGE

Then, perhaps at our third production, I was approached by a patron who was there to see the play. He told me that, although he had no prior experience in theater, he had always had an interest in set building and maybe even set design. He was a mechanical engineer by trade and an artist by avocation. At that moment, I thought to myself, "Build sets, maybe, but design them? I don't think so, buddy!"

Thankfully, he visited me again, showing me an album of his artwork. Among the pictures was one of a multi-colored, lifelike giraffe, probably ten feet tall, that he had constructed out of fiberglass.

I was sold. Ron Baldwin joined our volunteers, designing and leading the construction of our scenery for the remainder of our years at Center Stage and beyond. Ron turned out to be a wizard! There didn't seem to be anything he couldn't do, working his magic from show to show: a gigantic Buddha statue expertly sculpted out of Styrofoam for *The King and I*; the complete set of four "Audrey II" puppets – the biggest, large enough to swallow actors – for the play *Little Shop of Horrors*; an automatic revolving stage floor that we used for multiple productions; self-made mechanized rollers in the low ceiling of our small stage that allowed us to, instead of "fly" in multiple backdrops (for a show like *Gypsy*), "roll" them in – backdrops, by the way, which Ron designed and painted himself. Ron was more interested in building than painting, but when a set design required *detail* painting, it was just another skill in his bag of tricks. Our stage became a virtual laboratory of engineering magic.

Going forward, Ron, clad in comfortable overalls and flannel shirt, would become a daily fixture at Center Stage – a man who was proud of his gargantuan contribution to our theater and who continuously brought us new customers as he shared his handiwork with friends of his.

Fran and I loved our small space on Center Street because it required that we think out of the box, and with Ron on our team, we could do lots of things. For instance, we mounted productions of *To Kill a Mockingbird*, *Requiem for a Heavyweight*, and *You Can't Take it with You* in the round, with Ron's small crew creating suggestive scenery in corners of the space along with multi-level seating on the stage and on another open side of the room. We moved bookcases out of the way to accommodate the seating arrangement.

Our audiences never quite knew what to expect as the configuration of the space would change from play to play. Would the play be staged in the round? Or would it be on our small stage, with scene changes happening on the mechanical revolve Ron had installed? Would a small pit band for musicals be tucked into the back corner of our minuscule wings, or would it be behind a scrim, or would it be out on the floor next to a bookcase? They never knew what kind of magic Ron had up his sleeve for them.

In those first few years, Fran and I not only directed but sometimes we acted, not so much because we wanted to play parts but because we felt it was good business for our customers to see us do so. Sometimes, we acted because it was so challenging to find people the right age to perform in our productions that we did it ourselves. A few times, we acted in small cast plays because it seemed easier than trying to gather a larger cast. For instance, together we did the two person Neil Simon play, *Plaza Suite*, and I performed the one man play, *Give 'em Hell, Harry!*, based on President Truman. In a few cases, an actor dropped out of a play mid-stream, and Fran or I took over the role. Those instances were especially stressful.

In the meantime, early in the life of Center Stage, I had gone back to directing the Shelton High School Drama Club productions. During these years, the directing team for major musicals, whether with the Youth CONNection or the Drama Club, would be Gina and I or Mia and I rather than Fran and I.

We wouldn't have predicted it, but Fran steered the business side of the ship. Considering I was still working in education for the first seven years of Center Stage and not available during the workday, it's simply how it worked out. Also, I was at my peak creatively. My father once said, "A man is at his most productive stage in his fifties," which is certainly how it was for me. Fran would rather have been more involved on the creative side, but she would say at the time, "I am doing what I do, so that you can do what you do." It was a statement Ron Baldwin had made to me as well, and it was gratifying to have these two key people – my official and unofficial partners in theater – be so supportive of my creative drive and energy.

LESSON:
My father once said, "A man is at his most productive stage in his fifties," which is certainly how it was for me.

Even though she hadn't had a background in business, Fran attended workshops at every opportunity and became well-versed in the art of writing grant proposals. She also worked egolessly and cooperatively with board members who had accounting and business backgrounds. Without a doubt, as the executive director of Center Stage, she learned to become quite a businesswoman. It's safe to say that the success of the organization was due to two factors: the artistic quality of our productions and Fran's leadership on the business end of Center Stage.

Nonetheless, despite being immersed in the business side, Fran was still costuming every show, occasionally directing or choreographing, and giving periodic cabaret performances as well. It was quite a life. She did more than anyone could ever ask of her, and she never stopped until she retired.

THE BIRTH OF "FALL CAB"!

At the time, *Adaptations* was still running at Shelton High School as a fundraiser for the Drama Club, as it still is at the writing of this book. Gina had been directing an adaptation each year, and early in the life of Center Stage I was so taken with her thirty-minute take on *Hairspray* with the freshman class that I asked her to bring it to Center Stage. I was sure our audience would love it. Since the adaptation was not long enough to fill an evening, she gathered a cast of twenty-something-year-old friends and also directed an adaptation of *RENT* for the second act.

The production was such a hit, in fact, that we decided to do a fall production with teens every year at Center Stage. The adaptation of *Hairspray* morphed into a cabaret event that would be known as the Teen Musical Theater Workshop or "Fall Cab" as the participants liked to call it. It would be a cabaret-style review for high schoolers, presenting two or three numbers from a variety of musicals. Mia joined her sister in directing the productions, and I was fascinated to realize a few years later that it was the performance opportunity our teens loved and looked forward to most. I was almost jealous actually. Here I was directing splashy productions on the Shelton High School stage in the spring and summer, and the very same kids looked forward to Fall Cab each year with greater anticipation and excitement. There was something very magical about Fall Cab, though – an energy and an excitement that Gina and Mia instilled in the event.

Actually, it's no wonder that Fall Cab quickly became just about everyone's favorite show. It brought together talented kids from a variety of high schools. One year, we had participants from as many as twelve schools. Rehearsals took place only on Saturdays and Sundays so as not to conflict with school activities, and Gina and Mia often treated the kids to a jumbo box of Dunkin' Munchkins before rehearsals. Nothing said autumn like Fall Cab since our teens previewed their performance on UNICEF Day at arguably Shelton's most popular attraction, Jones Family Farms. Also, each October, a cast Halloween party was included in the rehearsal schedule. So, it was an amazing social experience where kids made new friends from near and far, shared common experiences and feelings, and had loads of fun.

Not that Fall Cab was a walk in the park for our teen performers. I'd call it more like musical theater boot camp. Once rehearsal began, it was all business. Gina and Mia had the highest expectations, and considering they were presenting numbers from a variety of musical theater styles, it was an amazing learning experience. And we couldn't argue with it from a business perspective. The production cost very little money to mount, and there was never an empty seat.

These early Fall Cab productions gave birth to a very important group of teens. Three Shelton cast members teamed up with three "Bunnells," investing themselves in our work at Center Stage in a way we could never have anticipated.

I would come to call Stephen Chueka, Samantha Melvin, Casey Perruzzi, Melissa Rampton, Katherine Sedlock, and Justin Zenchuk "the Big Six," and, despite being high school students, their contribution to Center Stage was critical in the most positive sense of the word.

An evening at Center Stage called for a full staff. There were guests to be seated, coffee and cheesecake to be sold, not to mention books, and a full length play that required a crew behind the scenes.

These six teens were on hand to take care of any and all of the above tasks. They each gravitated to an aspect of theater that interested them most – lighting, costuming, scenic painting, hair and makeup, and more. And every now and then, one or another of them would appear as an actor in a regular season production.

We told the Big Six that we never expected to have all of them on hand, and that we could afford to pay only two of them per performance. We would soon learn that they couldn't care less whether they were paid or not; they simply wanted to be involved. Almost always, the six would be on hand every Friday and Saturday night, and the two on the schedule would be paid while the other four volunteered their time. Because of their genuine passion for theater, they were happy to assist with whatever needed doing, which included making cappuccinos and selling books. And because these six young people were so dedicated, we sometimes made theater classes available to them free of charge. So, besides learning about the behind-the-scenes world of theater, hands-on, they had the opportunity to hone their skills as performers in the classroom.

Their work behind the scenes resulted in all six developing into highly skilled performers, all of whom played principal roles for us at Center Stage, and two of whom, as adults, would become our successors as directors of the Shelton High School Drama Club.

We were fortunate, once more, when this group of very special teens committed themselves to us in those early years at Center Stage. Their contribution was significant to say the least.

It's worth mentioning that during these early Center Stage years, neither Fran nor I nor our two daughters drew pay. Fran and I didn't draw a salary until our third or fourth year, and Gina and Mia directed and choreographed shows without pay for at least five years. As a family, we devoted ourselves fully to the goal of making Center Stage a success.

That said, so many volunteers gave of themselves without compensation – not only Ron Baldwin, but anyone who ever helped Ron build, paint, or decorate scenery, as well as adults and teens who assisted with costume organization and alterations, ushering, selling refreshments, gathering props, and a host of other tasks. Seeing all of the wonderful volunteer help we received through the first year or two, my mother would often remark with her signature reaction, "Shocking...just shocking!"

I remember Don Opatrny, understanding Ron Baldwin's immense value to Center Stage, felt that Ron needed to be paid and urged me to discuss it with Ron.

"He doesn't understand me, does he?" Ron asked.

"No, I guess not," I said with a level of chagrin.

"Besides," Ron added. "If I wanted to get paid, you wouldn't be able to afford me!"

I knew he was right. Ron continued freely giving his services for years to come.

Even our friend and box office manager, JoEllen Lisi, while one of the few paid employees on our small staff, worked all performances for free for well over a decade before a great board chair, the late Susan Coyle, insisted JoEllen should be paid for her services.

These are a few examples of how incredibly giving people like Ron, JoEllen, and the Big Six were instrumental in helping Center Stage to succeed. It's no secret that volunteers are the backbone of any nonprofit. There were scores of people, too numerous to mention, who came together to make our work in theater happen through the years. As anyone in the world of amateur theater well knows, we wouldn't have succeeded without our wonderful volunteers.

ACT I, SCENE 13

Perhaps two years into the life of the theater, our business manager felt strongly that we needed to become a nonprofit. As he was about many things, Don Opatrny was right. Fran and I hadn't considered that option upon opening Center Stage. Instead, in our excitement, we forged ahead, opening the business without considering all options.

As a nonprofit, we could apply for grants, and any donations patrons gave would be tax deductible. Don felt the bookstore couldn't survive, considering the competition that came from large book retailers like Barnes & Noble and Borders, not to mention a *little* book business known as Amazon. Clearly, more people were shopping online, especially for books.

We didn't like agreeing with him on this matter. We had invested a lot of time and money into the book business end of our place, and we felt very attached to it. But we also realized that in order to make a small independent bookstore succeed, the owners need to really "work" it. We were far too busy producing seven productions a year to give the bookstore the attention it required. With each passing month, we were selling more and more theater tickets and fewer and fewer books.

As we organized and put our non-profit status in place, we slowly phased out the bookstore, not ordering anything new and selling what we had on the shelves for half price. It hurt to watch the bookstore go south. After all, of our one hundred and fifty thousand dollar investment in opening the business, at least sixty had gone into purchasing our book inventory and shelves. There's no nice way to say it, except to say it was a sixty thousand dollar personal loss for Fran and me.

As we progressed into non-profit-ness, Don's self-admitted tendency to maintain control of multiple aspects of the business combined with some sticky inner politics precipitated by our new board of directors resulted in us unfortunately parting company with him. This was one experience of several during our years at Center Stage that we wish had worked out differently. Some things just seemed destined to happen.

I am happy that we were able to maintain something of a friendship with Don because, without a doubt, he always had our best interests in mind.

Upon becoming a nonprofit, we rolled our Youth CONNection summer production into the Center Stage season in order to make life a little saner for us, if we can ever call the theatrical life a sane one. We would also reduce our season from seven productions to six and then eventually to five plays. Along the way, we often offered cabaret weekends. For cabaret events we broke down the theater seating and set up tables and chairs, allowing customers to bring their own refreshments. In those early years, we had a wide array of events from an Elvis impersonator to a jazz trio to a comedy night to a Beatles tribute band to a Renaissance event, featuring a fire eater and a full course meal. I don't know how we did it. And when we needed something else to fit in, Fran, Mia, and other alumni of our shows provided great cabaret entertainment.

A growing community of actors performed in our productions, from alumni who had been in our high school and summer plays, now in their thirties, forties, and fifties...to seasoned actors who were now auditioning...to newbies whom I had recruited from one place or another. The headshots of the growing number of actors would adorn the walls of the space, giving Center Stage 1.0 even more of a theatrical ambiance. It reminded me of seeing *The Fantasticks*, the longest running musical in the history of New York theater, at the Sullivan Street Playhouse in Greenwich Village where the walls were decorated with the pictures of the many actors, some of them famous, who had appeared through the years in the play. Like the Sullivan Street Playhouse, the pictures on our walls were a testament to an emerging history that was part of the Center Stage story.

SAYING GOODBYE TO MOM

As had always been the case since Fran and I began directing in 1976, there continued to be an inextricable link between our personal and theatrical lives. As stated, my mother had been attending multiple performances of each production, rarely missing a Friday or Saturday night performance. For the most part, it was the only time she left the house after the death of my father. All dressed up in her signature colors, red and black, and sitting in a reserved seat in the front row, Mom became a favorite of our patrons and subscribers.

So typical of life in the theater, going out for a bite or a drink after a show was integral to our lifestyle – and Mom loved joining us. We were regulars at a local diner after just about every performance. We became friendly with the owner, and he loved to host anywhere from a dozen to forty of our cast and crew night after night. We were on a first name basis with all of the servers, and it was great fun, with the group of us closing the place at 12:30 or 1:00 in the morning.

For me, I will always remember Mom ordering Belgian waffles with whipped cream and strawberries or red Jell-O (and she wasn't pleased when they only had yellow!). And even though she was in her eighties, she kept us in stitches on those evenings.

I recall expounding one night that, given the hectic pace of our life, when Fran and I went on vacation, we wanted to go somewhere like an island, where there was nothing to do but rest, relax, and read.

With perfect comic timing, Mom added, "...and have sex!"

The entire table cracked up!

"Oh my God, Mom," I said. "Is that what you and Dad did on vacation?"

With an impish smile she responded, "Yes, and I was a *willing* participant," sending the entire group of us into even greater peals of laughter.

I relate this story because theater touched every aspect of our lives, including my relationship with my mother when she neared the end of her life.

LESSON:

...there continued to be an inextricable link between our personal and theatrical lives.

A lover of entertainment and film, my mother was a glamorous lady. I remember Saturday nights when I was a boy, and she and my dad would go out to balls and dinner dances. My brother Edmund and I would sit at the kitchen table while she put on her makeup, and when she came out of her bedroom a short while later, decked out in a gown, a mink stole, and sparkling rhinestone jewelry, she'd pose as if she were an authentic Hollywood starlet. The mothers of other boys in the neighborhood were normal moms; ours was a movie star!

Attending our plays allowed her to retain some of that glamour in her old age. In her eighties, black had become her color, and more often than not, she sported her bright red jacket topped off with a gold necklace at every show.

It was during a performance of *Little Women* when our daughter Mia, who was playing Jo March, noticed that her grandmother was asleep. Mia expressed her concern to me later that night. "It's completely uncharacteristic of Gramma to fall asleep at a play," she said.

For us, that night began a slow descent downhill in my mother's health. We went into a cycle of hospital stays, which led to a three-month stint in a nursing home. Mom was never the same after that. Once she was released, another cycle of emergency visits to our local hospital took place, and in the summer of 2009, my brother and I were advised to bring her to Hospice in Branford.

That summer, I visited Mom every day at Hospice. At night I was in rehearsal for a Youth CONNection production of *The Music Man* – ironic that as she neared the end of her life, we were repeating the show Fran and I began with.

SUMMER, 2009

My cell phone rings on Saturday morning. It is Edmund. "Gar, how do you feel about me sitting in the pit for the last show tonight?" he asks.

"That sounds great."

"Yeah...you know, I didn't feel I could realistically make the commitment, what with Mom and all. But I've never missed a summer show, and I've played The Music Man *with you before, so why the hell not?"*

"Yeah," I reply. "Like I said. I'd love to have you with us tonight."

Edmund also knows Mom herself has never missed a performance of a summer show before this production, and he needs to be there.

As Fran and I walk to the center of the stage to make the curtain speech, the audience greets us with a genuine round of applause. Looking out at the sea of faces, I begin. "Good evening, ladies and gentleman, and welcome to our closing performance of The Music Man.*"*

Fran stands beside me, my partner in theater and in life, but she won't be speaking tonight. This curtain speech will be mine, but Fran is my emotional support.

"I'd like to direct your attention," I continue, "to the two empty seats in the fourth row to my left. Many of you know that, historically, those two seats were reserved for my parents."

The audience grows somber as they no doubt hear my voice wavering.

"You might also know that my father passed away four years ago. Tonight, though, on behalf of my family, especially along with my brother Edmund who is in the orchestra pit, I'd like to dedicate this performance to our mother, our sweet Lily, who is currently a patient at Connecticut Hospice in Branford."

A collective sigh rings through the auditorium. Fran edges closer to me and takes my hand in hers.

"This is the first summer production my mother has missed since we founded the Youth CONNection in 1983. In fact, until the last few months, Mom never missed a show that Fran and I produced since we began directing more than thirty years ago. For this production, I chose not to sell the two seats my mom and dad sat in throughout our career. Thank you for your kindness, and we hope you enjoy the show."

Two nights later, I arrive home at 10:00 p.m. after "striking" the set, the all-day task of tearing down and disposing of scenery.

My cell phone rings. It is Hospice. Mom has passed, they tell me.

We immediately head for Branford with Fran at the wheel.

"She waited until the show was over," Fran says.

I nod. Unable to control my emotions, I sob.

The loss of a mother is a moment, no matter how you prepare, no matter how many journal entries you write, no matter how much talking you do, that you can never be fully ready for.

When we arrive at Hospice, Edmund and his wife pull in at the same time. We embrace as brothers...bonded and blessed to be Lily's children.

A solitary ceiling light illuminates our Lily. She is an image in white, swaddled in an immaculate sheet, and even her graying hair appears snow white. Her eyes are closed and her face, in the soft light, is serene. I feel that I am seeing Mom in her authentic form... her pure form. Hospice has attended even to this spiritual detail, and I think of a quote by Rainer Maria Rilke I had recently discovered, "Love and death are the great gifts that are given to us; mostly they are passed on unopened." I hope, when it comes to my dear mother, I haven't left these gifts unopened.

A few days later at the wake, as I receive heartfelt condolences from a friend, Mia taps me on the shoulder. "Look, Dad," she says. There before us in the entranceway I see a long line of our high school and college kids from Center Stage, perhaps fifty or more young people, all decked out in black with red highlights (ties, headbands, scarves), a tribute to our Lily. I swallow hard and it's impossible to hold back the tears.

It is a moment I will never forget. As our wedding had been directly linked to our work in theater, the cast of *The Music Man* in attendance at Trinity Episcopal Church in 1976, so too was this newer cast of *The Music Man*, clad in red and black, in attendance at Riverview Funeral Home to pay their respects to our mother in 2009.

CENTER STAGE 2.0

As we approached the end of our five-year lease, we were encouraged by our board and other advisors to try to negotiate a better lease going forward considering we had done no negotiating when we opened Center Stage on Center Street. The landlord, unfortunately, would only reduce the rental cost by a small amount, and we felt it was best to move to a new location. The truth was, we had outgrown the space on a few levels, both seating capacity and the scope of what we were doing on the small stage.

Along with our small board, we met with a select group of good people in the Shelton community to help us locate another possibility. Ultimately, a member of the committee and future board chair, Sue Coyle, was good friends with a businessman who owned property where several closed car dealerships were located. The plan was that the property would eventually become a shopping center, which it is, in fact, today. Sue asked her friend if he would allow us to use the space as an interim location for a period of a year or two while we found a permanent solution to our problem.

We would nickname this location Center Stage 2.0, the second of the three locations that Center Stage would inhabit.

We moved to the old Frascatore Cadillac-Oldsmobile building on Bridgeport Avenue in Shelton in the fall of 2010. Before we knew it, we had a contingent of a good one hundred actors, volunteers, and theater patrons assisting us in moving our entire operation from Center Street to Bridgeport Avenue. It was truly a beautiful example of a community rallying around an organization it cared about.

On the day of the move, Center Stage 1.0 was a hub of activity as lines of people passed chairs, lighting instruments, and more up the stairs to be loaded on a convoy of trucks, vans, and cars which transported our gear to Center Stage 2.0.

When the building was all but empty, Fran and I sat down, just the two of us, and we cried. Our five years in the space had been exciting and exhausting, both physically and emotionally. We had seen our bookstore die and our theater thrive. Saying goodbye was difficult, to say the least.

Today, the Center Street building is a great local restaurant, and whenever Fran and I dine there, it is a nostalgic experience. Mainly, besides remembering the many wonderful experiences at Center Stage on Center Street, we find ourselves shaking our heads in disbelief that it ever happened at all.

Gina and Mia had been in the midst of rehearsing Fall Cab at Center Stage 1.0, but we weren't quite sure the vacant car dealership would be ready. Although we had set dates, we were in the dark at that point. The car dealership building had been vacant for months, and the plumbing and electricity had been shut off. Ron Baldwin and a small team of volunteers went to work building a stage, working at night with battery powered flood lights. I can't remember who hung our lighting grid, but somehow it happened. Given the move and the progress inside the building, it was as if we were standing in the midst of a miracle.

With Fall Cab only about a week away, Fran was on the phone with utility companies. When the United Illuminating company explained to her it was impossible to restore electricity to the building in such a short span of time, Fran told them that their response was unacceptable, that we had fifty teens who had a show to perform, and that it was non-negotiable – they would have to power the building before opening night. It was a perfect example of the old theatrical adage, "the show must go on." It might have been only a day or two before opening night that power was restored to the building. With Fran's persuasiveness, the city building inspector signed off on the use of the building, and our Fall Cab cast was in business. Talk about going down to the wire. It's interesting to note that Fall Cab had rehearsed for weeks in a different space – at Center Stage 1.0 – and would perform in front of an audience at Center Stage 2.0 with hardly any rehearsal in the new space.

At the time, Fran texted a quote to Sue Coyle, then a board member, who had secured the use of the building and helped us get started on Bridgeport Avenue: "We're more than friends; we're kind of like a small gang," and Sue replied, "We can never ask for another favor from anyone in this town."

The two women had a laugh after a stressful week, but Fall Cab opened on time!

At some point after leaving Center Stage 1.0, with the assistance of one of our finest adult actors, Jim Lones, we revised our logo since "books and beans" were no longer part of the equation. At the time, Jim was working in business with a graphic designer whom he asked to assist with the logo. With Jim's help, the artist revised our original design, keeping the white lettering "Center Stage" against a black background with the white lights, and now adding the word "Theatre" set on a slant in an eye-catching red script. That revised logo became our brand going forward and served us well.

I recently thought of logos while watching a wonderful documentary about the composer John Williams. Upon seeing the *Star Wars* logo, it occurred to me that it has become iconic. The evocative design, composed of simple block-style lettering outlined in yellow, the S connecting to the T in the word "star," set against a black background is so distinctive that if the same design were to use two different four-letter words, let's say "Slow Down," film fans would still understand they were seeing the *Star Wars* logo. I feel that's the mark of a great design – one that really works. Similarly, residents of Shelton and the region were likely to immediately make an association to Center Stage the moment they saw the design and the blend of the elements in the logo.

It's important to remember that, during these early Center Stage years, I was not only working full-time in the school system, but I was again directing the Drama Club shows. I would arrange the Center Stage season in a way that didn't conflict with the high school show.

As we began our time at Center Stage 2.0, our stress level was approaching the breaking point. Working two full-time jobs was taking its toll on me – and on us. We had some volunteers, but we needed more help. Our board chair suggested that we take some time off, maybe six months or even a year, while we caught our breath. Despite our level of stress, we found the suggestion, well meaning though it was, completely unacceptable. Fran and I knew we were riding a tidal wave of momentum, and we felt if we took a break, the momentum might be lost. Consequently, after Fall Cab, we forged ahead with our season.

THE PROS AND CONS OF CENTER STAGE 2.0

The building was an amazing facility for us. The main car showroom was spacious to say the least. While we had somehow crammed one hundred seats into the Center Street space, we could now fit almost two hundred people comfortably. And the new stage that Ron Baldwin and his team built was three or four times the size of the Center Stage 1.0 stage, giving us a lot more flexibility for scenery and staging options.

A second smaller showroom had wall-to-wall paneling and

served as our lobby, creating an elegant ambiance. The car dealership was equipped with a service garage, a vast space, the size of a football field, which gave us unlimited storage space. It was also our scene shop where, while one show was being performed, Ron Baldwin and company could build our next set and, in fact, even erect it in the garage when it served him to do so.

The building wasn't perfect. Being run down, there were several places where the ceiling leaked into our space, particularly in the dressing rooms where we interspersed buckets across the room. Luckily, the ceiling didn't leak over our audience. Another drawback was that there were only two single-use restrooms in the main part of the building. To move intermission along, I would literally usher patrons back into the dressing rooms where there were two more restrooms. "This is our cast, getting ready for Act II," I would quip in the process.

But it was hard to ignore the many plusses. Bridgeport Avenue in Shelton was becoming its own Boston Post Road, so there was a high volume of traffic passing by the building. The front of the theater space had floor to ceiling glass windows, which meant that at night when we were performing a play, cars passing by could see the actors on the stage from the road.

The result is that tickets were selling like hotcakes, and we were sold out or packed to near capacity for each and every performance. Personally, I felt I did some of my best work at Center Stage 2.0, especially in mounting dramas like *A Few Good Men*, *Twelve Angry Men*, and *On Golden Pond*.

Despite the temporary nature of our stay at Center Stage 2.0, we have many memories of our time there – some of them sweet and some painful. As we were preparing our first Christmas show, we received heartbreaking news. On a Friday night, the brother of an important Center Stage performer had been killed in a tragic car accident.

With rehearsal scheduled for the morning after the accident, I called our cast member and told her we would cancel, but she implored me to hold the rehearsal, feeling it would help her to attend. That morning was one of the most profound experiences I have ever had. We began by trying to review some harmonies, but given the dire circumstances, we couldn't continue with "business as usual." Before we knew it, the small group of us sat on the stage and talked about life and death, alternating between laughter and tears in the process. It was a rehearsal that I don't think any of us will ever forget and one of the most important memories of our years doing theater for me.

Concurrently, Gina and Mia were preparing their teens for the latest edition of Fall Cab, and before the opening night performance, they held a candlelight vigil with the cast in memory of a former Fall Cab participant and a longtime vocal student of Gina's who was also killed in the accident. It was a heartbreaking moment in our history, and one we and those young people who performed with us will never forget. Once more, our theatrical life proved to be about much more than the nuts and bolts of mounting shows. It was during heart wrenching times like these that we Scarpas realized that those who participated in our shows were our extended family...a family of choice...a family that we wanted and needed to be there for.

ACT I, SCENE 14

Though our time at Center Stage 2.0 would be relatively short, it made me wish that Bridgeport Avenue could be our permanent location. I couldn't help wishing that some miracle would happen, that our own Mr. Bogardus would manifest himself and give us the space for good, as the transformed curmudgeon had done in *The Bells of St. Mary's*. But no such angel would appear to us.

A miracle would occur during our time at Center Stage 2.0, though – a Christmas miracle, in a manner of speaking. Thinking of old films, we had presented a stage version of the Christmas classic, *Miracle on 34th Street*, that first winter. At the cast party after our closing night, I felt a renewed love for Christmas, a holiday I had become somewhat jaded about over the years.

As we celebrated that night, one cast member accompanied Fran on his guitar in an informal and impromptu version of "O Holy Night," a song she had become known for. As the two began, the buzz of activity at the party calmed down, and we all listened to a pure and simple rendition of the hymn. Moments later, a parent of one of our child performers sat at the piano and began playing carols as the children's cast gathered for another unplanned sing-along. It was truly an old-fashioned Christmas that warmed my heart.

But, despite the Christmas cheer we experienced, no Mr. Bogardus would emerge. The fact is that Sue Coyle's friend who owned the building had cancer and sadly died approximately a year after our arrival. His death hastened our departure from Center Stage 2.0 because things began to move faster with plans to knock down the building to make way for the new shopping center.

SEARCHING FOR CENTER STAGE 3.0

By my count, besides Fall Cab, we had delivered eight plays and at least two cabarets at Center Stage 2.0 before moving to a more permanent location. A committee was again formed to assist with finding a space. Talk of moving out of town was on the table, but Fran and I felt that, given the hectic pace of running a theater, we wanted to remain in town. Shelton residents made up the majority of our customer base, which wasn't to say that we didn't have patrons from out of town.

As it would happen, a local grade school had been vacant for a few years. Ironically, not only had our daughters and our grandson attended Lafayette School but so had my mother in the 1920s and 1930s. It felt like it was meant to be.

Along with two other nonprofits, the United Way and TEAM, we moved into Lafayette School in 2011. Once again, scores of volunteers of all ages came to our assistance in undertaking the Herculean task of moving a theater from one location to another. For us, Lafayette School would become Center Stage 3.0. Although we would have loved to stay on Bridgeport Avenue because of the high visibility and the volume of traffic on the road, we had confidence that Lafayette would be our permanent location, and Center Stage, in fact, is still housed there today.

A rent was negotiated with the mayor, only a third of what we had paid at Center Stage 1.0, and in this case, it included heat, electricity, and a custodian for the common areas, like the lobby, hallways, and restrooms. As much as we had loved our time at Center Stage 1.0, we now had, perhaps, ten times the space at a fraction of the cost.

Even better, plans were soon underway to rename the building, dedicating it to a local politician. It would take a few years to come to fruition, but Lafayette would eventually be renamed the Richard O. Belden Cultural Center in 2017. State Representative Richard O. Belden (1934 – 2007) had been as big a supporter of our work in theater as anyone in Shelton. While he was alive, Mr. Belden loved our productions, especially with teens, and it seemed he never missed a performance at Shelton High School, always staying after the curtain call to offer his congratulations to Fran and me. We couldn't have been happier that the building was named in his honor.

Once again, we were moving into a building that had not been a theater. The gymnasium would become our performance space, but there was no stage. When my children went to school there, portable staging had been used for school assemblies, but that wouldn't serve our purpose. We had the play *Harvey* scheduled for October of 2011, only a few weeks after our arrival, and it continued to be our practice never to skip a beat. Without a stage, our actors delivered the show from the gym floor in what is known as the three-quarters, while the audience sat on temporary risers on three sides of the action. As soon as *Harvey* closed, we hired two professional carpenters to help build a stage under Ron Baldwin's direction, once again, in just a matter of a few days. After all, we had no time to waste considering Fall Cab was up next on our schedule.

The school building really served our purpose well in so many ways. As we prepared to build our stage, the question was: what would be the best orientation for our stage in relation to the seating of the audience? Would we put it at one end of the gym where there was a basketball hoop? But Fran and I conferred and decided that it would serve our purpose better if we planned the theater space as a horizontal rather than a vertical orientation. Along the long wall of the basketball court where the team benches had been placed for games, there were three or four small rooms – storage areas, no doubt for gym equipment. Our vision was that these rooms be situated behind the stage and serve as dressing rooms. And placing the audience in a horizontal orientation would mean that the furthest any patron would be from the stage would be only eight rows back. On the other side of those storage rooms was a hallway with bathrooms, creating an even more expansive and practical backstage area.

The plan worked perfectly. The basketball hoops were removed from the backboards on the far left and right and behind the audience, and we fastened enlarged photos of past productions to the backboards, giving the space a nice theatrical ambiance, considering we couldn't completely hide the fact that it had been a gymnasium.

At Center Stage 3.0, when patrons walked in the door, they entered what would be our lobby which we eventually raised the funds to renovate, giving it a modern, theatrical vibe. The theater was immediately to the left, and our box office/administrative office, formerly the principal's office, to the right. In the backstage hallway, there was another small room which became what we would call our Wig Room. More and more, we were utilizing wigs in our shows, as we had observed on Broadway where most if not all performers wear wigs. Over time, we amassed several hundred wigs. We installed peg boards on the walls and hung the wigs for easy access. The Wig Room featured a large mirror where Fran would meet with each performer and make sure her wig was freshly styled and ready to go. It was in the Wig Room where Fran worked her magic on cast members, not only with their hair but with their hearts, creating a caring and loving environment, as only she can.

Continuing with our use of the school as a theater, we kind of spread out across the building, sometimes having to negotiate with the mayor since it remained a city building. The cafeteria became our scene shop where our sets would be constructed. The adjacent kitchen served as wood storage, a walk-in refrigerator became a shoe storage space, and a large kitchen storage closet became a hat storage room. We simply seized every inch of space we could.

We found empty classrooms to store other important items. One classroom became our prop room, where we set up shelving and organized everything from antique cameras to glassware;

another pair of classrooms became furniture storage; another pair, costume/wardrobe storage; and still other classrooms were used to deliver our theater education program or to rehearse when scenery needed building and painting details on the stage. The school nurse's office, at first, was used as a small rehearsal room or a space where we held auditions and board meetings. Eventually, with the help of a grant, we purchased three or four industrial level sewing machines and turned the nurse's office into a costume shop. With the guidance of our friend and costume consultant Richard Harding, we were doing more and more costume work utilizing volunteers, like Diane Chuba and Linda Gallo, who were skilled sewers. We even constructed a full set of maid's costumes for our 2018 Youth CONNection production of *Annie*.

LESSON:

It was in the Wig Room where Fran worked her magic on cast members, not only with their hair but with their hearts, creating a caring and loving environment, as only she can.

Considering Center Stage 3.0 was a city building, sometimes the mayor would need to take space away from us because he had a new organization moving into the building or because he felt we were spread out too much. His decisions, in these cases, led to some heated discussions in the boardroom when one board member or another thought the mayor was being unfair with us.

"Look," I would say, "before the mayor reduced our space, this was the best deal in the universe. Now it's only the best deal on the planet!"

Even when we lost some space, we adjusted and the building continued to serve our purpose quite nicely.

Come December, we staged an adaptation of the film *It's a Wonderful Life*, which would be our Christmas show that year. A year later, we decided on what would become, for some years, a tradition.

After *It's a Wonderful Life*, we began to alternate two shows from one year to another at Christmas: *A Center Stage Christmas*, a holiday variety show usually hosted by Fran, and *A Christmas Carol* with music by the great Alan Menken, famous for his work with both Disney and Broadway. Both shows offered up plenty of heart and Christmas spirit.

Our previous Christmas shows had always featured at least a few children, but this rotation of Christmas shows would be a wonderful mix of children, teens, and adults, with participants ranging in age from seven to seventy. For me, it had been that production of *Miracle on 34th Street* at Center Stage 2.0, and the homespun cast party afterward, that set in motion a desire on our part to look for and produce plays which featured intergenerational casts. We loved seeing scores of children grow up performing in these two rotating shows. This is what we have always felt community theater should be.

MRS. JONES! MRS. JONES! MRS. JONES!

A highlight of *A Center Stage Christmas*, besides Fran's warmth and beautiful singing, was a skit I borrowed from the Boy Scout Gang Show where I had begun performing as a child. As the skit went, a teenager would enter the auditorium and interrupt the show.

In the midst of Ed Strang announcing the next performer, the teen would wander down the aisle holding a maple tree sapling and interrupt the performance. "Mrs. Jones...Mrs. Jones...Mrs. Jones..."

Somewhat nonplussed, Ed would then say, "Pardon me, young man, but we're trying to do a show here. Is there something I can help you with?"

"Well," the somewhat nerdy young man would say, "Mrs. Jones ordered this tree and asked that it be delivered to this address."

Ed would ask if there was a Mrs. Jones in the audience, and

when no one responded, he would apologize, suggesting that maybe she was sick or delayed, and send the young man on his way. Twenty or thirty minutes later, the teen was back calling for Mrs. Jones, only now the tree had grown...and the same repartee took place again between Ed and the teenager. The young man returned again and again becoming more and more bewildered by the tree's growing size. When the audience exited the church basement where the show was held, much to their surprise, the voice of the boy calling Mrs. Jones from above could be heard. When they looked up, he was sitting on the bough of a giant maple tree outside the church.

In our Christmas shows, I played the part of the tree delivery boy, donning a flannel jacket and a comical hat and glasses, a la Jerry Lewis, and instead of a maple tree, I entered with a baby Christmas tree which grew and grew as the night went on. In our case, the host of the show was Fran, and our audiences delighted in the improvised dialogue between me and my wife as we tried to make each other break character, like a skit between Carol Burnett and Harvey Korman on the famous television show. At the end of the evening, I stood atop a twelve-foot ladder next to a giant evergreen tree outside of the theater.

To this day, people still mention the skit to me seven years after our retirement. The legendary Ed Strang would be proud!

Ironically, Fran is remembered from those shows for her magnificent singing, and I am remembered because of my silly skit. I don't mind a bit, though.

A NEW TRAGEDY

All Christmases weren't happy, though. Early in our stay at Center Stage 3.0, we were faced with another tragedy during a run of *A Christmas Carol*. On December 14, 2012, a Friday, along with the rest of the nation, we were devastated upon hearing tragic news of the Sandy Hook Elementary School shooting in nearby Newtown, Connecticut. Fran and I had a critical decision to make about our performance that night. Should we go ahead with the show or cancel it? Was it disrespectful to have a performance considering the tragedy and its close proximity to us? We decided, though, that the play's themes of kindness and compassion and its message of love was one our audience and all of us needed to hear on this night of all nights.

It wasn't easy for anyone involved, but our cast, from the youngest child to the oldest adult, bravely forged ahead. And when our children, in one scene dressed as angels, sang the deeply moving lyrics by Lynn Ahrens: *"Let the stars in the sky remind us of man's compassion. Let us love till we die, and God bless us every one!"* there wasn't a dry eye in the house. Alan Menken's sublime melody and Lynn Ahrens' poignant lyrics became a prayer for all of us to contemplate that evening.

Like the rehearsal a few years before when our cast faced the deaths of a cast member's brother and another friend, our theater was a place of healing and comfort.

During the next few years at Center Stage 3.0, we put our energies into upgrading our lighting system. We added a computerized lighting control board, and we acquired lighting instruments that Long Wharf Theater in New Haven was discarding since they were also upgrading their lighting system. My understanding was that Long Wharf would be the beneficiary of used lights from the Juilliard School of Music. In this way, one theatrical organization helps out another. We were honored to be part of this plan that trickled down, in a sense, from Juilliard to Long Wharf to Center Stage, and we were grateful to receive lights that were far superior to what we owned. We also finally paid our friend and colleague, Fred Santore, for the sound system that he had graciously set us up with in 2005.

At this point, Fran and I wanted to revise our season schedule. Going forward, our Youth CONNection production at Shelton High School each summer would kick off our season. A non-musical would follow the summer show, then our Christmas show in December, another musical in February with an age-appropriate cast, and finally, another non-musical in April to end the season. It was a formula that had evolved over time and worked well for us.

THE END OF SELLOUTS AT SHELTON HIGH SCHOOL

We had noticed, during these Center Stage years, an interesting phenomenon. While our Center Stage audiences continued to grow, we had stopped selling out shows at Shelton High School, both Drama Club and Youth CONNection productions. In truth, not only had we not sold out any Shelton High School shows in some years, but we were also not even having what might be deemed near sellouts. Our best sales were approximately eight hundred patrons. While that's a nice crowd, it was odd that, after selling out for so many years, we suddenly weren't. Tickets were easier to acquire since, with growing technology, customers could buy their tickets online – or, in the case of our Youth CONNection production, just call our box office and reserve them. It wasn't as if our productions at the high school had fallen off in quality. If anything, I feel they were just as good as ever if not better.

LESSON:
What I came to realize is that we had become our own competition.

So what was the problem? One supporter offered that our audience members, populated largely by senior citizens, were dying. It was certainly true that a great many theatergoers are seniors. I had noticed that to be true at professional theaters like Long Wharf or the Roundabout Theatre in New York where, well into our fifties, Fran and I felt like we were the youngest patrons. Middle aged people are often caught up in the lives of their children and don't have the time and energy to be regular theatergoers even if they enjoy plays.

But I didn't really feel that the problem was patrons dying. My hunch was that as seniors became too old to come to the theater or passed away, new seniors naturally took their place.

What I came to realize is that we had become our own competition. Before Center Stage, when we were staging only two shows a year with the Drama Club and the Youth CONNection, local patrons didn't want to miss either one. But when our number of productions increased to eight or nine a year, people had the luxury of becoming pickier. It was my hunch that they might see a show advertised and think, "I'm not that interested in that one, but the Scarpas are always doing a show. I'll catch the next one."

A CHANGE IN THE PIT

Another difficult, if not controversial, decision we made during the various incarnations of Center Stage was to move from live musicians to recorded accompaniment tracks, something that happened in stages. During a rehearsal for a Center Stage musical, something hit me. The actors were all adults, and I started to have difficulty justifying why we were paying musicians but not actors. As a community theater, we couldn't afford to pay actors. We were also aware that a number of the musicians who played our shows also volunteered to play for free in civic orchestras. My own brother, in fact, played in two.

At the time, for a show at Shelton High School, we had been paying each musician fifty dollars per rehearsal and performance, a small amount of money indeed. For six rehearsals and four performances, it worked out to five hundred per musician. With a large orchestra of twenty musicians, though, that came to ten thousand dollars, a good quarter of our overall show budget for a musical on the high school stage.

Fran and I were faced with one of the most important artistic decisions of our Center Stage years – the decision that it would be in the best interest of the theater not to pay musicians. When I sent our roster of musicians an email explaining this plan, only a small number agreed to keep playing for free – people who had been with us since the beginning, like Kathy Bizub and Peter Sanders, as well as my brother and a few other loyal musicians who just loved playing our shows.

At the time, one of the major licensors of musicals, Music

Theatre International, came out with a resource known as OrchExtra, a computer program meant to be used in conjunction with live musicians. The software needed an operator to keep time using a miniature keyboard, and in the process, OrchExtra would fill in the instruments we didn't have.

Actually, this was technology that I had already seen in action. A former performer in our productions, David Kaeppeler, now a professional conductor, invited Fran and me to see a production of *The King and I* starring Sandy Duncan that he would conduct at the Bushnell Center for the Performing Arts in Hartford. After the performance, we complimented David on the great orchestra. David explained to us that it was actually only a handful of musicians. "The rest," he explained, "was technology!"

Similarly, we saw another former student in a touring production of *Miss Saigon* at the Oakdale Theatre in Wallingford, and when I asked about the orchestra, once again it was explained that it had been a combination of a few musicians who toured with the show, enhanced by technology. Even more recently, we saw a production of *The Scarlet Pimpernel* at a professional theater on Long Island. I didn't ask about the wonderful full orchestra we heard because, when I examined the program, I saw only five musicians listed. It was clear to me that once again, technology was utilized.

Our problem with OrchExtra was that it was very tricky to operate. If the keyboard operator made the slightest mistake in timing, it seemed there was no way to recover. Normally, when a single musician makes a mistake, he can rest for a measure or two and then jump back in. No such recovery seemed possible with OrchExtra.

Then, an actor in one of our shows made me aware of a company out of Utah called the MT Pit, who created recorded accompaniments for musicals. These were high quality tracks that sounded like live musicians. Accompaniment tracks we had heard and even used in cabarets in the past tended to have a computerized sound since they were created using synthesizers. But the MT Pit used samples of real instruments, and their sound was magnificent. The MT Pit tracks cost us approximately two thousand dollars to use, so there was still a significant savings.

Besides the fact that the MT Pit tracks saved us money and sounded like we were using a Broadway orchestra, the tracks had other advantages as well. The performers in our shows started working with the tracks from the very first day of rehearsal. In the past, our live musicians needed their own rehearsal period, and our performers didn't sing with the pit band until very late in the process, often not until dress rehearsals, of which there were only three. A major advantage of the MT Pit tracks was that, by the time we got to production week, the cast knew exactly what they were going to hear from the "orchestra" so there were no musical challenges or glitches.

During this period of time, it was very occasionally brought to my attention that people missed live musicians. I understood since I too missed them. My love for conducting was so great that I hated giving it up. Additionally, I was sorry to stop using the handful of musicians who had been loyal friends to us for decades. But I was also keenly aware that I was aging, and the use of tracks relieved a great deal of stress and took a lot of pressure off of me.

In our world of running a full-time theater, with overhead costs and mounting at least three musicals a year, we had various things to consider, including what were the best decisions for the performers, for the programs we were running, for the theater, and not least of all, for our health and well-being.

Without a doubt, our most loyal musicians were unhappy not to be playing our shows anymore, but we felt we had made a choice that was necessary for us at the time. I hope they forgive me and remember the good times we had. Certainly, I loved conducting as much or more as anything I had ever done, so it was something I sacrificed as well.

ACT I, SCENE 15

Speaking of technology, Gina and Mia had introduced their own brand of technology to our rehearsal process, which was a game changer.

Gina, for instance, is very gifted when it comes to singing harmonies. Consequently, she would make recordings of all harmonies for our casts, and that included tenor and baritone harmonies which she was able to sing as well as the alto and soprano parts. Each cast member would be given these harmony tracks during the early part of the rehearsal period thus eliminating the need for long music rehearsals, something I had run for years with the cast gathered around the piano and me plunking out the harmonies. Gina's method was far more efficient, and with only occasional brush-up rehearsals, the harmonies in Fall Cab and our Youth CONNection productions were flawless during those years.

Additionally, at the time, Mia introduced what became known as *the dance blog* – a video recording of the choreography, so that cast members could work on the dance numbers at home. In the midst of earning a Master of Arts in Teaching from Sacred Heart University, she was assigned the task of using technology in a new way. With us Scarpas immersed at Center Stage as we were, Mia decided to approach the assignment in a way that would make rehearsing plays more efficient, and the dance blog was born. Being a stickler for detail, Mia also had a stage manager or dance assistant keep a binder with a detailed log of the placement and formations of cast members. If, at an early rehearsal or even a dress rehearsal, a cast member was off their mark, Mia would say, "Check the binder." Gina adopted the dance blog approach as well, and it would become a standard part of rehearsing for all Scarpa productions going forward.

Even before Center Stage 3.0, Gina and Mia had created a rehearsal culture where cast members would meet an hour before rehearsal on their own to review the choreography. One or another cast member would take a leadership role in organizing and running these dance reviews.

These innovations in rehearsing elevated the quality of our productions.

During those years, as I've said, I directed our summer shows with one of our daughters instead of Fran partnering with me. I had always felt that our Youth CONNection shows were of the highest quality, but this use of technology, along with the high standard that our daughters continued to uphold, upped our game in an important way. While Fran, so busy with the business end of things, wasn't as involved on the artistic side, she was still costuming each and every show brilliantly.

As a family, we were especially proud of our Youth CONNection productions during this era: *Thoroughly Modern Millie, Annie Get Your Gun, Legally Blonde, The Drowsy Chaperone, Les Misérables, Peter Pan, In the Heights*, and *Children of Eden*.

Add to the harmony tracks and the dance blog the fact that Gina and Mia implemented rehearsal rules that the cast received on day one, covering everything from attendance to appropriate rehearsal attire. Not that we hadn't always had these expectations, but now they were delivered to cast members in writing.

What had been a husband-wife team had now become a

father-daughter team, and in the case of Fall Cab, a sister-sister team. In all respects – a true family affair.

The reality is that Gina and Mia had grown up in the theater, and they helped us achieve a whole new dimension of efficiency that brought us into the twenty-first century in preparing a play for production.

LES MIS REDUX

When I think of the growing efficiency of our rehearsal process, I am reminded of what became our second Youth CONNection production of *Les Mis* in 2014. At the time, I decided not to tamper with anything, keeping the set design, the lighting, and especially the staging essentially the same as our 2002 version. As the saying goes, *If it ain't broke, don't fix it.*

In this 2014 version, the cast was older – the leads by an average of four or five years – since this time college students were eligible. Also, these performers had grown up in the theater with us, taking classes in acting, singing, and dance for years. And they had benefited by our growing use of technology to prepare a cast for performance. We now had the rehearsal period down to a science. Our cast had years of experience with us, and they knew what was expected of them in rehearsals and how to deliver.

To illustrate, on the night of the final dress rehearsal, during the finale of Act I, our atmospheric effects (haze and fog) had set off the fire alarms, and in the process, we had to evacuate the auditorium while firemen in full regalia employed gigantic exhaust fans to air out the building.

Rather than wait for an hour or two to rehearse Act II, I decided to send the cast home early to get a good night of rest. It's a decision that most directors don't typically have the luxury of making. We could only make this decision because of a combination of how well our cast was prepared to perform and the fact that the technical elements of the show were in such great shape. The importance of this kind of preparation will be discussed in a later chapter.

A CONTAGIOUS COMMITMENT TO QUALITY

During the Center Stage 3.0 years, with a more expansive and versatile stage space, Ron Baldwin was certainly at his creative best. He had developed a small and efficient crew over time, which included Jim Welch, a highly gifted carpenter who would go on to build scenery for the Shelton High School Drama Club for years to come; his talented wife Linda; Robin Hartel, a childhood friend of mine; Mike O'Mara, a man who not only acted on the stage but devoted himself to the building of the scenery, Bob Garber, a retiree who was all too happy to assist us; and Mark Cummings, a faithful and dedicated member of the crew. This was a dream team of dedicated and gifted volunteers that any theater would love to have, a crew who cared about the quality of our productions as much as we did.

Fran recalls an exchange with Robin Hartel where Robin was scrutinizing a painting detail that she wanted to fix. "That's way up above," Fran said. "The audience won't even notice that." Robin replied, "But *I'll* notice it!" Robin's words encapsulated how all of our volunteers felt about bringing our shows to life.

In the world of amateur theater, set building and painting often goes down to the wire. With this dedicated team, I had no such worries. Like they say, *It takes a village.*

Additionally, during crunch time, we could often depend on parent volunteers to answer our call and assist with set building, painting, and decorating.

As we felt great about our summer shows, we Scarpas rode a giant wave of success with our February age-appropriate cast musicals as well. Between the talented actors who performed in these shows and the all-around high quality production value (scenery, costumes, lighting, props), audiences were treated to outstanding evenings at the theater. Between 2013 and 2017, productions of *Big River, Guys and Dolls, Fiddler on the Roof, Man of La Mancha, Hairspray*, and *My Fair Lady* were sold out for the full run and several required that we add extra performances. As had always been the case, Fran costumed each of these diverse plays beautifully. Perhaps *Man of La Mancha* in 2015 was performed on our best set ever, one which I feel could have been on any professional stage in the country, including in New York.

As an example of the quality of our work, when Gina and I staged *My Fair Lady* in February of 2017, Mia, who had been performing professionally, brought a fellow cast member to see our show – a woman who had, a few years before, appeared in the Broadway revival of *Les Misérables*. Sitting in the audience, looking at the preshow set before them, illuminated with warm, dim lights, Mia's friend remarked, "You understand that many of the regional, professional theaters you and I will be auditioning for this season won't have scenery and lighting nearly as good as this."

In emphasizing production value, I don't mean to minimize the talent of the actors who graced our stage. We are grateful for all of the performers who passed through our doors, but I would propose that talent certainly is not unique to our theater. I have been to a great many productions rendered by high school drama clubs and community theaters that fell short, in my opinion, not because of a lack of talent but because of other factors.

LESSON:

...mounting a show is a ton of work whether you get it right or not, so let's get it right.

Often, when one of my Drama Club students would tell me they had seen a show at another high school, I would ask them how it was. "The girl who played the lead was amazing," they would sometimes answer, to which I would reply, "I didn't ask how the lead was, I asked how the show was. How was the scenery? How fast were the scene changes? How was the lighting? How about the costumes? How was the choreography executed? How was the orchestra? How good was the worst person on the stage?"

These were the details we Scarpas were interested in.

When you direct amateur and especially high school theater, you see all kinds of things. The way we always looked at it is, mounting a show is a ton of work whether you get it right or not, so let's get it right. The last high school show I saw was a mess. It wasn't that the kids weren't any good. There were several who were very talented, but the direction and production of the play was substandard.

I joked after, saying, "It was as if the director not only had no experience, but had never even *seen* a play before."

Would the school hire a football coach with no clue? What would the interview be like?

Q: Do you have prior coaching experience?
A: No, I don't.
Q: But you've played high school or college football?
A: No, I've never played the game.
Q: But have you studied football? Plays? Formations? Offense? Defense?
A: No, never.
Q: We assume you have, at least, watched football.
A: No, I've never seen a single game.
Q: Perfect! You're hired!

Watching this production, I felt the director was like the fictional coaching candidate I've described. I don't mean to be hyper-critical because, when an amateur group produces a Broadway musical, as I've indicated, they are truly doing the impossible even if they're doing it badly. In our world, at our first cast meeting, I would explain to our casts, especially our teens, that we were about to embark on an experience of accomplishing the impossible. High school students love such a challenge, and, with trust in their director, they'll surprise everyone with what they can do. After one of our productions, in fact, our cast gave us a plaque with a quote by Walt Disney: "It's kind of fun to do the impossible," which we displayed prominently on our desk at Center Stage.

It's important to note that we didn't always get it quite as right as we would have liked, but it was never through lack of effort or knowledge, but rather due to a myriad of other variables that we couldn't always control.

Our last years at Center Stage 3.0 were both gratifying and challenging. Mia had departed to seek professional theater work. Gina was doing a great job as the head of our education department. She and Fran had essentially revamped and updated our learning opportunities, now bringing our program for kids into the public schools in Shelton since the importance of the arts is often diminished, unfortunately, by school budget constraints. But Fran approached school officials and soon began delivering programs right in our public schools: *On Stage at Perry Hill* in our lower middle school and *Musicals Alive!* in all of our elementary schools. The principal at Perry Hill School required that we submit a detailed curriculum to her, so we enlisted Mia, with her degree in education, to write a curriculum that included goals and objectives.

At one point, we had over two hundred kids taking classes at Center Stage. Gina even took the magic of Fall Cab and created a similar event for younger kids which was called Musical Theater Workshop Junior or Spring Cab.

A special memory I have of Gina occurred at the end of a theater camp show. Gina took the stage to thank the families in the audience for sharing their children with us, and without warning one of the small campers ran and hugged Gina. Immediately, the entire camp population, dozens of kids, joined that small camper for a group hug, an outpouring of love that Gina couldn't have expected. It was hard for me to hold back the tears.

CHALLENGES

Besides the great shows and our wonderful education program, though, we found ourselves experiencing stressful dynamics with a few board members. In speaking to a few directors of other nonprofits, we were told that these challenges weren't unusual. All I will say about it is that these were especially difficult challenges for us. Allow me to add the caveat that perhaps we weren't cut out to have a board of directors. Fran and I had directed productions for twenty-nine years before opening Center Stage. By the time we turned Center

Stage into a nonprofit, we had been directing for thirty-two years. We had functioned for more than three decades without answering to anyone but ourselves. Now we answered to a board.

Since my objective in writing this book is to celebrate our years in theater, I will refrain from adding any details. I could probably write a book on non-profit boards, but for my purposes here, I would like to highlight what, in my mind, are the qualities of a good board member.

The best board members are those who have no agenda and no reason to volunteer other than to serve the needs of the organization. We had a number of such board members through the years. Ultimately, I feel we were fortunate that most of those who accepted an invitation to be on our board did so with the best of intentions.

For us, the late Sue Coyle exemplified all of the qualities of an outstanding board member. Even when she became board chair, I felt it was a position she didn't really want for any personal gain of her own, having too much on her plate in life and in business, but I believe she took the position strictly for the good of the organization. A Shelton businessperson, Sue was able to take a few hours from her realty business each week and meet with Fran and me every Thursday morning, making fundraising and other organizational plans with us, something no previous board chair had been at liberty to do.

With Sue Coyle at the helm, our board meetings were positive, organized, and purposeful. During her first year as chair, we raised over a hundred thousand dollars, the most we had ever raised. We had previously been hugely successful with a fundraising program called "The Great Give," run by the New Haven and Valley Community Foundations. Sue instituted a second fundraiser which she called "Funding the Future," and between the two programs, we did extremely well.

LESSON:

When you're an artist…walking away from your art form is easier said than done.

Fran and I probably decided we wanted to retire at least three years, if not more, before our retirement actually became possible. In fact, it wasn't uncommon for a caring friend to ask us when we were going to retire, given the staggering pace at which we were operating. I remember Erik Hansen, our protégé who makes his living working on Broadway plays, paying me a visit and asking, "How long do you and Fran think you can keep this up?" No one could understand better than Erik how hectic our life was. A board member, at the time, asked me the very same question. When you're an artist, though, walking away from your art form is easier said than done. Add to that, neither we nor our board had given much thought to a succession plan.

In 2015 and 2016, we challenged ourselves by producing two plays from a trilogy featuring a deaf protagonist, *Mother Hicks* and *The Taste of Sunrise*. In the author's introduction to these plays, she explained that while a theater could certainly have a "hearing" actor play the role and teach him American Sign Language, she strongly recommended finding a deaf actor.

When an age-appropriate deaf actor showed up at the audition, I was exuberant. "God loves me, and God loves Center Stage," I exclaimed in the lobby after meeting Joe Ronan. While it has not been my choice to mention actors by name in this volume, I mention Joe because the choice of the play, *Mother Hicks*, along with Joe's unlikely but auspicious arrival on the scene as the sole but perfect candidate to play the central male character inspired us to implement initiatives and programming at Center Stage that wouldn't have happened otherwise. It was quite an experience rehearsing with Joe, and not always having someone to interpret, we found ways together to communicate through lip reading on his part and our own brand of signing on ours. In the process, we learned as much from Joe about the deaf community as he learned from us about theater, and we even offered accessible performances.

I remember going to see a Broadway revival of *Spring Awak-*

ening presented by Deaf West, a professional theater company which utilizes hearing and deaf actors, with Joe. While buying tickets at the train station, we suggested to Joe that handicap tickets were available. Joe chose to purchase a full price ticket, explaining to us that he wasn't handicapped but that he merely spoke a different language than we did.

If we hadn't retired when we did, Fran would have instituted closed-caption technology, making all Center Stage performances accessible.

With the help of Joe Ronan and Diane Gamse, a teacher of the deaf who had worked with us on the *Mother Hicks* plays, we began to offer a class called *Acting Using American Sign Language* (ASL) in our education program. These classes resulted in our students signing during song selections in youth performances and even one of our teens becoming so interested in sign language that he would minor in ASL at UCONN. And it was particularly touching in June of 2019 to see our students sign a song at our retirement celebration.

ACT I, SCENE 16

In the meantime, during our later years at Center Stage 3.0, in that we were hoping to retire, we hired guest directors – primarily two seasoned directors, Scott Brill and Marty Marchitto, who had acted under our direction when they were high school and college students. We were trying to get a feel for what might work upon our leaving. Would it be best to have multiple directors like many theaters, or to have one primary director as had usually been the case in our years at Center Stage?

Even though we had expressed our wish to retire, our board leadership seemed unable to help us make it happen, so much so that, for us, it added to the frustration of those later years. When Sue Coyle finally stepped in as board chair in 2017, she was determined to get us to retirement.

STRATEGIC PLANNING?

An interesting thing happened at the time. As a non-profit organization, we began a process known as "strategic planning" for the second time in less than ten years. As it is the practice, we hired a consultant to the tune of ten thousand dollars to guide us in planning for the future. The consultant astutely identified a succession plan as the organization's critical need. In retrospect, it seems like the fee paid to the consultant didn't turn out to be money well spent.

The truth is, upon founding Center Stage, we hadn't considered a succession plan – an error on our part. Now faced with the reality, Fran and I had a concept of what the future could be. Fran, a great lover of ballet, had watched a documentary about George Balanchine, founder of the New York City Ballet. A concept presented in the documentary is that, today, the New York City Ballet "beats with the heart of Balanchine." Fran and I loved the idea of Center Stage beating with the heart of Gary and Francesca Scarpa. Perhaps it was hubris to have such a wish. I don't know.

There were undoubtedly differences between the two organizations, not the least of which was that Balanchine never actually retired. His leadership of the New York City Ballet came to an end because he died. When our time in the theater came to an end, Fran and I were very much alive.

We had suggested one of our guest directors, Marty Marchitto, as a possible successor. In addition to having performed in shows under our direction as a young adult, he had been our choice to be our successor at Sacred Heart Academy in 1993. Now, years later, Marty was in all ways a great candidate. He had earned a certificate in theatre from the Yale School of Drama as part of a post-graduate program, then went on to earn his M.F.A. in theater from the University of Illinois Urbana-Champaign. As a theater professional, Marty had a resume with tons of experience directing at various theaters, which included directing plays and teaching at several colleges. His experience also featured a long list of set, costume, and lighting design work he had done for professional theaters across the country.

That combination of directing and design experience made him, for Fran and me, a tremendously versatile and viable person, capable of taking Center Stage into the future. Also, in my mind, it might not be long before our two most skilled set builders, Ron Baldwin and Jim Welch, both older than me, might want to slow down or pack it in. Two members of Ron's crew had already died and another had aged out. Everyone else was in their seventies.

Marty, we felt, was someone who could lead the way, not only with the direction of plays and musicals but also with set design and construction when the time came.

In September of 2018, after Sue Coyle and a few key board members met with Marty, she introduced him to the entire board, and they agreed that he was the right man for the job. Fran and I were grateful that a plan was finally in place. We would mentor Marty into the job during his first year. Fran would come off the payroll as of January 1st, 2019, only coming in for periodic meetings with Marty, while I would stay on until the end of June, working with Marty to bring our last season to a meaningful end. A cancer survivor, Sue had a relapse, but operated from home, holding meetings with us when needed and continuing to serve the organization devotedly as she had always done.

As it happened, the work we put into a succession plan wasn't really implemented. We had planned on hiring two people to replace us (which only made sense) plus a part-time production manager. In the wake of Sue's relapse and eventual death, the plan would not be implemented, a production manager would not be hired, and Marty would be left to cover both of our positions.

OUR FINAL RETIREMENT

In that last year, though, while mentoring Marty into the position, Fran and I tried our best to enjoy our final months at Center Stage. We began our last season with a Youth CONNection production of *Annie* which we chose to co-direct. It had been a long while since the two of us had partnered on a musical. Since we had founded the Youth CONNection, we wanted to work together on what would be our last summer musical. It turned out that our ensemble was composed of a lot of younger teens. Their inexperience presented a challenge, compared to a good many of our earlier Youth CONNection productions which featured casts top heavy in college students, but our wonderful young cast reminded us of our early days as directors with the Shelton High School Drama Club where we had to really guide and teach our cast members. We especially loved this cast because we knew it was to be our last musical. It was really like old times, except that as directors we were now forty-three years older than the two kids who directed *The Music Man* in 1976.

During that final season, we had Scott Brill direct *Blithe Spirit* and *A Christmas Carol* and Marty direct *Anything Goes*.

Fran and I would collaborate one final time, co-directing a play, *I Remember Mama*, in the Spring of 2019. For this production, we had what we will always remember as a "dream cast" – a multi-generational group of actors who put all of their trust in us from day one. This was a cast with whom we shared memories of our history in theater and with whom we were able to bring closure to our career.

One of the stories I told them was of the engraved pewter goblets the cast of *The Music Man* had given us all those years before, with which Fran and I toasted on our wedding day, and how those goblets had disappeared, probably during one of our many productions of *Fiddler*. It's poignant to remember that in the context of the play itself, Golde enters, hands the goblets to her son-in-law, Motel, and says, "Motel, be careful with these. My mother and father, may they rest in peace, gave these to us on our wedding day." Our advice today would be to heed Golde's warning to be careful with the precious gifts we are given in life.

After our closing performance of *I Remember Mama*, our cast surprised us with new pewter goblets, engraved with our first and last productions: *The Music Man, 1976 / I Remember Mama 2019*. Fran and I were reduced to a puddle of tears.

LESSON:

Our advice today would be to heed Golde's warning to be careful with the precious gifts we are given in life.

And now our season had ended, and our time for retirement had come. This time it was going to be a real retirement. Some kind of party seemed in order, but what should it be? In 2012, I had retired from the Shelton School System after thirty-five years.

As a regular practice, I was honored at a banquet with a half dozen other fellow retirees.

Personally, I felt we needed closure with a meaningful celebration to end our career in theater, and being a little bit of a type A personality, I didn't want to leave that up to chance. Consequently, I turned the matter over to our daughters. I explained to Gina and Mia that they should plan whatever they felt would speak to us, and we wouldn't find out what that was until the evening of the event.

This celebration wouldn't be a banquet, though, but rather a performance on the stage at Shelton Intermediate School, where we had presented a few Youth CONNection productions during summers when the high school was undergoing renovations. It was attended by over three hundred people – actors of all ages, volunteers, and patrons – who wanted to bid us farewell.

The evening started with two slide presentations, one which showed a photo of every production we had ever directed in Shelton, with musical underscoring. The second one was a pictorial history of our life in the theater, narrated by our daughter Gina. After a few short speeches by Marty Marchitto, our successor, and a representative of our board of directors, the rest of the evening was filled with musical performances. Brett Boles, not only a veteran actor but also a composer, wrote a song especially for us entitled "Your Light Shines On" which Gina taught to our young performers for the evening.

Gina then took the microphone, singing a moving and powerful rendition of Gloria Estefan's "Coming Out of the Dark," with forty of her students, dressed in red and black (my mother's signature colors), singing background.

Mia and Brett, with two girls from our education program who are sisters in real life, sang a song from the musical *Children of Eden* – "Close to Home" – which, in this context, symbolized the life Fran and I and our daughters, as a family, had shared in the theater. Fran and I couldn't hold back the tears during this song.

After the musical presentations, Fran and I had our chance to speak, reflecting on our four decades in the theater. I remember having a lot to say – but as I've always said, I've never met a microphone I didn't like!

Gina and Mia ended the evening, bringing the house down with a rousing rendition of the song, "That's Life," made famous by Frank Sinatra – because, after all, theater had been our life, and now we would indeed be moving on.

After the performance, there was a receiving line where those in the audience were able to wish us well in the future. It was a perfect night.

A few weeks later, on June 30th, I had my last day on site at Center Stage 3.0. For me, leaving our building for the last time was bittersweet and somehow surreal. It was completely without pomp and circumstance. After all, we had already had our retirement celebration. My closest friend tells me that when he retired from Sikorsky Aircraft, on his last day, everyone in his department formed a double line and high-fived him as he left. With a staff of only three people in our office, there was no such goodbye for me. I felt strangely alone that day, walking out of our air-conditioned building for the last time into the sweltering summer heat, the quiet ending of a forty-three year career in the theater.

Exactly three weeks and one day after I left Center Stage that day, Sue Coyle, sadly, passed away. Her obituary chronicled her success in the business world and her many contributions to the community, not the least of which was that she had co-founded Relay for Life in Shelton and was instrumental in creating what would become known as The Valley Goes Pink in our region. Her obituary also modestly stated that Sue "loved being involved in Center Stage and helped develop it as a great cultural asset for the town of Shelton." In my mind, she did that and so much more!

Of the various deaths Fran and I had faced during our Center Stage years, Sue's death was one of the hardest. Though we knew it was imminent, there are some people you simply can't imagine no longer being a part of your life. I know I speak for many when I say that Sue was such a person. Sitting at her funeral that July morning, I couldn't help contemplating how brilliantly and unselfishly she had served the organization and how, in the process, she had become a cherished friend. We would miss her.

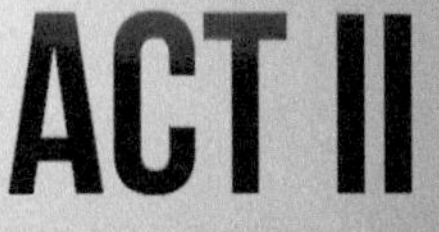

ACT II

ACT II, SCENE 1

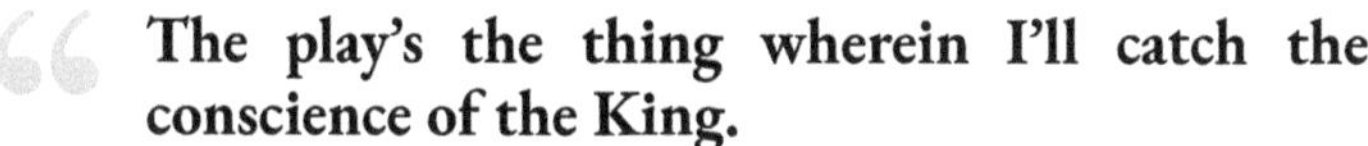

> **The play's the thing wherein I'll catch the conscience of the King.**
>
> WILLIAM SHAKESPEARE, PLAYWRIGHT

When Shakespeare wrote these immortal words for arguably his most famous character, Hamlet, he was talking about the immense power of a play to move people, and for Hamlet, the power of a particular play to be a means to an end.

I would eventually discover that, for me, the play was indeed *the thing*, something that had always been true, even when I wasn't aware of it. In the process of directing a given production, the play I was working on became the center of my universe. It became my obsession...my *raison d'être*. Everything I did, in my mind, served the best interest of the play.

It was never my inclination to rest on past laurels. I spent little if any energy thinking about a past theatrical triumph. Right from the beginning, my goal was to make the play I was working on the best that we had ever done. That wasn't always possible because the talent and experience level of the cast and the availability of skilled set builders, for instance, changed from one production to another. Nonetheless, it was still my goal.

Over time, I would come to the conclusion that the director, as visionary, is the artist who brings a play to life. The others: the actors, set builders, lighting technicians, costumers, etc. are the colors on the director's palette. Someone has got to be in charge. In our world, I was that person. It certainly could have been Fran, but she was all too happy to relinquish that role to me. While necessity very occasionally dictated that she be the point person for a production, she wasn't completely at home at the helm. From the start, we both realized that I was. When I would eventually direct with my daughters instead of Fran, they knew it to be true as well. Mia, in fact, would address me as "Boss" in rehearsals or speak of me as "the Boss" when referring to me.

As an artist, it was important to me to direct plays that I was excited about and which served the theater group I was working with. I simply had no interest in what plays high school drama club members wanted to do. I had heard of high schools where directors welcomed input from students on the choice of plays. I had also worked with and known community theater groups who had play reading committees. I found that many students and members of reading committees were often interested in plays that served themselves – plays in which they saw themselves playing roles. For me, it was all about what play I was motivated to devote my life to and how well I thought it served the needs of the group in terms of participation.

During our years of directing, I felt it was important that I, as the point person, made such choices without the input of others, with the exception of Fran – or when they came of age, Gina and Mia – who had been my partners in this world. For the high school Drama Club or the Youth CONNection, particularly, I tried to choose plays that had a good number of ensemble numbers (to allow for a large cast) and a good distribution of male and female roles. More often than not, classic musicals are top heavy in male roles. And I reiterate, most amateur theater groups are top heavy in female talent.

EVERYONE'S ON THE SAME PAGE

Preparing a play has two distinct periods, both wonderful – the rehearsal period and the performance period. Being a creative person, I thrived on the rehearsal process.

At Center Stage, particularly, going from one play to another, we would typically hold auditions for our next play on the Saturday after opening night of our current offering. I remember a conversation with an actor before a performance of *A Few Good Men* back in 2010. On our second performance night, considering I had auditioned candidates for our next production, *The Man Who Came to Dinner*, that morning, he said, "You're all done with us now, aren't you? You're on to the next one." In response, I quipped, "Yup, I've got a new girlfriend now!"

The exchange was all in good fun, but I realized that the actor understood me, and his remark sparked a realization in me. For me, the play was indeed the thing.

In mounting a production, I had the good fortune to be working on what I feel is an incomparable collaborative project. There is a great beauty about producing a play. It is a multidisciplinary creative experience, blending acting, music (presuming it is a musical), visual art (scenery), lighting (which is certainly, in and of itself, an art form), and history (at the very least, in the creating and finding of period costumes and props).

Inherent to the project is a very specific timeline. We found that for a musical on the big stage, a seven-week rehearsal period worked well for us. For a musical on our smaller stage, six weeks, and a non-musical, five weeks. There is such a thing as too much rehearsal. We learned, early on, that there comes a point when the actors and the play itself *need* an audience. With proper planning and effective rehearsing, a play is put before an audience at just the right time.

That said, the mounting of a play has a very specific deadline, known as "opening night." It's not just any deadline, but a very exciting and exquisite one, albeit an inflexible one as well. With tickets having been sold, it's very difficult if not impossible, logistically, to move that deadline back.

Personally, I can't think of any other endeavor where, at the end of a short time, the collaborators of a project have anything nearly as wonderful to show for their labors. The progress that takes place in a short span of time is mind-boggling: actors, some of whom may have little or no experience, have grown by leaps and bounds; effective scenery has been created; details like costumes and props have been added; a lighting design has been implemented – all in the name of bringing quality amateur theater to the stage.

The closest thing outside of the arts I've ever been able to think of is the building of a new house. Similarly, there must be an allotted time period to complete the project. But, even in that case, once the project is completed, there aren't hundreds or thousands of people who come to see it and show their appreciation through applause. I can think of no other endeavor outside of the world of the performing arts where creators are shown immediate and direct appreciation for their work.

Never during a rehearsal period have I ever wished I was doing something else. For me, in the midst of a rehearsal, time ceased to exist. Rehearsal began at 7:00, and in the blink of an eye, it was 10:00. I was never, at the end of a rehearsal, glad it was over.

As a director, I expected to see progress at each and every rehearsal. Throughout the process, I wanted to see similar progress with other aspects of the production like scenery and costuming. Opening night was always looming in the not-too-distant future, putting just the right amount of pressure on us to get things done.

Considering my focus and, yes, even my obsession as an artist, there were often hard decisions to make. I will go into more detail about casting later, but I tried very hard not to let normal human emotions like sentimentality or friendships enter into my casting decisions. Let me be clear. It was *always* my goal to cast people who served the needs of the play best, no matter what anyone might have thought or said. Never did I promise a person a role in advance. If I knew and loved the person(s) I cast, great. If I didn't, great as well – as long as I believed they could get the job done. In casting, it's basic math to say everyone can't get what they want and, subsequently, feelings are often hurt. I would quickly come to the conclusion that there was no way around it. When it comes to casting, it's simply the nature of the beast.

With all aspects of a production, the buck stopped with me. There were times when I made unpopular decisions. Considering I was working with volunteers, I knew it was important to be diplomatic and judicious in communicating with them. Still, there were tense moments. One year at Sacred Heart Academy, a unit of scenery was built for *The Sound of Music*, which I deemed unacceptable. It was the exterior of the von Trapp home, and the proportions were odd, making it look cartoony instead of like a realistic structure. It was a difficult decision, but I felt it needed to be rebuilt. The parent in charge of set construction was miffed. "Gary, if I ask these guys to rebuild it, they may quit," he warned. "What'll we do then?"

"If they quit," I replied, "I'll have a new crew in here tomorrow night." Yes, I was young and perhaps more brash than I should have been, but the reality was that our existing crew rebuilt the unit to my satisfaction.

In a similar situation, the proportions were *way* off for a pair of rectangular columns built for our 2002 Youth CONNection production of *Les Misérables*. Once again, I told the guys who built them that the columns would need to be rebuilt. I recall that one of the dads, a carpenter by trade, reacted with a look of incredulity. His eyes said, *You've got to be kidding*. The columns were rebuilt and the carpenter never returned. Perhaps his disappearance was a coincidence, but I don't think so.

I understand. These men had what Fran and I would come to call a "good enough" attitude. The thinking was, *This is just an amateur production, and what we've done, no matter what it looks like, should be good enough*. It's the same "good enough" thinking

I faced early in our directing career when a principal questioned why we needed to spend money on period costumes instead of having the kids costume themselves from their own closets.

LESSON:
...there's simply something about mounting a major production that is uniquely exhilarating.

But the real truth is – our quest for quality and perfection, for the vast majority working with us, was exciting. People wanted to be a part of that creative energy.

Whether we are talking about students or adults, it had everything to do with being part of something bigger than themselves – because there's simply something about mounting a major production that is uniquely exhilarating.

FACTORS FOR SUCCESS

I would come to talk about the vital factors that contributed to our success with our casts, especially our student casts. "I have never," I would tell them, "been associated with another project where everyone seemed to be on the same page – where the person in charge had a clear vision, and where his team wanted to do everything in their power to help make that vision a reality."

As a teacher, I had never seen a staff fully united under the principal. There always seemed to be pockets of dissension. "In a high school like ours, if the principal had a clear vision and every member of the staff was behind him, ours would be the best high school in the state if not the country," I would explain.

I'm sure those pockets of dissension exist in all walks of life. But there seemed to be something about theater where, just about every time, our cast and volunteers were of a mind to do everything they could to bring our vision to fruition.

I feel it was the result of accomplishing what I came to call "the impossible." In the midst of what is often the humdrum routine of daily life, participants loved being involved in such an extraordinary endeavor – in a big idea. Most everyone we encountered in the world of theater wanted to climb on board the journey of excellence we always strove for. I also feel that Fran and I had a special chemistry that motivated people to give us their best every step of the way.

ACT II, SCENE 2

> **Auditions are like a gamble. Most likely you won't get the part, but if you don't go, you'll never know if you could've got it.**
>
> ROBERT DE NIRO, ACTOR

As I dive into a chapter about auditioning, I can't help recalling seeing *A Chorus Line* on Broadway many years ago, and the powerfully dramatic opening number, "I Hope I Get It." The title of that opener is an anthem for anyone who loves performing on stage and has to go through the process of auditioning.

There are few activities that can create more nervousness and anxiety than auditioning for a play, especially a musical, and there are few examples of courage, from my perspective, greater than a high school student auditioning for the first time. It is my experience that, in the audition room, a person is somehow rendered extremely vulnerable. The reality of the matter is, auditioning is challenging for performers at every level, from high school students to professionals. So, it almost goes without saying that when any person walks into the audition room, it is a true act of courage.

When I think of the thousands of teenagers we auditioned

through the years, I think of that first college audition. Being so inexperienced, I had no idea what to expect. And I have no doubt that my nerves were as evident as the high beams of a car on a dark road.

In my case, though, I had grown up performing on stage. I had often sung on the spur of the moment without rehearsal with live musicians at weddings and other events. So, once I understood the audition process, I could navigate the situation with relatively calm nerves and good success.

For a candidate auditioning for a high school musical, it is, in many cases, the very first time the student has ever sung a solo in front of anyone. So many candidates have no confidence in this situation and sing at an inaudible volume. Often a candidate's knees tremble and her voice wavers while singing. Many of our students had never sung with a pianist and some had little or no ability to sing in rhythm. Still others would sing off pitch, clearly not in tune with the pianist. Fran and I always tried our best to be patient and compassionate with these students.

EVERYONE IS A SINGER / EVERYONE IS A DANCER

Regarding singing off pitch, during my years directing, I came to a rather controversial conclusion. I stopped believing in what many people refer to as "tone deafness." Tone deafness suggests that certain individuals, as a permanent condition, simply don't have the capacity to sing on pitch. Now, don't get me wrong. I am well aware that some people don't sing on pitch. Personally, I would describe tone deafness as a disconnect between a person's ear (hearing the pitch), the person's brain, and the person's voice. The signal, for some reason, gets short-circuited somewhere.

But I have had too many experiences with students, mainly boys, who appeared to be tone deaf but who, ultimately, weren't. In the world of high school theater (and community theater, for that matter), many more females audition than males...so, for a high school drama club, boys are at a premium. I often joked that if a boy had a pulse he'd be cast. That wasn't always true, actually, because now and then a boy was so introverted, we didn't feel he was ready to be on stage in front of an audience. But would we cast a boy who was supposedly tone deaf but for all other practical purposes would succeed on the stage in our opinion? In many cases, the answer was yes.

I can name a number of boys who appeared to be tone deaf, but who would eventually sing on pitch. Several of them went on to sing major roles with us and with other theater groups.

The best example I can think of was a candidate whom I asked to audition for a production of *Pippin* we directed in 1990. This handsome high school junior was on the school cheerleading squad, and I couldn't help but notice him as he danced at a pep rally. Although he had never studied dance, he was as good or better than any girl who danced alongside him. Some people have inexplicable gifts, and he was one. I introduced myself and encouraged him to audition for our spring musical.

When he began singing in the audition, he was completely and utterly off pitch. I stopped him immediately, which was something I had come to do in such situations. Even though he had prepared his song, I didn't need to hear several minutes of off pitch singing. I took him over to the piano and asked him to sing a scale – do, re, mi, fa, sol, la, ti, do. He couldn't do it, so I just concentrated on one note – middle C. "Just sing this note," I urged him. I plunked the note and sang it for him to hear.

As he attempted the note again and again, incorrectly, I urged him by singing the word "higher" on pitch. His voice gradually and perhaps painfully rose to meet the right tone. We cast him in the ensemble, where he would sing in group songs with the entire cast. In such cases, I would ask a student to sing quietly while focusing on listening to those around him who were singing on pitch.

In this student's case, his love of theater and performance was so great that, in the ensuing months and years, he sought out the services of several prominent voice teachers, one in Connecticut and one in New York. He went on to train at AMDA (American Musical and Dramatic Academy) and developed into a talented singer who went on to perform in professional productions as well as in night clubs in New York and

Paris. What would have happened to him if we had written him off as tone deaf?

While this is the best example of my theory, it certainly isn't the only example. I can think of several others who went from so-called "tone deafness" to leading player. I think there are reasons for what appears to be tone deafness. Maybe the tone deaf person wasn't sung to as a child. Maybe he had been sung to by a parent who sang off pitch. Maybe in grade school, a misguided teacher discovering a "tone deaf" boy told him not to sing, shattering any musical confidence he may have had in himself. Any and all of these reasons could be devastating to a young person, giving him a life-long belief that he is incapable of singing.

Tone deaf girls were not as fortunate because we always had an abundance of female candidates who could sing, so often a girl who sang off pitch would be cut. But if, in the presentation of her song, a girl who wasn't a gifted singer (and believe me, there were many!) showed me she had acting chops – that she had an ability to "sell" the song effectively, she would be cast. Sometimes I would suggest to a female student that she try out for a play, only to hear her say, "I'd love to, but I can't sing." I would reply, "We need people who can act and dance as much as we need singers, so everyone we cast isn't Barbra Streisand. Let me be the judge of your singing ability."

LESSON:
If you can talk, you can sing;
if you can walk, you can dance.

I kind of adopted an approach I had observed in highly competitive drum and bugle corps competitions. I would tell our casts, "Everyone is expected to march in step, executing intricate drills. No one is let off the hook because they are uncoordinated. We expect you to dance with precision, and we want you all to sing on pitch."

Fran liked to wear a t-shirt that read: "If you can talk, you can sing; if you can walk, you can dance." The shirt showed two amorphous figures, presumably dancing, and the wording stems from a

Zimbabwean proverb which suggests that "the basic ability to move your body or make sounds grants you the fundamental potential to dance and sing. It doesn't imply expert-level performance, but rather the capacity for self-expression. It's a call to action, encouraging people to engage in joyful activities and overcome self-consciousness or perceived limitations."

This proverb beautifully expresses the nature of our work as directors of amateur theater.

Speaking of dancing ability, we eventually decided that everyone in our productions needed to dance. In our early days, we had designated dancers in our casts, not an uncommon practice in amateur theater. At Sacred Heart Academy, for instance, in our first year there, the dancing chorus was very clearly delineated from the singing chorus. It was probably at Sacred Heart, in fact, where we decided that we didn't care for that distinction. Certainly, some people excel more in the area of dance and movement than others, whether because of training or because of God-given ability. Still, with each passing year, we got further and further away from distinguishing our cast members as dancers or as singers.

Certainly, by the time Mia and Gina had come over to the directing side of the table, there was no distinction. Every cast member was expected to participate in a dance audition and, if cast, learn the choreography and dance in the production. Were some better at it than others? Of course. And those who were better were more likely to be downstage, center. But we feel it was a richer experience for all involved to learn to dance and to participate as equally as possible.

The fact of the matter is, we would learn that in the professional world of theater, performers dance who are not considered dancers. In fact, it is my understanding that in some Broadway productions, like a revival of *Anything Goes*, a tap-dancing musical, only some of those on the stage actually wore shoes with taps on the bottoms.

Under the direction of Fran, Mia, and Gina, everyone experienced what it means to dance on the stage, and we believe they are all better for having done so. In the process, given high expectations and fruitful rehearsals, my observation was that only the most astute audience members could tell the difference between the dancer and non-dancer.

REFINING THE AUDITION PROCESS

In those early years of directing, students had to find a song to sing and the sheet music for our accompanist, despite having very little ability to choose a song. We would observe in those early years students making ineffective song choices, perhaps hits from the pop world totally unlike the musical we were doing, and sometimes singing these songs badly. Or we would hear the repetition of particular songs, probably because one student had the sheet music and shared it with friends. Two that come to mind from the 1970s are Bette Midler's version of "The Rose" and "Day by Day" from the musical *Godspell*, both of which were sung more often than we would have preferred.

Some performers, I would learn, chose to sing the same song at audition after audition. One young man sang "Stars," Javert's song from *Les Misérables*, every time he auditioned for us throughout high school and college, replete with the same gesturing and movement, right to kneeling down on one knee at the end of the song. It seemed to serve him fine because he was cast again and again in character roles.

Speaking of "Stars," when our daughter Mia attended the Broadway Theatre Project, she took a class with Terrence Mann who originated the role of Javert in the U.S. premiere of *Les Mis*. He explained that he almost always used the same song when auditioning, so it's not as if it isn't done in the professional world.

Although in the early years we allowed a candidate to sing an entire song and also read from the script, we soon realized we could determine a candidate's singing ability within the first few measures. At a professional audition, a candidate is typically allowed to sing only sixteen measures (approximately thirty seconds), and sometimes only eight measures.

Probably by the time we directed our third musical, we realized we needed to assist students in the audition process, and we began holding audition workshops for our Drama Club members, explaining how to better prepare and present themselves. We talked about choosing a good song. We had seen girls sometimes choose songs arranged for the male voice, which presented a problem in relationship to key since a song written for a male isn't in a good register for a female.

LESSON:

...we could determine a candidate's singing ability within the first few measures.

We also suggested they dress to look their best for an audition. We urged students to get control of their nerves and to not get carried away talking too much in the audition room, thereby slowing down the process for us and other candidates.

Along the way, all kinds of things happened in the audition room to get our attention, things we couldn't have expected. I remember a candidate singing "The Mickey Mouse Club Theme Song," and as he sang the letters M-I-C, K-E-Y, M-O-U-S-E, he pulled cards with those very letters out of his pocket, displayed them, and threw them into the air while marching around the room. Silly, I know, but memorable nonetheless...although, of course, he didn't win a major role.

Another early candidate, a strong singer, chose "Somewhere" from *West Side Story* for her song. In the midst of singing it, she crossed the room, took me by both hands, and led me to the performance space, where she looked into my eyes and sang the rest of the song directly to me, holding my hands the entire time. It felt awkward and contrived to say the least, and it was something I would never allow to happen again. These were gimmicks that I wouldn't recommend.

In those early years, our pianist was a gifted student who could sight read anything. During these and similar auditions, her eyes would peek out over the top of the upright piano in disbelief, a memory that makes me and Fran smile to this day.

Speaking of pianists, sight reading is a skill essential for an audition but not one every competent pianist has. It was my experience that having a less-than-competent sight reader at an audition only complicated the matter and hindered a candidate's chance of giving a good audition. Here, a candidate is in an anxiety producing situation, and now we add a pianist who plays the song badly. Not good!

The situation asks a director to find a pianist who sight reads, and then the questions arise, *How much will the musician charge?* and *Can the budget afford it?* Considering auditions take place over the course of several days, and considering we had encountered only one student musician ever who could sight read, the answer to both questions was usually no.

Not long after this very adept pianist graduated and moved on with her life, we made some changes in our audition process. Given the challenge of finding an accompanist who could sight read, we decided to have candidates sing with a recording. It could be a recorded accompaniment (homemade or commercially available) or the soundtrack of a Broadway show. If the latter, we would simply turn the volume to a setting that allowed the candidate's voice to ring out and be easily heard. We strongly suggested that students pick Broadway songs instead of pop songs, which often didn't serve the purpose very well.

As far as members of the Shelton High School Drama Club went, we eventually decided to simplify the audition process, thereby making their lives easier and leveling the playing field. With so many students auditioning for the first time in their lives, instead of requiring them to choose their own songs, we chose songs from the show we were doing and made recordings on cassette tapes available to each candidate. Students picked up tapes from me in advance and began preparing. It made it easier and more efficient for everyone.

We would pick something in a moderate range and work out the specific vocal needs of major roles in a callback where the most talented students were "called" to a second (and sometimes a third) audition to determine major roles. In this way, no one could choose an inappropriate song. We also simplified the matter by making it a one-minute cut of the song. A minute was plenty long enough to determine a candidate's singing ability. We would hear longer versions of songs at callback auditions. We stopped using scenes in the initial audition and provided candidates with a short monologue from the play as an acting audition. Sometimes, we heard only the song in the initial audition and saved readings for a callback, commonly the way it's done in the professional world.

We made other simple improvements over time. Not long after that chaotic first audition for *The Music Man*, we began to require candidates to sign up for a time slot. I would estimate how many people we could see in a half hour (perhaps eight or ten), and we tried very hard to stay on schedule. In the Center Stage years, candidates signed up for a time slot online.

We even created a schedule for callback auditions. For instance, in the case of *Thoroughly Modern Millie*, it might look like this:

2:00 to 2:30 Millies (sing)
2:30 to 3:00 Jimmys (sing)
3:00 to 4:00 Millies and Jimmys (read)
4:00 to 5:00 Dorothys and Trevors (read)

In the process, it was generally our goal to give each candidate an equal opportunity to sing and read.

FAIR, EQUITABLE, AND EFFICIENT

Our way of auditioning people was colored by my own personal experiences auditioning. I remember an early college audition for a non-musical. It was another open audition, which apparently the professors at Southern were fond of at the time. I sat in the auditorium all night before finally being called up to the stage to read a scene where I only spoke one or two lines. Meanwhile, veteran members of the theater department were called up to read over and over again, reading different characters and long scenes. At one point, a veteran candidate read a monologue as if he was a modern television evangelist for no other apparent reason than to amuse the director and the other candidates. As he did so, I found myself contemplating that I wasn't being given a fair shot to win a role.

Ironically, I spoke to a friend from the theater department after the audition, complaining that the director had, perhaps, had people in mind for roles. His response was, "Gary, the director had this cast worked out when she chose the play last spring."

I will have much more to say about casting in an upcoming chapter, but we wanted to be as fair and equitable as possible, requiring everyone to sing for the same length of time and, when reading from the script was called for, to have a similar number of opportunities, inasmuch as it made sense to do so.

We would fine tune the audition experience to a highly organized and efficient process. I remember late in our career at Center Stage, as a callback audition was running completely on schedule, teasing the candidates as we called them in from the hallway, saying, "This is the most organized callback you'll ever attend, and if I'm wrong about that, please let me know who's running a more efficient callback."

LESSON:
...we wanted to be as fair and equitable as possible...

As the reader might have guessed, from the beginning we chose to hold "closed" auditions in order to help alleviate the nervousness of candidates. At one point, I experimented with an open callback audition, which had its positive points, allowing candidates to gain insights in interpretation from each other, but ultimately, after a few of these, I opted to go back to closed auditions even for callbacks.

In the audition room, I tried to streamline the process, asking a few questions to get a sense of the candidate's personality, but generally keeping the chit-chat to a minimum for the sake of time.

Thinking back to the young lady who had, years before, made me a character in her rendition of "Somewhere" and also considering that, in their nervousness, candidates might wander about the room...even coming directly up to the audition table, we created a performance space in the room, simply laying a blue line of masking tape on the floor. The candidates were instructed that they needed to stay behind the line, creating an appropriate distance from us.

Having spoken about the behavior of candidates, allow me to say more about my behavior as director in an audition. It became my custom to try to be as welcoming and supportive as possible in my demeanor, but not to react, positively or negatively, to the candidate's presentation of a song. This was easier said than done for several reasons.

First, when listening to a great singer audition, it was hard to mask my excitement, but I did my best. When hearing a weak candidate, while I wanted to be supportive, being too supportive could be a problem. I have been told about other directors who were more encouraging than I, who, after a student sang his song, said, "Hey! Awesome job! Really good!" The candidate left the audition feeling good about himself, only to be cut.

I didn't want any candidate to leave the audition having any idea of what was in my mind. It certainly wasn't my practice to tell a candidate how great they were and then cut them. And besides, talent alone doesn't assure winning a role because there are other important factors which come into play.

Consequently, I viewed auditions in an attentive but businesslike manner. In the case of callbacks, I would give candidates direction and when they successfully executed the direction, I would certainly confirm that they had.

Occasionally, after singing a song, a candidate would ask me, "How'd I do?" to which I would simply reply, "I can't discuss how you did at this time." In truth, it's an inappropriate question for a candidate to ask in an audition.

"FINDING" ACTORS

Once we opened Center Stage, the task of casting a play would become different for us. Except for two plays we directed with the Orange Players in the late '70s, we had always worked with high school and college students. With the SHS Drama Club, our pool of candidates was limited, besides age, to candidates who attended Shelton High School. While we drew from beyond Shelton with the Youth CONNection, our talent pool was still limited by age.

At Center Stage, though, most of the time we would be doing what is known as "age-appropriate casting." While at Shelton High School, an eighteen-year-old would play the role of a fifty-year-old man, as in the case of Tevye in *Fiddler on the Roof*, at Center Stage we wanted a fifty-year-old man to play a fifty-year-old man.

We experienced this as a different casting challenge. As it would sometimes happen, perhaps no fifty-year-old man auditioned, or among the fifty-year-old candidates, perhaps no one was right for the role. Consequently, I sometimes chose to recruit actors as discussed in an earlier chapter. I couldn't always afford to be limited to the candidates who initially auditioned. If the right person in terms of age, type, and talent didn't audition, I needed to *find* the right person and invite them to read or sing for me. We were, after all, running a business now. Our subscribers and patrons expected a certain level of quality from us.

In the midst of our goal to have an age-appropriate cast, I certainly wasn't going to have one cast member in a role who was clearly too young for it. Consequently, occasionally I found myself in the role of talent scout, something I feel I was very good at.

As an example, I have a very happy memory of recruiting an older gentleman right out of our audience. He would get my ear at intermission or after a performance and tell me how he and some friends at a local senior center had dressed up in drag in a comic skit for their variety show.

These conversations sparked an idea. I wanted a seventy-something-year-old to play a small role in an upcoming play, and I didn't anticipate anyone that age auditioning.

One evening, I asked, "Bill, have you ever been in a play?"

He laughed out loud. "Get the hell outta here," he said. "I could never be in a play."

"I think you could," I replied.

"Get out! How could I be in a play? I have no experience."

"If you can do drag at the senior center, you can be in a play," I teased.

Bill didn't seem to believe me, but at the next performance, he pulled me aside and said, "Were you serious about me being in a play?"

"Yes," I said. "I have a small part in our next production, *Requiem for a Heavyweight*. A doctor. It's one scene...two pages of dialogue."

Our patron would go on to appear in small roles in *Requiem* as well as *To Kill a Mockingbird*, *Gypsy*, and *The Miracle Worker*. And when he died a few years later, we felt like we had lost a member of our family. Displayed at his wake were his theatrical headshot and a few thank you notes I had written to him.

But this is just one example of dozens. I recruited at least ten teachers I worked with at Shelton High School to audition for us.

That same production of *Requiem for a Heavyweight*, a cast heavy in males, called for a middle aged female to play a small role. I remember taking the mother of one of our theater students aside and asking her if she had ever been in a play. "No," she said. "Why?" Was she ever surprised when I told her I wanted her to play the part of a hooker. She accepted the role, though, and did a great job.

When we did *Gypsy*, we only had one age-appropriate candidate audition for the three "over the hill" strippers, so, once again, I recruited the other two strippers from the mothers of our youngest cast members. One had once been a rock singer and the other had no prior performance experience.

A few years in, we would produce an adaptation of *To Kill a Mockingbird*, but there was no one right for the central character,

Atticus Finch. One night, a rare evening when we weren't rehearsing, I said to Fran, "Hey! I know who can play Atticus Finch."

"Who?" she asked.

"That guy from church, the lector."

"There are a lot of lectors," she said. "Which one?"

"The one who does the Christmas gospel every year. The guy with the accent and the voice of God."

"John?" she asked.

"I don't know the guy's name...but he'd be a perfect Atticus Finch," I said.

Oklahoma born and bred, John had never acted before, but he was the man for the job. We got him involved playing a small role in *Little Women*, and then he went on to give a superb, heartfelt performance in *To Kill a Mockingbird*. In retrospect, I'm not sure we could have found a better Atticus Finch if we had held auditions in New York. John would go on to play other important roles for us, and he made major contributions behind the scenes by helping us build scenery. I'm not sure I've ever known a kinder and humbler individual.

Our auditions for *On Golden Pond* at Center Stage 2.0 in 2010 yielded only two female candidates. The play has only two female roles – a mother and a daughter, made famous in the film version by Katharine Hepburn and Jane Fonda. But our two candidates, both good actresses, were too close in age to play mother and daughter. In other instances, I would have been on the phone calling thirtyish year old actresses, but I simply had no one I could think of. In this instance, I recruited a friend. I ran into her at her business, and in the moment, it hit me that she was the right age for the character. I asked her if she had ever been in a play. When she smirked and said, "No!" I replied, "Would you like to be?" After she laughed, I convinced her I was serious, and despite her doubts, she agreed to my offer. Together, we worked hard, she turned out to be perfect for the role, and our audiences thoroughly enjoyed her performance.

Time and time again, I would need to *find* actors to populate the casts of our productions. There was nothing I loved more than introducing someone to the stage...or bringing them back after years of being away.

But there were certainly instances of recruiting people who were talented and experienced. One example occurred when we produced the play *Big River* in 2013. We needed a talented actor and singer to play Jim, the slave seeking his freedom who befriends Huck Finn. Only two male candidates auditioned for the role. One of them was a pretty good singer but was without any experience. In his case, he had no confidence in himself. I didn't believe he was ready to play such a role, nor did he want any part of it. The other candidate was perfect in age, type, and acting ability, but he simply couldn't sing. Jim is a major singing role, and I hoped and prayed that, at a callback audition, this candidate could prove to us that, musically, he could be worked with. But it wasn't to be.

Consequently, I sent out email and social media messages seeking an actor to play Jim. It resulted in a first year college student being referred to me. The previous spring, he had won an award for best high school performance by a male in Connecticut. This young man was a phenomenal singer. The problem is that Jim is not nineteen years old. He is the father of multiple children, and I had hoped for a man of at least thirty years old. But in amateur theater, we sometimes have to surrender to the best choice that we have. In this case, this college student brought a magnificent portrayal of Jim to our stage, despite being too young for the role.

The fact is, I have an inherent belief that we can all act and be successful in the process. Do some people have a greater gift than others? Absolutely! But that does not negate the fact that we can all act. We have, all of us, been acting since we began to speak, pretending in our play as small children, often manipulating our parents to get our way, and wriggling our way out of awkward situations. We have spent our lives watching actors at work – if not on the stage then certainly on television and in film.

I have certainly met people who have said to me that they could never perform in a play. These folks can't imagine playing a role in front of hundreds of people every night. I would argue that it isn't that they couldn't be in a play, they simply won't because of their fears and insecurities. Are they capable, though? I would say, yes – all of us have qualities, with the proper preparation and guidance, that will assist us in succeeding on the stage.

LESSON:
…there are probably as many fateful reasons why each person comes to audition for their first play as there are people reading this book.

I think of a heart to heart talk I once had with a college student who wasn't cutting it in his chosen college major, engineering. He needed to choose a new major and was very disappointed in himself. "Have you ever spent a day with an engineer?" I asked. Puzzled, as if to say, "What's that got to do with it?" he told me he hadn't.

I offered, "I'm just asking because you don't really know what it's like to be an engineer. In my case, I became a teacher, which was an easy choice. I spent seventeen years, from kindergarten through college graduation, watching a teacher at work every day."

The only occupation we, as citizens of this country, have spent more time observing than a teacher is an actor. Add to that the fact that we are all thinking, feeling individuals, and yes, I think, for the person who will open his mind to it, each of us has an ability to succeed as an actor. I've simply never experienced working with anyone who had absolutely no acting ability.

To discover that potential, though, a person obviously has to audition. Like me, there are probably as many fateful reasons why each person comes to audition for their first play as there are people reading this book. It all starts with the audition.

ACT II, SCENE 3

Casting can be heartbreaking. Dealing with the disappointment is the hardest part.

STOCKARD CHANNING, ACTRESS

Following auditions, obviously, is the task of casting the play. If I had to choose a downside to being a director, I would choose the angst that goes along with casting, something, by the way, I believe I had a gift for. With the Drama Club, my least favorite day of the year was the morning I posted the cast list on the auditorium doors. Disappointing people is a heart wrenching thing to have to do. To see the sad faces of kids all day, some of whom were my own students, wasn't easy.

I'd like to say it was different with adults after we opened Center Stage, but I found that adults of all ages, even senior citizens, often seemed almost as disappointed as teens.

A play only has so many roles, and hard decisions have to be made. This is a reality that I think some candidates forget. Casting, of course, isn't personal but rather it's about the greater good of the play. As a team, Fran and I (and eventually our daughters) were in the position, unfortunately, of having to disappoint people.

PRECASTING? NOT EXACTLY!

It was always our goal, from the outset, to have the audition and casting process be as fair as possible. That said, as directors, we often knew many of the candidates who would be auditioning, especially in the case of the Drama Club or the Youth CONNection. It only makes sense to contemplate who might be right for one role or another. Using *Oklahoma!* as an example, we might think, *for the role of Curly maybe **a** or **b**. For the role of Laurey, perhaps **y** or **z**.* In a situation like a school where a director mostly knows who will be auditioning, we felt it was a good idea to think of two or three different people who were good for each role. If a new candidate emerged, all well and good...and, believe me, I can name many instances where that's exactly what happened. It made absolutely no difference to us. We simply wanted to put the best cast on the stage.

Let me use sports as an example. I think it's safe to say a high school football or basketball coach probably knows, going into a season, who his most important players will be. Allow me to use as an example Shelton's most celebrated athlete of all time, Dan Orlovsky, now a sports analyst on ESPN. It's safe to say that Dan was the greatest football player ever to attend Shelton High School. That assertion would be hard for anyone to argue with. An all-state quarterback who led Shelton to a state championship before becoming a star at UCONN and then having a career in the NFL, Dan was obviously the chosen starter from the time he was a high school sophomore. No one could call it favoritism.

But I don't need to use someone with pro-level skills to make my point. I'm sure the current coach at Shelton High School has a solid idea of who his key players will be next season. I will, in fact, wager that in the months before the football season, the coach knows exactly who his starting quarterback (as well as his other key players) will be, presuming the unlikelihood that new players don't suddenly show up on the scene.

Through the years, we never settled on a candidate to play a role before auditions and our minds always remained open to the possibility of an unknown candidate who might surprise us. And, in the process of imagining who might play what role, I never discussed the possibility (or probability) with a student. I didn't want to get someone's hopes up by suggesting they'd play a part in advance of the audition even if I had a hunch the person would win the role, only to disappoint the candidate later.

I also tried to avoid such discussions with adult actors at Center Stage, although they were more likely to try to broach the subject with me to see where they stood. Even with my own daughters, I never discussed whether they would play a role or not. I expected them to go through the audition process and receive news of casting when everyone else did. Our daughter, Gina, as an example, was called back for major roles for Youth CONNection productions of *Brigadoon* and *South Pacific* but didn't win the role in either case. In Mia's case, there were a few instances when she asked me if I would consider her for a certain role at Center Stage, and I replied that I probably didn't see her in the role but she was welcome to audition anyway.

Disappointing people, even my own daughters, was part and parcel of casting. I had to learn to accept this hard fact as a vital aspect of directing. To put it simply, to be performed, a play needs a cast – and assembling a cast creates disappointment. There is simply no way around it.

For years, we had to post the cast list on the auditorium doors, so receiving the casting news was a very public experience. Disappointed students had to stand side by side with students celebrating getting major roles. In the summers, we literally mailed letters, informing candidates of casting, making it more of a private experience of receiving the news, good or bad. As one alumnus of the Youth CONNection recently shared with me, "Waiting for the casting letter was like waiting for an acceptance to college."

With the arrival of the internet, we could set up a web page where the casting was posted. In the case of the Drama Club, it became our practice to post the cast online after school on Fridays, giving our candidates the weekend to experience and hopefully get over their disappointment.

Through the years, every now and then a few candidates who

didn't receive the role they hoped for would decide not to do the show. To me, a veteran performer choosing not to participate was a shame, and I often tried to dissuade the student from the decision, but I had to accept when someone wouldn't.

THE "BOX"

This issue prompted me to begin a practice. On our audition registration form, we began to include what would become known as "the box," which asked the candidate if he or she would participate whether it was a lead part or an ensemble role. Many kids wondered if it was a trick question. Some students weren't honest in their response to the box and checked that they would participate no matter what, only to drop out when not cast in a leading role. But it wasn't a trick question at all. I was simply trying to avoid disappointing someone by cutting them, only to have to contact that person after the fact because someone had dropped out. At the same time, I remember several candidates who indicated they would accept only a major role, and that's exactly how they were cast. Again, the object was to have the best cast possible.

I found adults at Center Stage to be generally more honest about answering the question, which didn't diminish their disappointment when not cast in the role they had hoped for.

At our first cast meeting, especially of Drama Club and Youth CONNection productions, I spent time addressing the matter of casting, explaining that disappointment is a normal human emotion, but cast members needed to put it behind them as quickly as possible and participate positively. Almost always, this is what they did. I can even think of high school seniors, who had hoped to play major roles, who were able to get over the disappointment and lead by example as veteran members of the ensemble. It warms my heart to remember these young people.

Within our family, as directors, we didn't always agree on casting. I remember, early in the life of the Youth CONNection, after a callback for *Bye Bye Birdie*, Fran wanted one candidate for Albert Peterson and I wanted another. That night we discussed it at length, each giving our reasons for wanting our person, finally deciding to sleep on it and resolve the casting dilemma the next day. Come morning, I said to Fran, "After sleeping on it, I feel you were right. We'll go with your candidate." She replied, "I feel the same way about yours. I think you were right about him." I don't recall how, but after laughing it off, we somehow made a decision.

It was sometimes so difficult to decide on a role that we had a second and, in a few instances, a third callback for a particular part. Other times, the candidates for a given role didn't seem to cut it, and we cast someone who had not been called for the role. A particular instance occurred at Sacred Heart Academy for *The King and I*. A freshman who gave a great audition had been called back for Anna but not for Lady Thiang. When our Lady Thiang candidates fell flat, we called the freshman into the room and had her read for the role, which she ended up winning.

If someone were to ask me what wins roles, *talent* might seem like the obvious answer, and it certainly is important. But I would have to say that, at the amateur level (and perhaps the professional as well) *confidence* and a *competitive spirit* go a very long way. In our family, we would come to call students who exuded those two qualities (along with talent) *barracudas*. Occasionally, we might have someone whose singing showed potential but who just didn't have the confidence and drive in an audition to convince us he was the person for the role.

When we had two or more similarly gifted candidates, which was often the case, we had to go simply with a *feeling* of who would be better for the role. I think of an audition for *Legally Blonde* with the Youth CONNection, and we couldn't agree on who would play Emmett. Fran and Mia preferred one candidate, while I preferred another. My candidate had never played a role with us, despite always doing a stellar job in the ensemble. I would come to tease him, saying, "You're the most talented guy who *never* played a role in a Youth CONNection production." (He did go on to play several very important roles in the years to come.) The night of the callback, Fran, Mia, and I must have debated for two hours about the role, unable to agree. I suggested calling back my candidate again because I felt I needed to see him one more time. For me it was very close (as it often is!), but ultimately I conceded to Fran and Mia, agreeing that their candidate might be the better fit. Having multiple possibilities for a role is a great problem to have. I have no doubt it's a reality on the professional level. That said, my candidate accepted a role in the ensemble and, like always, he performed at the very highest level.

THE "PRINCESS COMPLEX"

I found through the years that some people pigeon-holed themselves into one particular role and weren't open to other roles. In the process, if they were asked to read for a role that they weren't interested in, they gave only a half-hearted attempt. Allow me to add that actors, young and old, might not know what they're right for – or, at the very least, *can't* know what a director thinks they're right for.

I came to coin a term I called the "princess complex" where some females only saw themselves as the ingénue rather than the comic role or the villainous role. I remember actors dropping out, having won a role, but not the role they wanted. I remember a guy dropping out of a production because he had been cast in a supporting role, the antagonist, instead of as the main character. The candidate's girlfriend, also a performer, even told me I had made a mistake by not casting him as the leading man. "Why is that?" I asked. "Because he would have given you one hundred percent," she replied. I simply answered that I had almost never encountered an actor who gave me less than one hundred percent.

LESSON:

...actors, young and old, might not know what they're right for – or, at the very least, can't know what a director thinks they're right for.

In another instance, a girl who won a supporting role told me she wasn't going to accept a "second ass" part. Quite an inappropriate response, in my opinion!

Thankfully, many actors accepted roles of varying types and sizes. Without such people, there would be no such thing as live theater. I recently ran into the parents of a former Youth CONNection actor, and I found myself reminiscing about how their son seemed to fluctuate from one year to the next between chorus roles and major roles like Man in Chair in *The Drowsy Chaperone* or Captain Hook in *Peter Pan*. In the process, he participated fully and positively in both ensemble and leading roles. It's easy to see, I'm sure, why egoless cast members like this person were among my favorites.

Beyond talent and a competitive spirit, I would add lack of inhibition and open-mindedness as important factors in winning a role. In our family, we enjoy reminiscing about the auditions for my very last Shelton High School production, *The Addams Family*, and about one of the most uninhibited and creative kids we had ever directed. Only a sophomore at the time, this person was a true chameleon – certainly not an actor who pigeon-holed herself into a "princess" type of role. Whether auditioning for Morticia, Wednesday, Grandma, or even Pugsley, she gave a great audition. At the time, we certainly could have cast her in any of the roles, but we simply put her where we needed her the most, as Pugsley. Given her versatility and her willingness to play any role, she turned in a wonderful performance in the role. She would go on to play important roles in future shows with the Drama Club, the Youth CONNection, and beyond...and, in the rare instances when she wasn't cast in a major role, she was an incredibly valuable member of the ensemble.

I don't care who you are, as a person in the position of casting a play, there will always be critics – people who feel you've cast your "favorite." I don't suppose there's any way to change the minds of such critics. Anyone in our position knows what I'm talking about. Similarly, I often cast someone I wasn't close to or whom I had never seen in my life. A question I would ask the critics, given my desire to do great theater is, *Why would I want to cast anyone other than the best person for the role?*

LESSON:
I don't care who you are, as a person in the position of casting a play, there will always be critics...

I recall a social gathering at our house one summer with the cast of *Joseph and the Amazing Technicolor Dreamcoat*. The young man who had been cast as Joseph and I were talking, and I explained that I had been occasionally accused of choosing favorites or pre-casting, "But," I continued, "no one can accuse me of that in this case since I never saw you in my life before this audition." The actor replied. "You've seen me before." Puzzled, I asked where and when. "Two years ago, you cut me!" I was stunned. I explained that we seldom cut a boy. He shared that, at the time, he was painfully shy. He had somehow gotten over his shyness, he gave a standout portrayal as Joseph, and he went on to do some notable professional work after performing with us.

I can think of another actor who would go on to play a string of major roles with the Youth CONNection who was cut at her first audition. It may sound odd, but there's something I liked about these instances. To me, they illustrated a will to improve and succeed. In the case of this person, she was cut in her first attempt and then was cast in the ensemble in her second. It wasn't until her third audition that she was cast in a major role. I liked that she had paid some dues, learning and growing, before appearing in her first major role.

BASKETBALL STAR TURNED STAGE PERFORMER

I can recall countless other times when we cast someone in a major role who had no prior experience with us – and even no experience whatsoever!

I think of our 1982 production of *The King and I.* That fall before official practice started, the head basketball coach had invited some of us younger teachers to join varsity players in the gym to play "pick up" games. Heck, I was only thirty, and I had always loved playing basketball.

One afternoon, the captain of the team asked me what musical I was doing, and he told me he was thinking about trying out.

"That's great," I said, "but why have you waited until your senior year to audition?"

"I don't know," he said. "I've always wanted to, but I was afraid of what my friends would say."

"And now?" I asked.

"I don't give a damn what they think anymore," he said while dribbling and taking practice shots.

It made sense. As a senior, he was growing in identity and maturity.

"But let me ask this," he continued. "Can I play the King?"

His confidence and unfiltered brashness was amusing to say the least.

"It's your first time auditioning. I don't think you'll be playing the King," I explained with more than a touch of irony.

"But Mr. Scarpa," he said. "If you let me play the King, I promise you I'll give a hundred and ten percent at every practice."

He thought like an athlete. I liked that.

Come audition time, we watched the basketball captain give a not-so-effective audition.

The male talent that year was a little shallow, though, with most of our boys being underclassmen. Our only veteran senior boy, a gifted singer, would need to play Lun Tha, the singing role in the show.

As Fran and I sat on the carpet of our living room, reading and shuffling the applications of candidates back and forth, we both knew that we didn't have a King. It wasn't that our boys weren't talented, but they were too young and inexperienced, at the time, to play such an important role.

I pushed a paper in front of Fran and said, "I think this is going to have to be our King. It won't be easy, but we'll make it work."

She was baffled. "I don't even know who this kid is!"

"The basketball player," I replied.

Alarmed, she moaned, "The basketball player? Gar! Have you lost your freaking mind? He can't sing or act or anything. The kid's got no talent at all."

"It's a gut feeling I have," I said. "I grew up around sports, and I know this kid. He has a confidence and maturity that none of our other boys have. And I've done a little background checking on him. He's an achiever, on the basketball court, in the classroom, and in life. He succeeds in everything he does. And he'll succeed here too. It's who he is."

And succeed he did. I have no doubt it's the only play he ever appeared in, and he did so with great success. In the process, we had a great time directing him, even turning the "Shall We Dance?" polka into a quasi basketball footwork drill...a wonderful memory!

Because we had a limited pool of candidates in the amateur world, we sometimes didn't have a candidate who was perfect for a role, so we needed to choose the best option given talent, confidence, and experience. My story about the star basketball player is a good example.

With adults, it seemed like many of our best actors were in their late fifties and early sixties, and often we needed them to play roles where a forty-year-old would have been a more appropriate candidate. But among forty-year-olds, the pickings were mighty slim. I would come to joke that forty-year-olds were too busy taking their kids to dance classes and soccer games to act in plays.

Another important factor for the director of amateur theater (and I daresay for the director of professional theater) is prior knowledge of a candidate. In the world of high school and community theater, we directors often have prior experience working with many of our actors. We know who takes direction well and who doesn't. We know who thrives in front of an audience and who doesn't. We know who learns lines quickly and efficiently and who doesn't. I could go on, but you get the idea. So, is the audition important? Yes, it is vitally important, but it's not the only factor.

LESSON:
Gut instinct, by the way, is a vitally important factor in casting.

I think of a boy who played the role of Motel Kamzoil, the poor tailor, in our 1978 production of *Fiddler on the Roof*. The competition for male roles as usual wasn't as heavy as for female roles. While this young man won the role, we knew he would need a lot of work. We could see in the audition room that he didn't read that well from the script, but I had a gut feeling that he was the best candidate, type wise, for the role. Gut instinct, by the way, is a vitally important factor in casting. What we learned about our Motel was that he was entirely devoid of ego and took direction beautifully, ultimately giving a very funny and sensitive performance.

The following summer, the same young man would audition for another production of *Fiddler* which we directed with the Orange Players, but this time, in a similar shallow pool of young men, we cast him in a different role, the Russian suitor Fyedka. After the "read through," a cast member whom we had worked with in other Orange Players productions remarked to me, "It looks like you have a great cast except for maybe that Shelton kid." We assured him that our student would deliver, and, once more, he succeeded beautifully.

Theater is no different than anything else. In all lines of work, management wants to hire someone they have come to know and someone whom they can count on. On the professional level, I think of an example of a friend of mine who had been cast in three Broadway plays. There was an interesting common factor. In each case, it was the same director. Logic would say to me that the director enjoyed working with our friend and didn't hesitate to cast him again and again.

Similarly, outside of the world of theater, I had a related experience. When I left teaching in my early thirties and then decided to go back to the classroom, I called the principal of Shelton High School. Having prior knowledge of my teaching ability, he was all too happy to rehire me. Concurrently, in resigning from the yearbook company I had been working for, the manager asked me if I knew any sharp candidates in Connecticut who might be interested in my job. My hypothesis? Those in a hiring position like to hire a person they know can get the job done. It is the reason employers ask for references on a resume.

Casting decisions are complex ones. In the professional world, a director is faced with a plethora of wonderful choices. Often there are several good candidates even in the more limited world of amateur theater. I recall one girl who also played a succession of roles with the Youth CONNection, four in a five year period. Upon hearing a complaint about casting her again, I asked, "Should I not cast her because she's a great singer? Or should I not cast her because she's a great actor? Perhaps I shouldn't cast her because she never misses a rehearsal and is never tardy to one. Or should I not cast her because she is always the first to learn her lines and never needs to 'call' for a line?"

Ultimately, choosing roles relies tremendously on the director's concept of who he believes is right for a role, who he thinks is dependable, and who he thinks will succeed at the highest level. The director is the artist, and the choices he makes are unique to him. Two different directors, viewing the same pool of candidates auditioning, might very likely choose two different casts.

EVEN BETTE WASN'T A SURE BET

Not everyone knows that, before she was a star, the famous Bette Midler appeared in the ensemble of the original production of *Fiddler on the Roof* on Broadway, understudying Tevye's eldest daughter Tzeitel and eventually taking over the role. At the time, Ms. Midler was a virtual unknown.

There is a wonderful story about Bette Midler from one of my favorite books about theater, *Audition* by Michael Shurtleff, who was a casting director. Shurtleff talks about Midler's Mary Magdalene audition for *Jesus Christ Superstar*. By this time, he explains, she had, in fact, gained celebrity status:

Bette Midler sang "I Don't Know How to Love Him" like no one else: disillusioned, hurt, vulnerable, with the pain of a Mary Magdalene who had been made to believe again after she was determined not to because of the hurts she had experienced. (Director) Tom O'Horgan adored her...but eventually, I think, he realized this mature, voluptuous, womanly interpretation of the role would not fit in with his cast of hippies and flower children.

Ultimately, Shurtleff makes the following point:

I tell this tale to show that actors must not worry about why they don't get a role; they should only concern themselves with doing the best damn audition they know how to do. Midler did brilliant auditions for Superstar, *but she was not cast because it would have disrupted the casting of the rest of the show.*

Many times I have heard directors say about an actor: "That is the best audition we'll ever see of that role. Too bad we can't cast him." Their regret is genuine. But there has to be a balance in casting – the parts must fit like a jigsaw puzzle – and there are times when the best auditioners don't "fit."

An actor cannot concern himself with that; there lies madness. Just go ahead and audition well, cry a little when you don't get the role you want, but never ask why. The why is usually a series of imponderables over which the actor has no control.

For me, this passage sums up casting beautifully. The "jigsaw puzzle" Shurtleff speaks of is something the actor (or the caring parents of a teen actor) can't possibly conceive of, in part, because that puzzle resides inside of the creative mind of the director. And, presuming the director cares about the quality of his work, it has nothing to do with favoritism.

The reality is the director has a concept of what he's looking for. For *The Sound of Music*, he may be looking for the second coming of Julie Andrews or he may be looking for the very opposite of a Julie Andrews type. It is something the actor has absolutely no control over.

As I've said, in the world of theater, a director often comes under fire when certain candidates don't get what they want. I've also noticed that sometimes actors are notoriously bad at realizing what roles they are right for or even evaluating their own overall ability (acting, singing, and dancing). In the professional world, we have heard our daughter Mia speak of the matter as "knowing your lane."

Those who criticize, typically, are thinking of only themselves (or their parents are thinking only of their own child). Those who criticize are not witness to the other candidates who auditioned or to the myriad of factors, some of which I've mentioned, that come into play during the audition process.

In a sense I understood because I remembered a few instances when I myself had felt critical of casting decisions, knowing so little about how they were made at the time and thinking only of my own wishes. But being on the other side of the table, I could look back on those times and see why the directors had made their choices. An example is a college musical I auditioned for called *The Streets of New York* when I felt I was more talented than the actor who was cast as the romantic lead. Looking back on the choice years later, I realized that he was several inches taller than I was, and he had lighter features than I did. Today, my hunch is the director was probably more interested in casting a 5'11" actor with handsome Anglo features than a 5'7" actor with handsome Italian features, and the differential in talent (if there was one) probably wasn't enough to make him change his mind.

Sometimes when such criticisms filtered back to me, which they inevitably did, in my less patient moments I said, "I have forgotten more about casting than this person will ever know." Patient or not, being who I am and striving for excellence as I did, my focus was always on casting those I felt would help our productions reach the level of excellence we were striving for.

In the process, there were a good many candidates I would eventually disappoint because they couldn't win a leading role every time, just as a team can't win a championship every season. But disappointing people, as I've stated, went with the territory. There was simply no way to circumvent it. It wasn't too many years before I came to a realization: "Audition for me often enough, and I will eventually disappoint you." Not because I wanted to, of course, but just because of the ebb and flow of casting needs from one production to another.

Ultimately, patrons would compliment us on our casting decisions, somehow marveling at how we successfully chose the right people for the right roles. It was a matter we took very seriously to be sure.

ACT II, SCENE 4

> **I am a fan of rehearsal. I like doing it over and over and over and over until it looks like you never did it before.**
>
> BILL NIGHY, ACTOR

I would come to realize very early in my life as a director that I loved the rehearsal process. When I was in rehearsal, I was in a zone. Some actors may have found me intense, but I would explain that I was simply passionate. In our Center Stage years, adult actors would often tease me about my passion which I didn't mind at all.

When I was in rehearsal, my reality was that time stood still and I was very much lost in the process of working on a scene or a musical number. For me, a rehearsal would begin at 7:00, and in the blink of an eye, it was time to end the rehearsal two and a half or three hours later. To quote Beat writer William S. Burroughs: "I would say, in general, that for anyone who wants to get out of time, any kind of art is useful. That's what art is all about. That's what it's for, to get out of time." This wasn't the reason I did theater, but it was what doing theater did for me.

From the very beginning, directing plays was a trial and error process. Luckily, when it came to theater, I was a fast learner. Having had the good fortune to have appeared in more than one production under the direction of Thom Peterson in college, I learned good lessons about how a director should organize rehearsals and what expectations a director should have of his cast.

TO FAIL TO PLAN IS TO PLAN TO FAIL

When we got underway directing *The Music Man* in 1976, I began each week with a very detailed weekly rehearsal schedule designating half hour or full hour time slots to specific scenes or songs. Not only did I want to have a plan, but I also didn't want to waste people's time. It isn't unusual for a director to decide what will be worked on at the rehearsal rather than in advance. In such cases, everyone is called to rehearsal, and maybe you rehearse and maybe you don't.

LESSON:
Our philosophy was that every cast member was equally important.

In these early years of directing, I was told of one high school director who operated without a schedule. While the entire cast was called to every rehearsal, more often than not, cast members in attendance wouldn't rehearse. In the process, sitting out in the "house," cast members would naturally begin to socialize. I'm told the director would reprimand them, telling them that, as ensemble members, they weren't even needed.

Fran and I had a very different approach. Our philosophy was that every cast member was equally important. The ensemble, then, was *vitally* important to our success.

When talking to our casts, I would often use one of my patented sports analogies to illustrate my point. I would tell each and every one of our high school casts about a friend of mine who was a high school basketball star...about the night I watched him break a school record, scoring an unbelievable fifty-four points. My friend was on fire and simply couldn't miss. But his team lost a close game to an opposing team that wasn't very good with the score being something like 64-60. "What good was his scoring ability," I would point out, "if the rest of the team was only able to contribute six points?" For me, the goal was team, not individual, success.

My point was that, to be a winner, every member of the team needs to contribute. Using another sports analogy, I would ask, "While the quarterback of a football team may receive more publicity and acclaim than linemen, how can he succeed if his linemen don't block for him?" Not everyone is the star of the team, but everyone plays a key role, and championship teams are populated by role players who are doing their part to create success.

I would come to feel the strength of our ensembles was one of several factors that contributed to the high quality of our shows. Great leads come and go, but there is no reason why an ensemble can't be great from one show to another. And that happens in rehearsal.

LESSON:
...championship teams are populated by role players who are doing their part to create success.

So, with the use of a detailed schedule, we tried to organize our rehearsal time to be as productive as possible, with as little idle time as possible. And, with a detailed and effective schedule, very little time is wasted and much progress can be achieved for all involved.

THE REHEARSAL SPACE: SACRED SPACE

That said, if cast members had a little down time or arrived early, I expected them to be silent in the rehearsal space which I considered sacrosanct. Let me point out that the "rehearsal space" was wherever the rehearsal was taking place, and that was often in a variety of locales for a variety of reasons. Optimally, it was on the stage, but often, because of set building, painting, and decorating, the rehearsal space might be somewhere else: the chorus room, the school lecture hall, the main lobby.

With tongue in cheek, I would explain, especially about the auditorium at Shelton High School, "This room is my church, and theater is my religion. I expect you to show the same respect to me, my rehearsal, your fellow actors, and this space that you would show in church."

They knew I was kidding, but at the same time, they knew I *wasn't* kidding. And when an unaware person, perhaps a parent volunteer, happened into our rehearsal space, chattering away, I quickly made my way over to them and respectfully but firmly told the offender I needed him to be silent. Outside of the actual theater, with people passing by in a more public space like the main lobby or a hallway of the building, it was harder to enforce this requirement, which I typically found frustrating, being who I am.

When smartphones became the norm, we banned their use in rehearsals. I told cast members that they could learn how to become better actors and performers, not by texting and scrolling, but by paying close attention to the rehearsal before them.

A few other fundamental requirements for the rehearsal process are punctuality and regular, even perfect, attendance. As in almost any endeavor, some people live their lives ten or fifteen minutes behind schedule. When it came to our teens, many of them depended on their parents to drive them to rehearsal. I would explain that, while their parents might run late to everything else in their lives, cast members were going to have to get on their parents' cases to run on time for rehearsals.

And when a cast member was tardy, I addressed it each and every time. I would immediately approach the cast member individually and quietly remind him that he arrived *x* number of minutes late and that tardiness was unacceptable. The more vigilant I was about the matter, the fewer times it continued to be a problem.

Absenteeism was a bigger challenge than tardiness. In the early years, we seldom had a full cast rehearsal without at least a few absent cast members. Other commitments, sicknesses, and more nebulous excuses caused people to miss rehearsal. What I quickly realized was that, with five or six missing cast members, a rehearsal wasn't worth having. The staging or choreography would have to be retaught again for the benefit of those who had missed rehearsal. Certainly by the time Fran and I had children, I found myself with a new existential problem: Why am I here running a fruitless rehearsal instead of home with my wife and small children? It was at this point that I got stricter about attendance.

ATTENDANCE POLICY

We would put into motion an attendance policy. A cast member was allowed to miss no more than two rehearsals, which had to be cleared with me at the beginning of the rehearsal period. At this point, I began devising a schedule for the entire rehearsal period, which was typically six to eight weeks in length. At our first cast meeting, I would explain that my expectation was that everyone would have perfect attendance, but I understood that a cast member might have other irrevocable commitments – family obligations like weddings or religious holidays. I would need to be informed of those up front. A cast member telling me on a Friday that he had to attend a wedding the next day was unacceptable. "I assume the wedding invitation didn't arrive today," I would exclaim.

Could a student participate in our plays if she was in another activity which had practices or meetings at the same time we rehearsed? Usually the answer was no. I remember two different phone calls, one from a priest who ran a youth group and another from a cheerleading coach, asking me if we could share the student. In both cases, there were simply too many conflicts between the schedules for the two activities. My answer was, "An important life skill is choosing priorities. If participation in a youth group is this student's priority, I am perfectly fine with that choice. But since the two activities conflict, the student will have to make a choice." It may sound extreme, but I would offer that great theater doesn't happen without a major commitment from the participants.

If another advisor, like our band director, approached me in advance, we often worked out our respective rehearsal schedules in a way that would allow a student to participate in both activities. But it needed to be worked out beforehand.

Even in the case of week-long vacations in February or April, I didn't excuse students from rehearsals. With each high school play, one of the long vacation weeks fell into the rehearsal period, and I found these weeks to be the most productive of the entire rehearsal process. In most cases, being away for a week precluded a student from participating.

What about sickness, you might ask. That was a trickier one. If a student had already been granted two excused absences, we had to keep a close eye on this concern. We expected to be notified that a student was ill and couldn't attend rehearsal.

I recall a particular case of chronic absences due to illness. The student in question seemed healthy enough whenever I saw him, though. I felt almost certain it was irresponsibility, not illness, that was causing him to miss rehearsals. I wanted to say, "You're too sick to be in a play. You belong in a hospital." Even though I wasn't quite that blunt, it was one of those instances when I had to remove a student from a cast because of too many absences.

To this point, by the time Gina and Mia came over to the directing side of the table, we required a phone call in cases where a cast member was too sick to rehearse – and we also expected the call to come from the teen himself rather than a parent. We felt it was a good way to have them learn responsibility. Ultimately, though, sickness being a reason why a performer was removed from a cast was a rare occurrence indeed.

Finally, attendance at dress rehearsals was non-negotiable. Seldom was it a problem, but I remember a few cases where it was. Let's consider the basketball captain who played the lead in *The*

King and I. A week before we opened, he told me he'd be missing the final dress rehearsal because he would be attending a scholar-athlete awards dinner. While I was happy to hear of his accomplishment, I explained that if he wasn't at the final dress rehearsal, he wouldn't be playing the King on opening night. Logical fellow that he was, he asked, "But who will play the King if I don't?" I responded, "I don't know. I'll play it...or Fran will play it...or someone who is *not* you will play it if you miss the final dress rehearsal." I mean, how on earth would we possibly have had a fruitful final dress rehearsal for *The King and I* without the King? Ultimately, he chose our rehearsal over the awards dinner.

Let me add that the same attendance policy applied to adult actors at Center Stage, but I often found, unhappily, that I had to be more flexible while working with adults. Why? With a cast of forty or fifty high school students, there was almost always someone that I could replace an actor with. But with a smaller cast of age-appropriate actors, replacements were much harder to come by. That said, I voiced my expectations in the same way.

LESSON:

...great performances only happen as a result of great rehearsals...

If any of this sounds extreme, consider the following. Imagine rehearsing a scene that has five characters and two of the actors are absent. There is little if any point in conducting the rehearsal. The other actors' time would be better spent staying at home studying lines. The same is true of an ensemble rehearsal. With multiple people missing, it is a colossal waste of everyone's time.

We simply expected full dedication from every cast member, just as we dedicated ourselves fully to the process. I knew in my heart and in the depths of my soul that great performances only happen as a result of great rehearsals, an axiom that I preached over and over again throughout my career.

There is an old superstition about dress rehearsals, especially in the world of amateur theater. With the myriad of problems, technical and otherwise, that can go wrong in a dress rehearsal, the saying goes, "Bad dress rehearsal; great opening night!" It is a saying that I would come to strongly disagree with. Certainly, I understand the reason for such a superstition. It can give a cast hope after a disastrous and discouraging final dress rehearsal. But I always felt that, when we had bad dress rehearsals, I had somehow failed as a director. Either I had not effectively organized the technical side of the production, or I hadn't properly readied my cast for an audience. With a little experience, the latter of these two concerns was simply never the case. But the technical piece was sometimes a little harder to control.

I recall that after the first dress rehearsal of Fran's and my last Youth CONNection production of *Annie* in 2018, I addressed the cast, saying, "Right now, *Annie* is bigger than I am. But I promise you that by tomorrow night (our second of three dress rehearsals), I will straighten these issues out." Again, the problem wasn't that our performers weren't ready but that the set changes had been fraught with problems and the lighting changes sloppy. By assuring them that I would fix the situation, it helped assuage the cast's anxiety and uncertainty so that they could be worry free by opening night.

I personally wanted to avoid bad dress rehearsals, especially final dress rehearsals, like the plague. At the very least, our goal was for our cast to be performance ready a week before opening night. I would explain to our casts that with the great potential for technical problems, their performance readiness was the last thing we needed to worry about. It was their job and ours to make sure they were prepared. So I came to amend that superstition. "Bad dress rehearsal, great opening night," I would say, "I don't know about that one. But what I am *absolutely* certain of is this: Great dress rehearsal, great opening night!"

CONCENTRATION ON MEMORIZATION

Memorizing lines was seldom a problem for high school and college students who have young, keen minds, but once in a great while when an actor fell down on the job, I really got on his case. I remember one student who, well into the rehearsal process, didn't know the lyrics to one of his solos. I told the rehearsal group to take a five minute break, and I left the room with the intention of memorizing the lyrics myself. It was a song which I, in fact, did not know by heart. Upon returning, I pulled the actor aside and sang the song to him. Then I explained, "I just learned these lyrics in five minutes, so I have a suggestion for you. Go home and spend five minutes learning these lyrics before our next rehearsal. If you can't learn them in five minutes, take ten. If you can't learn them in ten, then take a half hour. But be sure you know them next time."

Something I became convinced of through directing and acting is that memorization is the result of knowing how to study lines and putting in the study time. I remember seeing Broadway legend Richard Kiley, famous for playing Don Quixote, interviewed about another play he was doing. The interviewer asked, "How did you ever learn all of those lines?" Kiley clearly didn't care for the question. "If you spent as much time as I do learning lines, you'd know them too," he offered. Clearly, he didn't want to be complimented on being able to memorize.

When I played President Harry Truman in the one man play *Give 'em Hell, Harry!* at Center Stage 1.0., I memorized ninety pages of text. Some nights, as I waited backstage while Fran made the curtain speech solo, I asked myself, "Is it possible that I really know all of these lines?" Probably a universal question that all actors ask themselves. I even kept a little black book with an outline of the play in my pocket as a safety valve in case I was ever at a loss. I never needed to pull out the black book, though, and with the exception of mixing up the names McCarthy (Senator Edward) and MacArthur (General Douglas) one night, I never made a mistake over the course of ten performances. Still, after a performance, like Richard Kiley, I wanted to be complimented on my portrayal of the character, not on my ability to memorize lines.

Adults found it more challenging to memorize lines than kids for several reasons. First, my experience strongly suggests that younger minds are better at memorization – that the older we get, often the harder it is to remember lines. Also, it becomes challenging to carve out time to study when a person works all day and rehearses all night. A professional actor in a Broadway show has a full-time job too – rehearsing. After his rehearsal day, he is free to study lines. Not as easy for an accountant playing a role in an amateur play. Still, there are some non-rehearsal nights for actors when they can and must spend time effectively studying their lines. During those Center Stage years, actors not knowing lines was probably the most common cause of stress for me as a director.

I could name dozens of instances where a cast member made me worry. I remember one in particular who played a small role in one of our plays. Needing a certain age and type, I had recruited him. In a small role, night after night, every delivery was an adventure. We were never sure what he was going to say...or even if he was going to deliver the line at all. One night, after a performance, I asked him how old he was. "Me?" he said. "Why, I'm eighty-six." It was news to me, as I would have guessed his age to be ten or fifteen years younger. At the same time, I thought to myself, *What did you expect from a guy this age?*

In another instance, someone was having line problems in a performance. This actor was about fifty and playing a very large role. Fortunately, he had the ability to get himself out of a jam, but watching him struggle was disconcerting to me. Toward the end of the first act, I turned to a high school student who had volunteered to run lights for the show. "See this guy, Kate?" I said. "He's flubbed more lines tonight in the first act of this play than *all* of the actors who performed in the SHS Drama Club and *all* of the actors who performed with the Youth CONNection have in the last ten years." It was true.

The problem with an actor not knowing his lines is he inhibits the progress of other actors during rehearsals. My goal as a director was for the scenes in the play to build in momentum, to have good pacing, to not have superfluous pauses between lines unless a pause served a dramatic purpose. It makes me think of a high school production of *Fiddler on the Roof* Fran and I saw when we were in college. After the show, I said, "The kid who played Tevye did a good job, right?" Fran just shrugged, "He was pretty good," she replied, "but he slowed the play down, and you could tell that he was thinking, 'what's my next line' between every delivery." I would learn quickly what she meant.

"SPEAK THE SPEECH, I PRAY YOU, AS I PRONOUNCE IT TO YOU..."

To take poetic liberty with Shakespeare's famous line, I would amend it to say: *Speak the speech, I pray you, as the author wrote it!* An expectation I had for actors of all ages was that they deliver the lines as written. This was important for a few different reasons. First, I felt an obligation to honor the words of the playwright. An author doesn't choose his words arbitrarily. Certainly, we wouldn't paraphrase Shakespeare's language. Neither should we paraphrase a more contemporary writer like Neil Simon. In an article in *Playbill* when Nathan Lane was doing a revival of *The Odd Couple*, he made this very cogent point. He said that one of the reasons Simon's plays are so funny is because of the way in which he words things, and paraphrasing lines diminishes Simon's comic brilliance.

In the world of theater, some actors are what I call "paraphrasers." Somehow, it isn't their inclination to memorize the lines as written, but to deliver them in their own words. Throughout my directing career, I typically found this methodology to be a problem.

From a practical perspective, I noticed that paraphrasers almost never say the line the same way twice, and are more likely, therefore, to get tongue-tied than actors who know the script word for word and deliver it the same way in every performance. Paraphrasing disrupts the pacing of a scene, and the other actors on the stage are often thrown by the new way in which their scene partner delivers his lines from one night to the next. For the actor on stage with a paraphraser, their thinking is usually, "What the hell did he just say and is it the cue for my next line?" It's simply unfair to the other actors not to know the lines as written.

My take? Paraphrasers are sloppy about learning lines and refuse to give this important aspect of preparing a play the attention to detail it deserves. Usually these actors are very talented individuals, but this practice of paraphrasing isn't good for the play nor is it good for the other actors. I'll take the actor who I can depend on to say the lines verbatim every day and twice on Sunday.

LESSON:
Paraphrasing disrupts the pacing of a scene…

That's not to say that the ability to paraphrase isn't, in fact, vitally important for an actor to have in his skill set. I would explain to novice actors that they needed to know what the scene was about and have the ability to put it into their own words because, in a pinch, it may be necessary to paraphrase – but only in a pinch!

As my daughter Mia, who has shared the stage with many actors, recently said, "When I'm on stage with an actor who really knows his lines and owns them, it helps me to eliminate stress and anxiety and stay fully in the moment."

TO WATCH THE FILM OR NOT TO WATCH THE FILM...

I could certainly write a separate book on the subject of preparing a cast during the rehearsal process...but let me add a few final points.

I have heard of directors of high school and community theater discouraging cast members from watching a film version of a Broadway play. For instance, for a production of *The Sound of Music*, the girl playing Maria is told not to watch Julie Andrews in the film. The rationale is the director doesn't want his actress copying Julie Andrews' performance.

To me, it would be like telling a student violinist not to listen to a recording of Itzhak Perlman. Or telling a high school basketball player not to watch Steph Curry or Caitlin Clark on television. God forbid that the student's performance is influenced by witnessing someone else's greatness.

I took the opposite approach. I expected my cast members to watch great performances on film, even required it. I didn't want them to copy the performance, and the truth is, most people couldn't copy it if they wanted to unless in their arsenal of gifts was the ability to do impersonations. But watching great performances helps young actors (and even experienced actors) grow in their ability to interpret the written word, to understand nuance, and to develop important techniques like comic timing and dramatic pauses, to give a few examples.

During the rehearsal period, I wanted actors to learn to tell the truth – not Julie Andrews' truth, but their own personal truth. I always loved this explanation of how to be a successful actor from one of my favorite all-time actors, James Cagney. I've seen a few different variations of the quote, but it goes something like this: "I take my mark, look the other fellow in the eye, and tell the truth." Working with hundreds of actors over the years, I learned that each one has his own personal truth to tell, his own uniqueness, which has little if anything to do with how someone else played the role.

LESSON:
Let's work hard in rehearsal, make decisions about what works well, and then lock it in.

Once an actor knew his lines and had created his character, we felt it was important to "lock in" the performance. That's not to say there couldn't be any alteration during the performance period if there was good reason. But we felt that consistency was vital. We felt the other actors on stage shouldn't be surprised by what their fellow actor was doing. I was told of a play at New Haven's Long Wharf Theatre, a major professional regional theater, where acclaimed actor Sam Waterston appeared to change his interpretation from one night to another. That might be fine for a seasoned actor like Waterston, but I don't think it's a good idea for an amateur actor.

I remember working numerous times with an actor who came out with new deliveries over and over again with an audience in front of him. Not necessarily new words, but a new inflection, a different emphasis or timing. He was someone who, in my opinion, felt the rehearsal process was a terrible inconvenience – who couldn't seem to motivate himself to be creative unless he had an audience in front of him. Also, when an audience wasn't as demonstrative as we might have liked, he took matters into his own hands, choosing to "ham it up" in order to win the audience over. My observation was that two out of every three *new* deliveries didn't work. My methodology was: Let's work hard in rehearsal, make decisions about what works well, and then lock it in.

GOOD COP / BAD COP?

There were certainly actors that I was unsuccessful at getting through to. Perhaps my directing style didn't work for them. A great thing about my partnership with Fran was that I could turn these actors over to her, since her personality and approach were very different from mine, softer and less intense. I might say to her, "Fran, I'm getting nowhere with So and So. How about if you take over with her and see if you can make any progress?" Most of the time that worked well for us.

Once or twice, I heard an actor refer to Fran's and my style of directing as "good cop, bad cop." Personally, I couldn't agree less. "Good cop, bad cop" suggests an intentional tactic meant to elicit a certain response. It suggests the two people are playing roles and using a strategy. If Fran and I ever seemed like we were playing the good cop, bad cop roles, it was strictly unintentional. The reality was that we were simply being who we are in real life.

Speaking of strategies, I don't feel we *ever* used a strategy outside of expecting excellence from everyone. We each communicated that expectation in our own way, as did our daughters who learned from us. I remember a story a young actor told me of a play he was in where there were two equal male leads. At the beginning of the play, each actor entered from opposite sides of the stage. Five minutes before the curtain on opening night, the director approached him in the darkness of the wing and told him he knew he was going to do a great job. He then told him that he was the better of the two major leads. I have a strong hunch that the director then crossed behind the stage and told the other actor the same thing. Fran and I never used strategies or, may I add, rivalries to psych actors up. We simply shared with them our own truth about the stage.

In retrospect, I feel Fran and I were a great directing team, and I'm grateful for having the close working relationship that we had. We recognized each other's strengths and established our respective roles early on. I was better at placing large groups of people in an aesthetically pleasing way, and she was better at moving them about. I was better at blocking scenes with actors, and getting them going with interpretation and creating their characters. She was better at fine-tuning scenes once the actors were in great shape. Even in the Center Stage years when we weren't working so much in tandem because Fran was too immersed in the business end, I would have her come in the week before dress rehearsals, look at the scenes, and give notes.

Considering I was typically the main director, I often had the final say on all matters related to our productions. Fran loves to tell a story from one of our productions of *Oklahoma!* when she had the cast show me her choreography for "Many a New Day." After the girls finished the number, I said, "Uhm...is that what they're going to do?"

Fran reacted with deep irony. "That?" she replied. "No...not that! I just taught them that for fun! C'mon, girls, let's show Mr. Scarpa the *real* choreography!"

It's a great story to remember, but Fran did, indeed, restage the number. In rethinking the choreography, she came up with a brilliant concept where, through dance, the girls created a "surrey with the fringe on top," using a fringed blanket for the canopy and parasols for the wheels. Fran had one ensemble girl make a maneuver to turn her skirt into pants, thereby taking on the role of Curly, inviting Laurey to ride in his surrey. It was perfect. Mia and Gina have similar stories about re-choreographing numbers. In each case, I hope the new choreography added to the overall quality of the show.

I recently listened to an interview with composer/lyricist David Foster, who most recently wrote *Boop! The Musical.* He was asked if he gives the director, Jerry Mitchell, input. The interviewer said, "For instance, I just saw the show and the sound was fantastic. But if it wasn't, could you approach the director with your concerns?"

Foster balked. He explained that the mounting of a major musical isn't a democratic process, that it can't be. He continued, explaining that the director can't seek opinions from ten different people. It just isn't realistic.

In my case, I was seldom directing alone, especially musicals on the Shelton High School stage. Rather, I was working in tandem with Fran or one of our daughters. Throughout our career, Fran's input was always invaluable to the process, as she would inevitably pick up on things I had missed. We seldom had creative disagreements or arguments, and when we did, we were always able to come to a resolution. When our daughters directed with me, once again, we were able to resolve any differing opinions we might have had. One of the many lessons from the stage is that artistic differences, from casting to lighting design and everything in between, have to be worked out for the greater good of the production, and when necessary, someone has to have the final word. That someone is the director. That someone was me.

LESSON:
...artistic differences, from casting to lighting design and everything in between, have to be worked out for the greater good of the production...

As a creator, there is nothing like the rehearsal process for me. To see actors developing their roles and growing into their characters was exciting and gratifying beyond explanation. We might look at it this way: the performance period is great fun, but the rehearsal period is where creativity and hard work combine to bring a play to life.

ACT II, SCENE 5

> **Talent is cheaper than table salt. What separates the talented individual from the successful one is a lot of hard work.**
>
> STEPHEN KING, AUTHOR

I have noticed, over the course of my life, that some people are in awe of talent. In a way, I can understand why people are impressed, but given the life that we led, we encountered so many talented people that they are far too numerous to count. An acquaintance of mine, in talking about a great performer who appeared in our shows when he was a kid, said, "If you have that kind of talent, you make it, right?" If only that were true!

One only needs to watch an episode or two of *The Voice*, *American Idol*, or *America's Got Talent* and there should be no doubt in anyone's mind that great talent is fairly common. But how many of them make it? And to get a little more philosophical, what constitutes "making it?"

A parent of two talented sons once said to me, "I don't think you realize how talented my boys are." I replied with something like, "I don't think you realize how many talented kids I have encountered through the years."

Let's just say that I appreciated people who were gifted actors, singers, and dancers. Obviously, I needed them to be successful as a director. As a basketball coach and friend once remarked about a highly gifted player, "He's going to make me a great coach again."

Yes, having talented people on a team is tremendously helpful. But I can't say I was ever personally in *awe* of them.

Fran used to tell me about one of her high school teachers who seemed a bit too enamored with her talent when Fran was a kid. It's something Fran, being who she is, experienced her whole life, which brought up for her an existential question. "Do people like me for who I am or do they like me because I'm a good singer?" Ultimately, Fran relates to people in such a warm, caring, and genuine way that most people love her for the wonderful person she is more than anything else.

For me, personally, my affection for performers has never had anything to do with their ability to sing a song or deliver a line on stage. Similarly, as a high school teacher, my feelings for students had nothing to do with their intelligence or scholastic achievement, but rather with their personal qualities.

Fran and I have spent our entire lives working with talented adults, teens, and children. Are some more gifted than others? Certainly. As it is true in the worlds of sports or music or any activity, some people have more God-given ability on the stage than others. For those of us who direct plays, especially those who, like us, do so for decades, encountering a talented person is far from a novelty. It was the everyday stuff of our lives.

EXTROVERTS vs. INTROVERTS

An interesting question we might ask is: are certain kinds of personality types more likely to be successful on stage than others? I find that many people associate talent with outgoingness, assuming that an extrovert is likely to be more talented than an introvert, but I personally can't agree with such a premise. I have known introverts who have succeeded greatly on the stage and extroverts who want no part of performing in front of an audience. I think of a dad I grew up with always urging me to get his son involved in the Drama Club. "He's so hilarious," my old friend would say. "The kid keeps us in stitches all the time!" I only got his son as far as participating as a stage crew member, moving scenery. While perhaps the life of the party in a small setting, he wasn't interested in performing in front of a thousand people.

Conversely, I can think of quite a few instances where introverts blossomed on the stage. I think of one cast member, a senior who approached me before an audition years ago. She had appeared in the ensemble of our production the previous year. She stopped by my room during my free period and timidly asked if she could speak to me.

"I just wanted to ask," she began, "why did you cast me in the play last year?"

I explained that, while I was aware of her diffidence, I felt that with more confidence, she could be a really good singer, and that it was clear to me from her reading from the script that she had an exceptional ability to interpret the written word; she just needed more energy. "What I want to ask *you*," I countered, "is why aren't you competing for a major role?"

LESSON:

...I can think of quite a few instances where introverts blossomed on the stage.

I encouraged her to come into the audition with more confidence and go for broke, which is exactly what she did, winning a speaking/singing role in the process. A few years later, I ran into her father, who introduced himself to me. "Mr. Scarpa," he said, "when my daughter was in your play during her senior year, she didn't tell me she had a role with lines and songs. I was stunned when I came to the show opening night. I just couldn't believe that was my shy little girl up there!"

This actress, now in her sixties, went on to direct high school theater for years here in Connecticut, and to this day, she acts in theatrical productions.

Another notable example is a boy whom we cut several times. As stated, I have often joked that if a boy has a pulse, he gets cast.

But this particular boy timidly sang his song and recited his lines at an almost inaudible volume. Despite my urging him to speak up and sing out, he couldn't seem to bring himself to turn up the volume and let us see what he was capable of.

His mother finally emailed, explaining that she wasn't "that parent" but also expressing how much her son loved music and how badly he wanted to participate. She asked what advice I could give him that would help him succeed. I explained that he would need to show me that I could count on him to perform with some level of confidence in a play. I further explained that I wasn't trying to sell anything, but that my daughter Gina had been having great success, time after time, in pulling kids out of their shells, so I suggested her son take vocal performance lessons with Gina. He did so, and Gina got him to a level where he could audition with an acceptable level of confidence. After being cast, he appeared in the ensembles of several productions before, within a span of no more than two years, he played a succession of major roles with us, succeeding at the highest level. Today, he sings his own original music in clubs in New York. In retrospect, he went from being too much of an introvert to be cast in a play (even despite being male) to being among the most talented boys we had ever directed.

The introverted kids we encountered who ended up demonstrating an ability to succeed on the stage are simply too numerous to mention. And the list of talented people of all personality types who have passed through our doors is a long one.

As I've said, I believe with the right mindset everyone can succeed as an actor. The same principle might not be as true for singing, although I've also stated that I don't think there's any such thing as a non-singer – just a person who somehow received the wrong messages in their musical development. With that said, even with guidance it's not likely that non-singers, generally speaking, will suddenly become high level soloists. I have only occasionally seen dramatic improvements happen because singing, I feel, is a more complex matter than acting.

As far as dance goes, like anything else, some people are naturals while others aren't. I have seen girls who have studied dance for more than a decade who are largely uncoordinated, and I've worked with highly coordinated, graceful girls (and boys for that matter) who never set foot in a dance studio in their lives.

So, yes, talent is an intangible that is difficult if not impossible to explain. How do we explain a pianist who is a child prodigy?

Another important question we need to ask is: What does a person do with his talent? To Stephen King's point, is the talented person willing to work hard to develop his skills to the utmost? Is the person open to learning and taking direction? Is she focused? We have seen many talented people where the answer to these questions was a resounding "no." Consequently, even at the amateur level, such people didn't necessarily win the roles they might have if these other factors were in place.

Considering the many young people we've directed, I never promoted a professional career in the performing arts. I would offer that talent is a minimum quality needed to succeed in the professional world of acting. There are many factors that are equally important, many of which are intangibles – things like perseverance and the ability to take rejection. When one of our better girls didn't win a role with us as a high school senior said to me, "How can I expect to succeed in a professional career when I can't even win a role in high school?" I replied, "How can you hope to succeed in a professional career when you can't handle rejection in high school?"

Quite a few actors whom we directed pursued the incredibly challenging path of professional theater with varying degrees of success or lack thereof. But it's not something we were particularly interested in.

In considering the professional world of theater, though, we might ask how important is talent? Personally, I'd say, if a person isn't at the very least a gifted actor, singer, or dancer – or better yet, all three – she is delusional in thinking she'll have a professional career. But is talent enough?

Using another of my patented sports analogies, of the many gifted basketball players at Division I colleges, only 1.2 percent are said to make it to the NBA. Clearly, talent alone does not win the day or guarantee success. And clearly, talent is not unusual or hard to find.

MY FOCUS

My focus, however, was on the production I was working on, not in steering people into professional careers and, to be honest, not even trying to bring people out of their shells for that matter. If either of those things or a host of other wonderful phenomena resulted, all the better.

A truly wonderful aspect of our work was that the positive outcomes grew organically from our work and always seemed to be good ones. Kids grew in confidence. They learned how to function at the highest level as members of a team. They learned responsibility and problem solving. They grew culturally. The list of positive outcomes is endless. I suppose that's why we stuck with it for more than four decades.

I feel that Fran, being who she is, was a little more focused on these outcomes than I was. Still, I was certainly aware of the various ways kids were profiting from the theater experience, which made it all the more rewarding to do the work we did.

What we also learned rather early in the game was that we weren't so much growing tomorrow's pool of professional actors as we were helping kids to have a greater appreciation for theater. Consequently, the vast majority of students who appeared in our shows would become theatergoers in the future. In that sense, participation in amateur theater is good for the overall health of the professional theater as well.

LESSON:

The list of positive outcomes is endless. I suppose that's why we stuck with it for more than four decades.

A relative of mine who worked in the administrative end of a professional theater once told me that he felt, in his world, people looked down on the world of amateur theater. "That's too bad," I offered, "because without us, they don't exist!" Appreciation for theater, more often than not, is sparked at the amateur level.

Another perspective I have about talent is this: Whatever level of talent a person in our productions possessed added to the greater good and was, in that sense, invaluable. I remember a coach I knew who spoke of players who had long ago graduated. Remembering many of the players, I asked about the skill level of one or another, to which the coach replied, "He stunk...he stunk...he stunk." I couldn't help but feel how unfortunate it was that he felt that way, and how counterproductive it would have been if we felt the same way. It occurred to me that, while there were hundreds of kids in our productions who may not have had enough talent to win a role with us, their contribution was still vital to the success of the production.

LESSON:
Whatever level of talent a person in our productions possessed added to the greater good and was, in that sense, invaluable.

The theater is a place where talented people of all levels come together to bring a play to life. Our perspective was that each and every cast member was as important as the other and that success was achieved by *everyone* feeling valued as an important part of the whole.

ACT II, SCENE 6

It's the little details that are vital. Little things make big things happen.

JOHN WOODEN, COACH

How perfect for a guy like me to include this quote from a legendary basketball coach in my book. Long before I ever imagined performing in a play, basketball was practically my whole world. My wife recently asked me what I imagined becoming when I grew up, and it occurred to me that the only thing I ever dreamed of being was, perhaps, a basketball coach. I could never have imagined becoming a theater director. Little did I know that the lessons I learned about success in basketball and other sports would serve me well in the theater.

In the world of theater, when we talk about the little details, it is "production value" we are often talking about. And when speaking of production value, we are referring to the overall quality of a production as determined by its various elements – things like set design, lighting, costumes, sound, props, and special effects. Production value dictates how polished and visually impressive a show appears. These factors are strongly influenced, in part, by budget. Production value is also influenced by a director's creativity and his knowledge of the craft.

As directors, we weren't always able to control the level of talent or the "rightness" of our cast members, but the production value of our shows was something we had more control over from show to show.

As mentioned, I was fortunate to perform in a play for the first time back in 1973 under the direction of Thom Peterson, a versatile artist who was not only a director and choreographer, but also a scenic and costume designer. He had, in fact, received his advanced training at the Yale School of Drama. After working with Mr. Peterson, I was, in a manner of speaking, spoiled, considering the production value of my first theatrical experience was very high, to say the least. It would set the tone for how Fran and I would approach theater going forward.

LESSON:

At the professional theater, the question for me was: given our budget and resources, how can we accomplish what I'm seeing here?

We were also fortunate to have our college friend, Ron Lindberg, also a protégé of Thom Peterson, design our set for that first production of *The Music Man*, and to also have access to wonderful period costumes which were designed by Thom Peterson and crafted by Richard Harding. When I say these costumes were Broadway quality, I do not exaggerate.

Over the course of our career, we always strove to improve the quality of our production value. Succeeding very much depended on the quality and skill of those assisting us, almost all of whom, by the way, were volunteers.

As a lifetime student of the theater, I always looked at other productions, professional and amateur alike, in relation to production value, both in what worked and didn't work. At the professional theater, the question for me was: given our budget and resources, how can we accomplish what I'm seeing here?

CARDBOARD MOONS

A favorite play of ours, *The Fantasticks* by Tom Jones and Harvey Schmidt, has a short speech delivered by El Gallo, the narrator, alluding to scenery but with a much deeper meaning:

Their moon was cardboard, fragile.
It was very apt to fray,
And what was last night scenic
May seem cynic by today.

El Gallo begins the speech by gesturing to a simple cardboard moon which, at the end of the speech he flips, transforming it into a hot, burning sun.

Scenery is a most important element in the theater, and every play has its scenic requirements – whether we are talking about a play that calls for a cardboard moon or one that asks for twelve different realistic scene changes that fill a fifty foot stage, which is what we had at Shelton High School.

Through the years, we always seemed to have at least a few volunteers who were capable of making the scenery I imagined come to life. With highly skilled and dedicated teens in our early years like the Hawley brothers and later the amazing Erik Hansen, leading to great parent volunteers, we were fortunate to often have great help on our productions.

And, similarly, we were truly blessed the day that Ron Baldwin expressed an interest in designing and building our scenery, especially considering that he would stay with us for all of our fourteen years at Center Stage before we retired.

I reiterate that, not only because of the length of time he worked with us but also because of his creativity and skill, Ron was truly our partner in theater and making Center Stage the success that it became. As an artist and engineer, Ron was an amazing collaborator. I don't think there was ever a time when I said, "Do you think there's any chance we could do..." when he didn't say yes. He and I had something in common. We both thought *big*! We could always count on Ron to bring scenic magic to our productions.

Consequently, our productions would have revolving stages and the various other innovations that our set construction team created, giving our productions the professionalism we were striving for. Audience members would repeatedly compliment us on the quality of our scenery.

A favorite memory goes back to 2013 after a performance of *The Drowsy Chaperone*. We ran into a group of our customers at the local diner after a performance, and one lady made special mention of the set. "I just couldn't get over the great scenery," she commented. "Does it come in a kit?" *Yeah, lady*, I wanted to say, *a kit from Home Depot*. Actually, I did tell her that the scenery was constructed by our skilled and dedicated team of volunteers.

Besides the building and painting of scenery, there was also the matter of moving scenery during a performance – an aspect that I oversaw. At other amateur productions, we saw disorganized, ineffective set changes that took several minutes per change, often adding an extra hour to the overall production. Older musicals like *Fiddler* or *The Sound of Music* run for three hours. With slow set changes, an audience might not leave the theater until midnight. Disastrous! For me, if our production ended at 11:01, our set changes were too slow. My vision was to incorporate set changes that took fifteen seconds or less.

"THROUGH TATTERED CLOTHES SMALL VICES DO APPEAR"

These words of Shakespeare, from his play *King Lear*, suggest that when a person is poorly dressed (in rags), their small faults and vices become evident. So too is it true that when an actor is not properly costumed, the flaws in a play are magnified. Consequently, from jump street, we were very meticulous about the costuming of our shows, paying attention to hair styles, shoes, and everything in between.

As is the case with scenery, each show has its own costume requirements, and we weren't about to have our productions look like a Halloween party or like the costumes were pulled from our cast members' closets.

As often as not, we sometimes witnessed very little attention to detail at other amateur productions. I remember a production of *The Sound of Music* where at Captain von Trapp's party, the director rented tuxedos but somehow thought it was acceptable for actors to wear modern Sperry deck shoes with the tuxes. How much trouble would it have been to find dress shoes for each boy?

In our case, Fran was our costume coordinator for the greatest majority of our productions even when she was immersed in the business end of Center Stage. It was she who made sure our actors were appropriately dressed from head to toe. She chose all costumes and accessories we rented or bought, whether authentic period costumes or modern garb. So, besides her contributions as co-director and choreographer, Fran had a high IQ when it came to costuming.

When I was directing with our daughter Mia, she had the final say on every costume as well. If Fran or any other costume volunteer put a costume in front of Mia that didn't work for whatever reason, Mia insisted the costume be replaced or modified. Having grown up in our world with our standards, Mia had high expectations when it came her time to direct.

We were certainly fortunate to have a close working relationship with master costume maker, Richard Harding. We rented the vast majority of our costumes from Richard's inventory – but when he didn't have what we needed, Fran went elsewhere – even to New York.

Whether purchasing replicas of armor for a play like *Pippin* or buying and collecting cowboy hats and boots for *Annie Get Your Gun*, we strove to dress the cast as authentically as possible.

On occasion, we even created our own costumes both early and late in our career. The Home Economics department at Shelton High School pitched in to make women's skirts for our 1978 production of *Fiddler on the Roof*. For our last Youth CONNection production of *Annie* in 2018, our volunteers, guided by Richard, created a set of maids' costumes.

And, reflecting on Richard Harding's beautiful costume

creations, often period costumes were able to be used for different shows. Recently, I posted a picture on Facebook of the lead female in our 1979 production of *Hello, Dolly!*, and a woman who performed with the Youth CONNection many years later commented, "Hey, I wore that costume in *The Music Man* in 2009!" It was a great costume in both productions!

In the amateur world we do the best we can with the resources and budget available to us. We were fortunate. We had Fran Scarpa and Richard Harding on our team! For decades, Richard made professional level costumes available to us at a price we could afford, giving our productions a *look* that we could be proud of.

DRESS THE STAGE

We sometimes saw poor choices in the furniture dressing a set. Even school desks and chairs in the midst of a period piece. So, using furniture as one example, my goal was always to have authentic looking furniture on my sets. During our Center Stage years, I formed a relationship with an owner of an antique store in a nearby town. The business was a consignment shop, so she allowed me to borrow anything she owned, and she would ask other owners to rent their pieces to me at a reasonable price. Fran also had a family friend who owned a similar business in West Haven and who was kind enough to loan us great pieces of furniture. Over the years, I made many trips to one of these furniture stores in my Plymouth Voyager, the two back seats removed to make room to transport a Victorian settee, a rolltop desk, or some other interesting furnishing.

I can remember several times when Fran and I visited friends whose home decor included antiques. "Oh my God, you don't want me here," I would joke, "because, before long, I'll be asking you to borrow your furniture for one of my productions." The truth was, I was only half kidding. In several of those cases, I did indeed ask to borrow an item.

During the Center Stage years, when we couldn't find an authentic piece of furniture – let's say a bed or an armoire, Ron

Baldwin or Jim Welch, my highly skilled set construction guys, built the unit for me.

If it seems like I asked too much, I am of the opinion that the wrong costuming and furniture take the audience out of the play. Just as I wouldn't allow an actor to upstage a scene, neither would I allow a *chair* to upstage a scene.

The same was true with hand props. I was repeatedly mesmerized at the professional theater by the authenticity of the props on the stage. With each passing year and with each professional production I saw, my attention to detail became keener and more magnified.

We often had prop coordinators, but being students or working people, they weren't always at liberty to hunt down the right items. They served more in an organizational capacity. Typically, it was I who visited antique stores, secondhand stores, and junk shops. I would ask my prop person to create a scene-by-scene list and ask the cast if they could provide any of the items on the list, to be approved (or not) by me. My daughter Mia still teases me about my obsessive attention to detail, citing a production of Neil Simon's *Lost in Yonkers* where a football was needed, but I wouldn't settle for a modern football, instead finding a 1940s vintage football online which I purchased. Mia also likes to remind me of the prop heavy set for *My Fair Lady*, which featured great props, including vintage gramophones and telephones, as examples.

LESSON:

Just as I wouldn't allow an actor to upstage a scene, neither would I allow a chair to upstage a scene.

When we directed *Carousel* with the Shelton High School Drama Club in 1996, it came to my attention that in Bristol, Connecticut there is The Carousel Museum. Rather than asking our volunteers to make plywood carousel horses for our production, I purchased a half dozen three dimensional replica horses from the museum. I believe they cost two hundred dollars each, which to some might have seemed an extravagant expenditure for a high school, but with the help of several moms of cast members we came up with a great plan. The horses came unpainted and would need to be skillfully painted for the performances. Our moms did a superb job fulfilling that task, and we raffled them off at each performance. Our patrons went crazy for the horses, not only allowing us to recoup our expenditure but making a profit for the Drama Club.

LIGHTING IT UP AND SOUNDING IT OUT!

If we take lighting, as another example, our auditorium at Shelton High School originally had perhaps forty or fifty lighting instruments when we first started directing, while a Broadway theater has several hundred. I had also been in high schools which, at the time, had only a dozen or so instruments, a very limiting number. Back in the day, for most school systems, the goal was to illuminate the speakers at an assembly, not to create moods and excitement in productions.

In our case, with the aid of the lighting people we worked with throughout our career, we always tried to *up* our lighting game, adding lighting instruments when the budget would allow or, at the very least, renting them. For musicals, especially contemporary works, we began to incorporate "moving light" in the early 2000s. Moving light is exactly what the name suggests – automated lighting instruments that have the ability to move to create various effects. A Broadway show uses dozens of "movers," and when I first saw them, I recall asking myself what I always asked, "How can *we* do this?"

My "go to" person was Hugh Hallinan who ran Bridgeport's Downtown Cabaret. Besides running the theater, Hugh was a lighting professional. In 2001, we rented six "movers" from Hugh. At our initial lighting meeting, he explained how these lights could enhance our productions, and with my input, he programmed the lights for us. At the time, I don't believe many, if any, Connecticut high schools were using moving light. I doubt that many high schools use them today. We would continue to use them for years to come when the budget would allow, giving our productions a true professional feel from a lighting perspective.

Another vitally important component of production value is sound. In our early years of directing, we hired an old college friend to do our sound. I was eventually approached by another old friend of mine from grade school who was interested in getting involved with theatrical sound. Fred Santore and I had graduated from St. Joseph's School together. I remembered that he had won the science fair when we were eighth graders...and with what else? A sound project.

In the blink of an eye, Fred was using portable body mics on our actors, something we hadn't previously had access to. Body mics were a game changer in making our actors audible to everyone throughout our cavernous auditorium in Shelton. Soon enough, Fred was providing sound for a great many Connecticut high schools, an aspect of theater that I consider indispensable.

THE PIT

To use another component, I'd like to say a few words about orchestras. Considering that most of our musicians did not make their living from music, we always strove to have the best orchestra within our means and our budget. I was grateful to have a core group of musicians who were adept players, who were dedicated to our cause, and who exhibited an enthusiasm for our young performers. As I've said, I filled in the harder-to-find musicians with the best people I could get – some of whom were from institutions like the Bridgeport Youth Symphony or even the Yale School of Music. When we opened Center Stage and budget became more of a factor, I found my way to the best technology so that the musical end of our shows was first rate.

Outside of costuming, I handled the other aspects of the production, although not without Fran's input. As she trusted me in saying a costume didn't work, I trusted her in giving me input in other production matters, whether scenic or lighting elements. It was a true creative collaboration. It wasn't unusual for Fran to tell me, "You have to talk to the sound guy about..." or "You have to have the lighting guy fix..."

It was the production value, the attention to detail, and a quest for a level of excellence which all combined to motivate our casts to give the best of themselves. For the few cast members who were difficult to motivate, I would point out that we were spending dozens of thousands of dollars (often in the range of forty to fifty thousand) putting professional costumes on their bodies, a fantastic set behind them, and an outstanding orchestra in front of them, and it was their responsibility to give the best performance they were capable of delivering. Since they had tangible evidence, as we prepared the production, that what I was saying was so, I always felt that each and every cast member gave a full effort to the production.

ACT II, SCENE 7

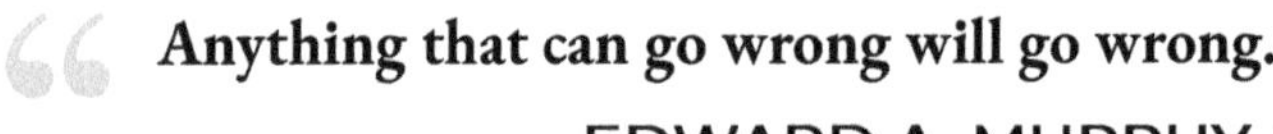

Anything that can go wrong will go wrong.

EDWARD A. MURPHY, JR.,
AEROSPACE ENGINEER

Who among us is not familiar with Murphy's Law? In American society, it's become something of a joke. Pessimism at its finest – but in the world of live theater, it sometimes feels like a given that things will go wrong. Considering a play is happening in the moment before a live audience, where might Murphy's Law come into effect in the view of more pairs of eyes than at the theater?

That said, in preparing a play for performance, the goal is to minimize the instances of things going wrong through strategic and diligent rehearsing, conscientious memorizing of lines, and carefully planning all technical aspects of the production. Anyone who's ever appeared in one of my shows will no doubt attest to the fact that I am a Type A personality.

Consequently, Murphy's Law notwithstanding, as creators of theater, it was our hope that what could go wrong would *not* go wrong. That said, it was our goal during the rehearsal period to plan as well as possible a strategy for what to do if things *did* go wrong.

MAKING THE SAVE

For instance, I spent a good deal of energy communicating to actors that if someone went up on their line (forgot or didn't say it), someone else needed to save that person in any number of ways – by feeding the other actor their line ("Were you feeling that you wanted to say...") or simply skipping the line and jumping to the next logical line. Famous for using hyperbole, I would often explain, "If your fellow actor blanks on his line, jump to the next line...to the next page...to the next scene...or, if necessary, to the next play!" Of course, I was kidding, but the point was made.

LESSON:
...the only way an audience will know there is a problem is if an actor "tells" them...

I can think of many examples of *saves*, but I especially remember an actor in a production of *Twelve Angry Men* saving people in performance after performance. This was a production I was very proud of for many reasons, not the least of which was that I had twelve adult men of varying experience on the stage who all gave outstanding performances. It's a very tricky play, though, because twelve different people speak throughout, so it's easy to be confused about who has the next line. In the case of the actor in question, he had played many parts with us in high school and college, then went on to earn an M.F.A. in theater from a major university before doing some work in the professional theater. Ultimately, at about thirty, he was the youngest member of our cast, but certainly the most experienced. Any time an actor went up on a line, I could count on this actor to speak up and make a save. The audience never knew, but I did.

I always assured our casts that the only way an audience will know there is a problem is if an actor "tells" them via a distressed or confused facial expression or an interminable pause.

In the rehearsal process, there are various stages of memorization. During the first stage, the actors are "on book" (using their scripts). As a director, it was my responsibility to set a date when everyone would be "off book," which might be three weeks before opening night. During much of this time, actors could call for lines – a practice where, when they can't think of the next line, they simply say, "line," and the stage manager feeds them the first few words of their line so the scene can progress.

As we got closer to performance, certainly by dress rehearsal week (but hopefully a week or two before), actors could no longer call for lines but needed to save each other instead. To do so, actors have to not only know their own lines, but they need to have a working knowledge of their fellow actors' lines. Naturally, there are variables which affect this plan. Some actors are conscientious about knowing their lines while others are not. Some actors are better under pressure than others and simply have a greater facility to make the save when needed.

There isn't exactly a black and white solution. As a director, it was my goal to prepare my casts for such a possibility and, beyond that, I hoped for the best. I recall seeing the 2009 Broadway revival of *A Little Night Music* starring Bernadette Peters and Elaine Stritch. Ms. Stritch was in her mid-eighties, and as the evening wore on, it became painfully evident that Ms. Peters was repeatedly saving Ms. Stritch. In one sense, I felt like I had paid a lot of money to see a Broadway legend forget her lines, but in another sense, it was good to know that it happens even in the professional world. Again, our experience was that the older an actor was, usually the more difficult it was for her to memorize lines. Conversely, line problems seldom if ever occurred with high school and college students.

So, while there were occasionally line problems during our shows, in the vast majority of cases with very few exceptions, the audience never knew it. Someone saved the day.

DEAL WITH IT LIKE JOEL GREY

Beyond lines, though, a great many other things can go wrong. My practice was to prepare my casts for random problems by telling stories of things I had witnessed go wrong on stage – like at a performance of a little known musical Fran and I had seen years ago on Broadway called *The Grand Tour*. In a two person scene between Broadway legends Joel Grey and Ron Holgate, a large piece of scenery suddenly fell from the rafters above the stage and came crashing to the floor about ten feet upstage of the two actors. Miraculously, it didn't land on one or both of them, preventing what would have certainly resulted in serious injury. We in the audience were understandably stunned by the crash. Mr. Grey and Mr. Holgate, interestingly, remained calm. Because they are human, the two men needed a few seconds to process what had just happened. Then, without breaking character, Mr. Grey made a gesture with his thumb to the piece of scenery. The two men walked over to it, picked it up, carried it into the wing, and marched back to their places where Mr. Grey delivered his next line. Before another word could be spoken, the audience erupted into a rousing ovation. I would explain to my cast members that the ovation was the result of an audience appreciating the fact that the actors were in control. A problem occurred and the actors handled it!

LESSON:

…it's the actor's responsibility to fix *anything* that goes wrong on the stage so that the audience feels safe in the actor's hands.

We wanted our actors to learn that no matter what, the audience was our invited guests, and we want them to feel comfortable. Our message in using the Joel Grey example was simply: it's the actor's responsibility to fix *anything* that goes wrong on the stage so that the audience feels safe in the actor's hands. "Something is wrong? Don't worry, audience members – we got this!"

We would amass a good many stories of things going wrong and being handled over the years from our own productions, which Fran and I would add to the story of *The Grand Tour*. An early example occurred in our Youth CONNection inaugural production of *West Side Story*. At the end of *West Side Story*, to avenge the death of his friend Bernardo, Chino shoots and kills rival gang member, Tony, the central male character. In the classic climax of the play, as Tony is running to the arms of his beloved Maria, Chino steps out from a dark shadow, and fires his gun. In one performance, the blank gun simply didn't fire. Our Chino pulled the trigger, only to hear a faint click, completely inaudible to the audience. Chino pulled a second time and then a third and fourth – "click, click, click, click." At that point, the actor made a decision, using his voice and a little onomatopoeia he yelled – "POW!"

The audience couldn't help but laugh. Audiences almost always laugh when stunned or surprised. The truth was, in previous performances, some in the audience had laughed at the firing of the gun when it went off without a problem. Even when I had seen a Broadway revival of *West Side Story*, the startling explosion of the gun had prompted at least a few audience members to laugh. In this case, Chino's "POW" had elicited a tidal wave of laughter. What happened then is something I am proud of to this day. The Jets and the Sharks, then, came running into the scene from different directions. Our actors entered with the same dramatic seriousness of purpose that they had demonstrated during every previous performance, quickly drawing the audience back into the tragic and somber moment of the scene.

I could probably write an entire book about things that went wrong through the years, but I'll mention only a few others. Sometimes the thing that went wrong had nothing to do with our cast or crew. In a Youth CONNection production of *Godspell*, as our Jesus took a dramatic pause, an audience member called out, "Well, say something," causing the rest of the audience to laugh. Inappropriate behavior on the patron's part to be sure. The actor's job is to stay in character and not react, which is exactly what our Jesus did.

In a Center Stage production of a play called *Art*, an audience member passed out in the middle of a monologue being delivered by one of our actors. The situation required that we stop the play, call 911, and have the man taken out on a stretcher. A half hour later, after the situation was resolved, we resumed the play. Our actor began his monologue from the beginning, and upon its conclusion, he was given an ovation, the result of his having braved the unexpected situation and then gotten back to business as if nothing happened.

Sometimes something goes wrong with a unit of scenery or a prop. At a performance of *The Music Man* at Sacred Heart Academy while our Harold Hill was doing a scene with another actor, a draft of air must have blown across the stage from the hallway stage door, causing a tall, scenic tree made of lightweight material to blow over and slowly float to the ground like a helicopter landing on a tarmac. After waiting a second or two, our Harold Hill simply said, "Wow, *fall* has sure come early this year!" and then he lifted the tree and stood it back up. The audience loved how he handled the situation and responded with a thunderous round of applause.

In a production of *Evita*, a cast member walked into a piece of scenery backstage, causing him to be injured badly enough for us to call 911 and send him to the hospital. The EMTs' arrival and the exit of the student in an ambulance all took place in the wing of the stage without the audience's knowledge...or most of the actors, including our daughter Mia who was playing the title role! In the very next scene, the injured student needed to be on the stage as an assistant to Eva Perón. Fran grabbed another member of the cast, and said, "You have to go on as a replacement. Just follow Mia and do whatever she says." Mia, not having any idea, crossed stage right to meet her assistant, only to find another castmate. Our replacement just smiled and whispered, "Your mom gave me this box and said you'd tell me what to do." Mia took over from there, and as our Che sang a song about Eva called "And the Money Kept Rolling In," Mia led the actor who had never been in the role before, telling him what to do next while remaining in character. The audience never knew.

The list of things that can go wrong is endless, as are the memories – stories that anyone who has ever been on the stage remembers for years to come. What an actor does in these instances, how he handles these situations, are part and parcel of what makes live theater such an exciting experience.

ACT II, SCENE 8

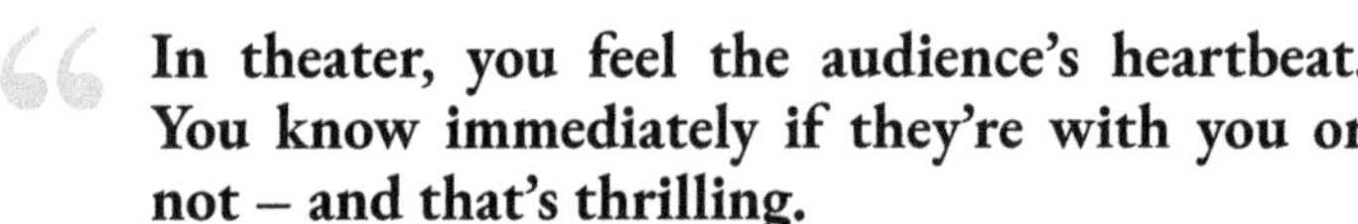

> **In theater, you feel the audience's heartbeat. You know immediately if they're with you or not – and that's thrilling.**
>
> MERYL STREEP, ACTRESS

Through the years, I have often had the pleasure of seeing film and television stars on the Broadway stage – Al Pacino, Judd Hirsch, Vanessa Redgrave, Sammy Davis Jr., Stockard Channing, Anthony Quinn, and many others. We might ask why they do it, especially knowing that, on the stage, such Hollywood stars make only a small fraction of what they earn on television and in film. The answer is pretty simple, though. The interaction with a live audience is something that so many actors want to get back to because, in truth, there is simply nothing in the world quite like it.

In considering Ms. Streep's quote at the top of this chapter, I hearken back to our heralded production of *Fiddler on the Roof* in 1978. Something magical happened at our second, third, and fourth performances. Our audiences were so in the moment that they spontaneously clapped in unison during scene change music. It was an audience behavior that spoke volumes about their enjoyment of the production. And what were the chances that three audiences in a row would behave in the same exact way? Outside of that production, I've never seen such a phenomenon, not in the many productions we directed nor in the hundreds we saw in the amateur and professional theater.

The audience's reaction is a critical aspect of the theatrical experience. Just as I became a student of professional theater, beginning with our first plays, I became a student of audience behavior as well. There is, in my opinion, a certain protocol and etiquette we expect from audiences in the live theater. To use a simple but rather obvious example, at the end of a song or scene, it is customary for the audience to applaud. And quite a wonderful custom! If the audience doesn't applaud in these instances, there is either a good reason or there is something radically wrong. Perhaps the song or scene was so dramatic that it rendered the audience silent. Great! It very well may have been the intention of the playwright or composer to leave the audience stunned. Conversely, perhaps the actor(s) failed to move the audience to applause or, as is sometimes the case, the members of the audience are ignorant of their responsibility to participate in the creative process of theater. Not so great!

Theater is a give and take relationship between actors and audience. The actors on a stage are real people, and it is my opinion that audience members have a responsibility to participate in the performance. I have seen some people at the theater behave as if they were at home, watching actors on a screen, an activity that doesn't require the viewer to participate.

GET YOUR FEET OFF THE STAGE, SIR!

As an example, I recall a man sitting in the first row of our theater, who put his feet up on our stage as if it were an ottoman in his living room. Similarly, even at Long Wharf Theatre, a prominent professional theater in New Haven, I witnessed similar inappropriateness. The audience at Long Wharf, at the time, was seated on three sides of the playing area. The playing area itself wasn't a raised stage, but simply a designated area on the floor of the theater, but with clearly defined geographic lines. Often, the floor of the playing area was given a realistic treatment (e.g., a hardwood or linoleum floor; a carpet). At a performance, from my raised seat in the twelfth row, I spotted a patron stretched out in his seat in a most relaxed posture, his feet crossed comfortably in front of him, clearly in the playing area. I wanted to shout at the guy, "You're not home in front of your television, sir! You're at the theater!"

I understand that some people are not theatergoers and don't fully understand their role.

But as people who create live theater, as directors and actors, it is our hope that our audiences will be active listeners, that they have an attention span, and that they will applaud when it is appropriate to do so, laugh when the jokes land, and feel deeply when a scene or song is meant to elicit such a response. We hope, as a minimum expectation, that they will have the courtesy to sit up straight in their seats.

LESSON:
…there are fundamental expectations of an audience.

I understand that a director can't control who comes to see a play, whether they are experienced theatergoers, or what their response will be. I also understand that how favorably an audience responds depends largely on the quality of the performance, as well it should.

That doesn't negate the fact that there are fundamental expectations of an audience. At a recent high school play I attended, I observed a problem we faced in our early years working with kids. Students in the audience were shouting out the names of their friends on stage. It's a behavior that might be acceptable at a talent show but not at the performance of a play.

An actor on the stage is playing a role – a character with a name. The actor has rehearsed the role for weeks. Let's say he is playing Tony in *West Side Story*. To have his high school friends calling to him by his real name does nothing to help him succeed, nothing to enhance the audience's enjoyment of the play, and is an utterly disrespectful behavior at a play. In our curtain speech before Drama Club productions, I typically asked the students in the audience to refrain from calling out the names of their friends, and a simple request from the stage almost always negated that behavior.

This issue reminds me of an instance where my curtain speech didn't work, but it is a story I love. Given this rude behavior, I would prepare my casts as well. One of my students, only a freshman, had tried out for and been cast in the ensemble of our production of *Funny Girl* back in 1987. He was a freshman football player, and I had noticed that upperclassmen in school had taken quite a liking to him, although I wasn't sure if that was the most positive thing for him.

During one performance, my freshman appeared in a scene with the central character, Fanny Brice. He played a non-speaking character, a porter in a train station along with more than a dozen other actors. It was an occasion when my curtain speech didn't achieve its intended result. In the middle of a sold out audience, a pocket of varsity football players began to shout his name at the top of their lungs. Obviously, their behavior angered me, but my actor simply stayed in character and didn't react. A person in the audience couldn't have guessed whose name the football players were calling out if they didn't already know him. By staying in character, the freshman quelled the rude behavior of his friends in the audience. I was proud of him, and seeing him in public once in a while all these years later, I remind him of that performance and how well he handled the situation.

CELL PHONE HELL

A person doesn't have to be a high school student to exhibit rude or inappropriate behavior. At a community theater production we attended in affluent Greenwich, Connecticut, someone's cell phone rang during a performance of *The Laramie Project*, a very heavy play, and the person answered the call and carried on a conversation from the audience. That level of rudeness is something I seldom witnessed, thankfully, but cell phones occasionally rang at Center Stage through the years, despite our request that patrons silence them.

It reminds me of stories about Broadway legend Patti LuPone. In one instance, during a 2008 performance of *Gypsy*, Ms. LuPone apparently chastised a patron who was taking photos with her phone's camera. In another, at a production of *Shows for Days* in 2015, when Ms. LuPone noticed a patron texting, she is said to have walked into the audience and snatched the person's phone. There are varying opinions on Ms. LuPone's behavior in these instances, but my point is that, even on Broadway, we can't be sure patrons will act appropriately...and, personally, I can relate to her frustration.

Early in the game, I noticed that people don't react as well when there are seats between them as they do when they are packed together. While musicals typically sold out, non-musicals sold many fewer seats. On opening night of our first non-musical as young directors in 1977, we had fewer than a hundred patrons. That small audience, scattered across our twelve hundred seat auditorium separated not only by multiple seats but multiple rows, didn't respond as well as we had hoped. I realized that most people that night felt too inhibited to laugh at punch lines and comic situations, as opposed to sitting in a sold out theater where laughter typically was a contagious chain reaction.

LESSON:
People don't react as well when there are seats between them as they do when they are packed together.

For future non-musicals, using chorus risers, I would erect barriers in the middle of the auditorium to prevent patrons from sitting far away from the stage. Eventually, I made our large stage into a small one hundred seat theater, setting up seating right on the stage along with a defined playing space and a set. Now, having created an intimate theater, each performance was a sell-out, and it was a game changer.

A CHEMISTRY LESSON

Another observation is that each and every audience has a chemistry of its own. I particularly noticed this phenomenon at Center Stage where we offered ten instead of three or four performances of each play. Given two audiences of the same size, on one night, the audience might be rolling in the aisles with laughter, and on the very next night, we could hear crickets outside through the brick walls. I couldn't distinguish any difference between the two performances – just two different audiences. And the fact that we didn't get as much laughter didn't mean the audience didn't think the play was funny or didn't enjoy it. As directors and actors, we try to understand. We speculate. We might say, "It's Thursday night. People have to go to work tomorrow," or "It's Friday night, and the audience is tired after a long work week." But we'll never actually know.

I remember reading an article about Eve Ensler, author of the very funny and moving *The Vagina Monologues*. Eve not only wrote the play, but performed it for a period of time as a one woman show in New York and on tour. She said in the interview that she had to give up any attachment to how the audience reacted or did not react. I would imagine that, having created the theatrical piece herself, she had a heightened sensitivity about the work, but knowing how unpredictable or fickle audiences can be, she simply created a mindset where she refused to let it get to her. Of course, in this case she was dealing with material that is highly controversial. Personally, when I saw Eve's play in New York, I felt like I was on an emotional roller coaster: laughing at one monologue, crying at another, and feeling as if my heart had stopped beating at still another.

To Eve Ensler's point about remaining somewhat detached in relation to an audience's reaction, I have learned that, even when an audience isn't demonstrative, it doesn't necessarily mean they are not enjoying the play. I recall a couple – loyal subscribers for our entire career – who were sitting in the first row of a production of *Little Women* at Center Stage 1.0. I was crammed into the stage right wing, leading a small pit orchestra, and from my vantage point, I could clearly see the couple in the front of the audience. Their faces were impassive throughout, during both comic and heartbreaking moments. I felt certain they weren't enjoying the play. At the end of the night, they waited for me and the cast to give us their congratulations. "What a wonderful production," the husband commented. "We just loved every minute of it!"

Despite my various criticisms, the vast majority of people who attend the theater *do* understand the etiquette, and we were grateful to have had many patrons through the years who were wonderful members of our audiences. Now and then, I would notice a patron who seemed to pick up on every comical line, no matter how subtle, and greet it with laughter. Such a patron often ignites the same reaction in others, making them feel comfortable laughing out loud. I would often tease these customers and invite them to come back the next night.

There is nothing more exciting than when an audience is *alive* and engaged...when there is an electric current that ricochets from the actors on stage to the audience, back and forth. This immediate feedback is one of the most beautiful things about performing on stage. It is, as stated, the reason many film actors return to Broadway.

The fact is that watching an actor on stage is very different from watching an actor on a screen. The latter can't see your behavior or hear your reaction. The former can. Live performers, actors and musicians, are living, breathing beings. Being an audience member at a live performance of any kind is not a passive experience. Far from it. Theater is meant to be an active give and take between actors and patrons. The performing artist depends on it.

I love a video clip about audiences that I recently happened upon with Broadway legend, Carol Channing. "Laugh, for heaven's sake, if it's funny," she said in her endearing albeit raspy drawl. "Clap if you feel like clapping. That's a sophisticated theater audience. We give to one another. It's a tennis match – back and forth."

It was always our firm belief that, as creators of theater, as directors and actors, our ultimate responsibility was to our audience. Conveying that concept to our casts was paramount for us. It was gospel. I didn't hesitate to remind our actors, of any age, that people paid money and left their homes to see our productions. I would often remark to our high school casts at our final dress rehearsal, "We're throwing a party tomorrow night, and we're expecting twelve hundred guests. I want to make sure they have a good time!"

LESSON:
Theater is meant to be an active give and take between actors and patrons.

Even a smaller audience deserves our best effort. Fran, while performing in *Nunsense II* at the Seven Angels Theatre in Waterbury years ago, performed in front of only seven or eight people one night due to inclement weather. Fran remembers that the cast still gave one hundred percent that night, and were, in fact, grateful that the few brave souls chose to attend. We owed it to our audience, no matter how large or small, I would explain, to prepare ourselves in the rehearsal process to give the best of ourselves on the stage.

Without an audience, quite simply, there is no theater. One depends on the other.

In a book called *The Courage to Create* by psychologist Rollo May, the author explains that patrons at theaters, museums, or concert halls are not only witnessing the creative process, but they are, in fact, an integral part of it. When I read May's explanation, it immediately resonated for me, and I knew it to be true from my own experience in the theater. "...In our appreciation of the created work...when we engage...we are experiencing some new moment of sensibility. Some new vision is triggered in us; something unique is born in us. This is why appreciation of the music or painting or other work of the creative person is also a creative act on our part."

ACT II, SCENE 9

I think there should be a rule that everyone in the world should get a standing ovation at least once in their life.

R. J. PALACIO, CHILDREN'S AUTHOR

Going hand in hand with audience behavior is the curtain call at the end of a play, another wonderful custom in the theater. The curtain call is an extension of the play and should be approached as such. It is also an opportunity for actors to take a well-deserved bow. I can't think of another art form or activity where people receive immediate positive feedback like in the wonderful world of the performing arts. There is nothing quite like it. We always found it gratifying to watch cast members from seven to seventy glow in the light of applause and a standing ovation.

We had experience staging all kinds of curtain calls. For instance, in *Hello, Dolly!*, the curtain call is meant to be a full-blown production number, complete with cast members singing and dancing onto the stage en route to their bows. The score of the musical is written with vocal parts, leading up to the high point of the curtain call when Dolly herself bows to the title song of the show.

In *West Side Story,* conversely, because of the somber way in which the play ends, it may be more appropriate to have a curtain call without music and, perhaps, even without the actors bowing. If memory serves me, the musical score of *West Side Story* doesn't have what is typically referred to as curtain call music. It's been a long time since we produced *West Side Story*, but it may be that the curtain call takes place in silence – very unusual to be sure. In our productions of *West Side Story*, we had the cast simply stand as a group on the stage without bowing, while the audience was on its feet each night, applauding enthusiastically.

Either way – whether a highly theatrical curtain call or a more somber one – it is as important a moment in a production as any other.

The audience not only participates in the curtain call, but they are entitled to it. Realizing the time and talent it takes to mount a production, people who attend live performances want to show their appreciation.

In order to receive the right feedback, there are certain requirements. The curtain call needs to begin as quickly after the last scene as possible – hopefully within mere seconds. If an audience has to wait a minute or more, the reaction will be diminished. The audience will not understand why, but I assure you that the wait will kill the momentum. In such a case, a standing ovation is highly unlikely.

LESSON:

The audience not only participates in the curtain call, but they are entitled to it.

The curtain call needs to continue the mood of the play. The 2000 Broadway revival of *The Music Man* included a curtain call where the entire cast marched onto the stage in band uniforms and played trombones (apparently all cast members were given trombone instruction during the rehearsal period). What a surprise! It was simply the most entertaining curtain call I have ever witnessed.

The curtain call needs to be highly organized with everyone

knowing exactly what they are doing. Being an extension of the performance, it has to be staged in an aesthetically pleasing way. The ensemble, as they bow together in lines, must do so in unison. We would tell our cast members to look to the person in the center and not bow until that center person had looked to his right and left.

It's important that performers savor the moment of their bow. In the world of high school theater, this was a skill that had to be taught. Some people seemed to have a tendency to run out on stage and take a half-bow, hardly breaking stride in the process. I required them to plant their feet and to bow while counting to three in their heads. Watch a classical pianist like the famous Yuja Wang bow if you want to see someone who knows how to savor the moment.

There is a standard way most curtain calls are organized, starting with the ensemble and/or smallest parts bowing first and working up to the leading character(s) in order of importance. The curtain call music is composed with this plan in mind. This music, by the way, is almost always a medley of some number of songs from the show. Occasionally what that bowing order should be may be a little hazy because it's hard to say certain roles are larger than others, and the decision of who bows when is left to the director. But, to use a prior example, the last person to bow in *Hello, Dolly!* is obviously Dolly Levi herself.

I have attended high school performances where, after the last person bowed – using my example – Dolly Levi – the director felt it was a good idea to have the stage crew bow last. For me, this choice suggests that the stage crew are the most important members of the troupe.

LET THE UNSUNG HEROES BE UNSUNG HEROES

Typically, what I've observed in these instances is that the stage crew's bow is messy, not being performers. It is a practice that I never allowed. Those on stage crew needed to understand their role as "unsung heroes" and, as such, a bow was inappropriate.

Similarly, the team managers for a high school football team, while their role is important, don't expect to see their pictures on the sports page of a newspaper or their names in the headlines.

Believe me when I say that we valued the vital contribution behind-the-scenes volunteers made to our productions, especially stage crew members. In fact, I can't say it enough. The pride they took in making efficient, lightning fast set changes added to the overall quality of our shows and cannot be undervalued. And in some cases, it was a stage crew member who saved the day. In our 2002 production of *Les Mis*, a boy made a save that has become a bit of legendary folklore for those of us who witnessed it. A friend of a friend who was a steel worker made us a large (and heavy) gate where a crucial scene takes place outside the home of Jean Valjean. The truth is that a gate made of steel was probably overkill for a unit of stage scenery, but it sure looked great. One night at the end of the scene, somehow the gate came unattached from its supporting column and came crashing to the floor. Our stage crew member didn't miss a beat. In a display of superhuman strength, he lifted the gate from the floor and carried it off stage.

It's a lot of fun to remember stories like this one and the wonderful efforts of our stage crew members through the years. But a curtain call is designed for actors, not behind-the-scenes personnel.

Someone might argue, "Give the kids a bow. It's just a high school play." Again, it was our goal to achieve a high level of artistry, from the first note of the overture to the final bow of the curtain call. My former student Erik Hansen, as a Broadway professional, knows this better than anyone.

A nice custom in the world of staging curtain calls is for the actor who takes the final bow to acknowledge the conductor and the orchestra by gesturing to them and then gesturing toward the lighting booth at the back of the theater. When the lead actor lifts her arm to the back of the "house," she is, in effect, acknowledging all of those important people who volunteered behind the scenes. I don't mean to minimize the great contribution of stage crew members, but there are ways to show appreciation for them, and a curtain call *isn't* one of them. Thank them at the cast party.

Throw a parade for them! Forgive the hyperbole – but, please, don't give them a bow!

For the cast, I feel there is a positive psychological element in participating in a curtain call. Through the years I witnessed that special glow, especially as kids experienced their first curtain call. Perhaps it is because, in life, we get so little positive feedback or at least none so powerful as an audience of hundreds of people offering a heartfelt positive reaction to a performance. Where else can a person receive the kind of feedback that a curtain call offers?

THE CURTAIN CALL IS THE ULTIMATE FEEDBACK

This convention that is part and parcel of theater is also a reason why we chose never to participate in theater competitions. We didn't need an award because we had already experienced the *highest* kind of positive and genuine feedback theater people could hope for – a curtain call...often a standing ovation. I am not against competition, which can be a good thing in the right setting. Objective competition. Shelton plays another school in football and wins by a score of 24-12. There can be no question of who the winner was. The score is an objective measure that tells the tale.

But theater is quite a different matter. Now, we are looking at *subjective* measures. A friend who judged one of these competitions explained to me that only a few of the judges see a given high school show, and then, with the use of video clips, they make their case to a larger panel of judges. Ultimately, like reviews, what we have here are mainly the opinions of a small group of people.

My other issue with amateur theater competitions is that the participants are not on a level playing field. Some schools or community theaters have a much higher budget than others; some have a better facility. This is less true – if true at all – in the world of sports.

And then there are amateur theater competitions where people go online and vote for the "best actor," "best ensemble," "best musical," etc. – a veritable "people's choice" if you will. Most of those who vote, in these instances, not only haven't been to another theater or seen another of the nominated actors or productions, but they may not have even seen the actor or production they've voted for. Nonsensical!

I always liked a witty quote by Hungarian composer Béla Bartók: "Competitions are for horses, not artists."

"What about the Tony Awards or the Oscars?" you might ask. These are awards programs that have an economic end at their core. Film actor George C. Scott, upon winning an Oscar for the movie *Patton*, called the Academy Awards "a public display with contrived suspense for economic reasons."

If a new musical on Broadway doesn't at least get nominated for a Tony, it is likely the "kiss of death" for the show. Such was the case with *Big, the Musical*, which we Scarpas enjoyed very much. Given the Tony snub, *Big* closed after only six months. Certainly winning such an award in the professional world can change the trajectory of a play's success or an actor's career. Simply put, in the world of professional entertainment, awards drive ticket sales and profits, and in doing so, are *vitally* important. The same is hardly true on the amateur level. By the time the competition takes place, an amateur production is long over. Obviously, it wasn't meant to have a long run.

The amateur and professional theater are simply two different animals. Competitions may have their place in the latter. Broadway actors and creative teams are being paid a living wage. Productions have multi-million dollar budgets. Financial backers have made critical investments in shows. The playing field is far more level. Whether actors like them or not – and despite what Béla Bartók or I may think of competitions, they serve a purpose in the professional world. Paychecks, investments, and budgets change the game.

In my last years with the Shelton High School Drama Club when I was receiving a bit of pressure to enter such competitions, I explained to our casts: "If another drama club would like to play us in softball, I'm all about it. But I'm not interested in someone's subjective opinion of what we've accomplished here."

This topic is probably one that many people in amateur theater disagree with me about, but I'm at peace with that. In trying to convince me to change my opinion on theater awards programs, I have had people tell me that the kids who participate in these competitions feel no jealousy and are all "pulling" for one another. I don't buy it. One such person who used to say that to me changed her tune more recently when her own teen was heartbroken at not having received a nomination.

Look, here's what I know. People are human, and jealousy is a human emotion. I wasn't about to participate in a competition where one of my actors was nominated and another was not.

Personally, I didn't need some judge to tell me what was good and not-so-good about my shows. Having just spent weeks of my life in the intimate experience of rehearsing the play, I knew its strengths and weaknesses better than anyone. And besides, once a production has closed, what purpose does a critique serve?

I always cherished the good feeling our participants had when we closed a show. My thought was, *Why tamper with that?*

Even in the world of sports, I remember that after a basketball game, there was the culture of feeling bad about ourselves when we lost. On a thirty minute bus ride home after a loss, the team was expected to sit in complete silence contemplating the loss. As the losing team, we may have played our hearts out. Or, perhaps the other team was simply better. Either way, the message was clear – *Feel bad about yourself! You lost!*

It was a phenomenon I never witnessed in theater. From my very first experience to my last, show after show, year after year, each and every experience felt like we had won the state championship – and we didn't need to actually *win* one to feel that way. I found it to be the ultimate team experience where everyone felt like a winner every time. It was just the reality that came with working hard, preparing well, presenting our work to an audience, and experiencing the audience's appreciation via a custom known as a curtain call. Never once was there a losing feeling – only a winning one. In the process, unlike sports, there was never a reason to feel heartbroken or jealous.

Of course, a standing ovation isn't always a given. An audience that doesn't stand may have enjoyed a performance as much as one that does stand. There's just a different chemistry in that audience. There can be all kinds of factors on why an audience doesn't stand, from their not being a very savvy theater-going audience to a slow start on the bows beginning to the idea that some plays end in more or less upbeat ways than others. And, without a doubt, it could be that the performance just wasn't good enough to motivate the audience to stand. As I indicated in my chapter about audience behaviors, we can never completely know why one audience reacts differently than another, and that includes standing ovations. I have been at many Broadway plays where the audience failed to stand. My take is that Broadway audiences expect a lot, as well they should for the price they've paid.

A curtain call is the last word in a give-and-take relationship between audience and actor. It gives the audience an opportunity to show their appreciation of the talent and the work they have just witnessed – and to say thank you. As an audience member myself, I always relish that opportunity, and the more I enjoy a performance, whether on Broadway or at a local high school, the more I enjoy applauding during the curtain call. And, personally, I'm likely to be the first person on my feet!

LESSON:
A curtain call is the last word in a give-and-take relationship between audience and actor.

The custom of curtain calls is ancient and it's part of being a member of a civilized and cultured populace. In the worlds of professional ballet and opera, the prima ballerinas and divas are literally showered with bouquets of flowers during the curtain call. Accomplished performing artists understand how to enjoy their role in creating the moment that the audience yearns for at the end of a great performance. It was part of our work to help young people learn to fulfill their role in a gracious and sincere way, and in a way that helped put an exclamation point on a performance at the end of the show. Hopefully, along the way, we were teaching them how to become gracious audience members themselves.

ACT II, SCENE 10

> **Know your lines and don't bump into the furniture.**
>
> SPENCER TRACY, ACTOR

For the last "scene" of *Lessons from the Stage*, I've chosen to focus on the actor and the art of acting. Among the various creatives who bring theater to the stage, I feel actors are the most important. Storytelling is as old as humanity itself. A drama can come to the stage without any of the rest of the creative team – without playwrights or directors or designers or builders or costumers or prop gatherers. The one indispensable creative person is the actor. The actor, after all, can improvise a story, and while costumes, scenery, lighting, etc. are nice, none of them are completely necessary in bringing a story to the stage. After all, ultimately, what is theater other than storytelling?

It is the actor who puts himself in front of an audience. It is the actor's responsibility to bring the words on the page to life. And the words on the page are not always the greatest. In theater, television, and film, I have seen great actors make writing that is subpar work. Of course, when great writing is paired with great acting, we have the perfect combination.

Like anything, some people have a greater gift for acting than others. I suppose I could speculate all day why that is so without ever completely knowing why. It just is! Having dealt with hundreds and hundreds of novice actors in our career, time and time again, we saw that some of them simply had a greater God-given gift.

Without that gift, can a person learn to be a good actor? I've already indicated I am a strong believer that the answer is yes. That belief is based on the fact that inside every one of us is the ability to feel deeply, and given that ability, I believe everyone can learn to convey those feelings through acting.

I recently saw an interview with the famous Gene Hackman who was apparently abandoned by his father at the tender age of thirteen. When asked how that negative experience affected his future ability as an actor, Hackman felt it impacted him positively because, he said, it put him in touch with his feelings. Now, for someone else, such an experience might have quite the opposite result, but the important point is that Hackman felt that an actor needs to be in touch with his feelings to be effective.

Acting is a means of getting in touch with our feelings while playing someone else, and in that sense, I believe it can be very therapeutic.

Because we all have a complete range of emotions – from love to hate and everything in between – we are capable of bringing those emotions to the stage if we open ourselves to the idea.

In our world of amateur theater, we found ourselves in a teaching mode, not only with teens but also with adults whom we introduced to the stage or whose skills had grown rusty with years of non-use.

I would tell our young actors that in an eight week rehearsal period, we needed to give them the equivalent of a college degree in acting because, I further explained, the audience expects to be entertained and they ultimately don't care if you have little or no experience.

In regards to creating the character, I have often heard people say that an actor became the character. But I preferred to see it in reverse. I would tell actors that rather than becoming the character, they needed to think of it as the character becoming them. So, when I played Harry Truman, it wasn't possible to become Truman, but it was possible to allow Truman to become me. Speaking of presidents, a favorite example for me is Anthony Hopkins' portrayal of the title character in the film *Nixon*. As I watched his brilliant performance, I realized that rather than doing a straight-on impression of Nixon, Hopkins captured the essence of the former president without ever losing who Anthony Hopkins is. Simply incredible, in my opinion.

LESSON:
I would tell actors that rather than becoming the character, they needed to think of it as the character becoming them.

While this book isn't quite a textbook on the craft of acting, there are some fundamental skills beyond memorization that are worth mentioning – and not only the immortal Spencer Tracy's ironic advice not to bump into the furniture!

PROJECT YOUR VOICE!

I often told teen and adult actors that "volume is fundamental." It makes me think of a callback audition for a production of *Little Women* at Center Stage, and a candidate, after reading a scene, complained about me to several of the other actors who were called back. "All that guy cares about is volume," she bemoaned. Little did she know that several of the other candidates were Center Stage regulars who would relate her remark to me – not that it mattered.

But, yes, I do feel that volume is essential. I had stopped her several times and asked her to project more. And, no, volume wasn't all I cared about, but I had this really odd notion that an audience needs to be able to hear the dialogue. And that they shouldn't have to work to hear what's being said. Call me crazy!

"I'd rather be watching a bad actor that I can hear," I would tell actors, "than a good actor that I can't hear." I would sometimes relate a story of being at an amateur production where the actors, across the board, failed to project their voices. During the evening, I whispered to Fran: "What did he say?"…"What did she say?" It was frustrating to find it so difficult to hear the actors.

LESSON:
Volume is fundamental.

I have often observed that professional performances of straight plays seldom use amplification. In those instances it is clear that actors speak at a heightened volume. Anyone with working ears would realize this fact. I'm sure the practice of projecting one's voice goes back to ancient Greek theater. And even when we were using body mics for our productions, our sound engineer advised us to speak up as if we weren't.

Plain and simple: if the actors are not audible, the play is a failure.

PLAY IT BIG

Projecting the voice is key, but it's only part of the more important skill of playing it big. When we speak of playing it big, we mean that the actor uses his voice, body, and emotions in an expansive and a heightened way. There's an old saying in the theater, "Play it to the last row." Acting on the stage is not the same as acting before a camera. In the latter case, the television or movie camera can "zoom in" so the actor can give a more subtle portrayal of his character. But on the stage, it's the actor's duty to "zoom out" to the audience. Think of a Broadway theater with a mezzanine and a balcony. The people in the very last row of the balcony deserve the same experience as those in the very first row of the orchestra.

Doing that takes skill at playing it big. It makes me remember an acting class I taught at Shelton High School. I could see that several of the students had natural talent, but they were inhibited about playing it big. We would meet on the stage of our auditorium where we would work on scenes in close quarters.

But on this day, I sent the students into the middle of our large auditorium. "Sit in Row T," I said.

Projecting my voice, I said, "Everybody, I just want to show you something. I've been trying to learn to draw, and I think I did pretty well with this picture of a little old man I drew over the weekend. Tell me what you think."

And then I held up the picture of my little old man. The only thing is – I had reduced it on a copy machine to the size of a business card.

"What do you think?" I called out.

The kids started to giggle. "What is it?" they called back to me.

"What is it? I told you what it is. It's a little old man, obviously."

"But we can't see it," they replied.

"What do you mean you can't see it? Why can't you see it?" I asked.

"It's too small!"

"Oh...it's too small," I said. "I see. Well, how about this?"

I had also blown the drawing up and printed it on 11x17 paper.

"That's better," they said.

"You can see it better now?" I asked.

"Yes...it's still not that big, but we can see it."

"Oh...so it would be better if it was even bigger, wouldn't it?"

When I invited them to join me on the stage, we sat in a circle, and I said, "Your acting, you see, is like my small drawing. Your portrayal doesn't read. The auditorium is too vast for patrons to *see* it. Only a bigger drawing will read in this space. And, even then, it needed to be even bigger still."

Then a more important point. "Both of the drawings are the exact same work of art. One is just bigger than the other. One can be read and understood; the other can't."

I would also use examples from professional productions I had seen. One that comes to mind is *Catch Me if You Can* where I was blown away by the Tony Award winning performance of Norbert Leo Butz as FBI agent Carl Hanratty. Butz's performance was so appropriately big and so powerful that here's how I described it to my high school performers: "I was sitting back about twenty rows, and Norbert Leo Butz reached across the theater, grabbed me by the shoulders and shook me to my core!"

Another example I used was merely symbolic but fun. When Erik Hansen graduated from college his first job was with the national and international tours of the show, *Blast!*, a theatrical production that brought drum and bugle corps to the Broadway stage, as its website explains, in an "explosion of rhythms, colors, and sounds," winning a Tony Award for Best Special Theatrical Event in the process. When *Blast!* came to Connecticut, Fran and I went to see it at the Oakdale Theatre in Wallingford in support of Erik.

LESSON:
A stage performer needs to understand the space he is in, playing the emotion big enough to fill it.

Although *Blast!* isn't a play per se, I was able to find a great takeaway from the production. We were sitting well back from the stage in Oakdale's gigantic forty-eight hundred seat auditorium. While most of the incredibly creative performance took place on the stage, the musicians sometimes used the aisles. At one point, a cast member playing a contrabass bugle (the equivalent of a tuba) edged up to a little girl sitting in front of us, brought the bell of his horn to her ear, and played a musical excerpt for her, up close and personal. I marveled at the surprise and delight I saw register on the little girl's beautiful face. In relating the story to our actors, I would say, "Even though we can't literally go out into the audience, we need to play it big and become the bell of the contrabass for every person in the audience, no matter where they're sitting."

It's basic math. A stage performer needs to understand the space he is in, and use a combination of projecting his voice and playing the emotion big enough to fill it so everyone in the audience has as close to the same experience of the production as possible.

TELL THE TRUTH

A person might ask, doesn't the actor who plays it big run the risk of overacting? Possibly...but there is a solution for that concern. In the midst of projecting one's voice and playing it big, it's vitally important to tell the truth. Remember my drawing of an old man? Let's think of it as my truth! Whether it's the micro or macro version, it's the same drawing. Just because I have a large version that reads in a big space doesn't make it anything other than my drawing – my truth. And the blown up version also isn't a caricature of my drawing. It's exactly the same entity – big or small.

This is a very complex subject that can't be addressed in one chapter in a book like this, so I have to approach it broadly. Those who major in theater in college study acting teachers – sages – like Konstantin Stanislavski (1863 – 1938), Richard Boleslawski (1889 – 1937), Lee Strasberg (1901 – 1982), Uta Hagen (1919 – 2004), to name a few, to learn the craft of acting, not the least of which is how to tell the truth on stage.

That said, does a person need to study acting in college to be capable of telling the truth? I feel the answer is unequivocally, no!

Jane Fonda, for instance, studied what's known as "method acting" with Lee Strasberg. Her famous father, Henry Fonda, disliked method acting, apparently feeling it was self-indulgent. Many film actors of Henry Fonda's era – like James Cagney, John Wayne, James Stewart, Bette Davis, Clark Gable, and Rosalind Russell – did not formally study acting. They simply acted. And I think we can all agree that they were all great. Conversely, many of Jane Fonda's contemporaries did study. People like Pacino and De Niro, like Jane Fonda, studied method acting; Meryl Streep has degrees in acting from Vassar and Yale.

How one becomes adept at the craft is personal to each actor. Often it isn't through formal study with famous acting teachers or at prestigious universities.

Each actor has his own truth based on his unique characteristics. And a person doesn't necessarily need to suffer greatly or have experienced neglect (like Gene Hackman) or abuse to be able to convey emotion on the stage. All of us have a full range of emotions. I would explain to people that I don't need to have killed someone to play a murderer. I have felt hate in my heart, as well as all emotions – jealousy, fear, anger, surprise, disgust, grief – all of which are at my disposal when playing a role. A person needs only to tap into the emotions.

Can high school students in their inexperience express truth on the stage? The answer is yes. By the time the vast majority of people reach their teens, they've experienced the entire gamut of emotions. I'd go so far as to say that most teens want to tell the truth. They love the stage because it's a place where they can express a variety of emotions safely.

To make the point about telling the truth, I used to use a theater game. It was a "tug of war" pantomime. I would pair my students up and ask them to pantomime the game. Most of them didn't execute the task in an honest way. I remember choosing an athletic male from the group, grabbing a real rope, and having a tug of war. I was probably around fifty, and the student won. Out of breath, I then described my physiology to the class. "I'm out of breath," I began, "my heart is racing, I feel my temples pounding..."

After catching my breath, I repeated the game with the student, but in pantomime. When we were done, I exhibited and described the same physiological signs. "I'm feeling this way," I explained, "because I recall how I felt with the real rope. The physiology is the same, with or without the rope. By the same token – if I play a love scene on the stage, I remember what it felt like to be in love for the first time, and I remember how I felt when I fell in love with my wife. So, while playing the scene, emotionally and even physiologically, I feel the same as I did back then. The difference is that, when I exit the stage, I am no longer in love...because there is no real rope."

Telling the truth comes naturally to some actors, and to some it doesn't. Some people know how to play it big, but their whole performance is a lie – and it's evident to me when I'm watching an untruthful performance. I'm sure it is evident to most everyone – although I will say this. Many theater patrons love it when an actor "hams it up." Personally, I don't – but, in truth, I'd rather have an actor who hams it up than one who plays it so small that it doesn't read. Ultimately, I don't want either. I want an actor who understands the art of playing it big while simultaneously telling the truth.

In relation to this business of hamming it up or any other peripheral silliness we had sometimes observed at amateur performances, our strong message to our casts was, "Our goal here is certainly not to get ready for a Halloween costume party, but to prepare ourselves to present a play for an audience."

In the process, as a director my message was – first, last, and always – tell the truth! I would emphasize that an actor owes it to his audience to tell the truth. When I directed *Little Women*, in discussing the powerful song, "Days of Plenty," Marmee reflects on the death of her daughter and explains to Jo that she still has to go on.

In working through the complex emotions of the song and scene, we talked about the fact that people in our audience may have experienced the unimaginable loss of a child. We even spoke of someone we all knew who might attend the play. Our discussion focused on the idea that it was our duty to tell the truth, especially for people who have a direct experience with such grief.

LESSON:
...an actor owes it to his audience to tell the truth.

Finally, it's important to note that because each of us is unique, we all have our unique truth to tell. If I play Tevye in *Fiddler*, I will bring my truth to the role. Another actor will bring his. It's why I never had an issue with a cast member seeing a famous actor's portrayal of a role. The actresses who played Dolly Levi in several productions we directed are not capable of telling Barbra Streisand's truth. They have their own truth to tell.

This quote by esteemed acting teacher Stella Adler says it well: "The word *theatre* comes from the Greeks. It means the seeing place. It is the place people come to see the truth about life and the social situation."

The actor is the key person in bringing that truth to the stage.

LISTEN!

An actor can't tell the truth unless he is listening. We probably all know someone in our lives who is a terrible listener. It's no different on the stage.

A phenomenon I observed early in my directing career is that inexperienced actors sometimes have a tendency to do something I called "taking turns."

In this case, consider a scene where there are two actors on the stage. Actor B knows that she has a line after each line that Actor A delivers. So, she waits until he finishes his line and then delivers hers. In the process, she has hardly heard what he said because she's not actively listening.

Taking turns presents all kinds of problems. First, to tell the truth, an actor needs to hear what their scene partner is saying. Whether on the stage or in real life, when two people aren't hearing what the other is saying, there is a disconnect.

LESSON:
When actors actively listen to and truly hear each other, it solves a multitude of problems.

There are other reasons why listening is so important as well. If there is a line problem, it's easier to fix when both actors are listening to each other. In fact, I would offer to actors that if they're really listening, there won't be any line problems...because they've "heard" what was said, making it easier to reply logically.

When there are more than two actors on the stage, there is a greater risk of line problems. What does one do in a play like *Twelve Angry Men* when he isn't listening? It's much harder to "take turns" in such a case, making disastrous line problems more likely.

Taking turns also slows down the pacing of a scene in most cases. Again, I'm talking about the seconds between one actor's lines and another's.

When actors actively listen to and truly hear each other, it solves a multitude of problems.

Not having had formal training in acting myself, I remember the first time the topic of listening came to my attention. I was acting in a play with the Orange Players and one of the cast members related that she had run into a famous soap opera star on a New York bound train. Entering him into conversation, she asked him what advice he would give an amateur actor like herself. He answered in one word: "Listen!"

There is no art quite like *acting* and no artist quite like the actor. He has the privilege to stand before a crowd of people who want and need to hear a given story, and he has the responsibility to tell the truth of that story. I particularly love a quote that was recently shared with me. It's by Emily Habeck, author of *Shark Heart: A Love Story*: "...acting is paying homage to the visionaries who had the courage to go for it; acting is freeing the parts of oneself living secretly, ashamedly, in memory and regret; acting is living at the height of one's emotional possibilities; acting is crafting reality in the name of pretend; acting is the one time when no one suffers the consequences of truth."

In considering the importance of great acting to the theater, in rehearsals I would also come to discuss the importance of acting in the broader world of the performing arts, speaking of the singer as actor and the dancer as actor. Telling an emotional truth in an appropriate way was just as important for these artists, I would explain, as it is for a stage actor.

There are many factors that contribute to good – and even great acting. The aforementioned teachers and many like them of lesser fame have written volumes on the subject. Great acting doesn't happen by accident. Acting is a craft which can be improved upon in various ways: instinct, experience, education or, often, all three. When I think of the actor on a stage, I think of *The Wizard of Oz* because the actor is, in his way, a wizard. He is "The Great and Powerful Oz." Like Dorothy and friends, the audience strides down a long hallway to meet him. Suddenly, before them, they see the apparition of a large, demonic head, flames shooting from the floor as they hear him announce himself. They tremble in fear because they believe it is really Oz – so real is what they are seeing. As the omniscient Oz bellows, asking a series of questions, colored smoke and more flames explode thunderously around him.

We the audience participate in something known as "the suspension of disbelief," choosing to believe that the actor is that being, even though we know that this is an imaginary situation and the actor is playing a role. It is done so well, though, that for the time we are watching the play or the film or the television program, we forget our own humdrum lives and invest ourselves in the story before us. It is the beauty of the audience experience.

But then, in the midst of the excitement, Toto saunters over to a green curtain and, with his teeth, pulls the curtain open. The actor is two things at this moment. First, he is the apparition of The Wizard of Oz that Dorothy sees before her. He is also a man in a booth – a person who knows what levers to pull and what buttons to push in order to elicit a certain response from his audience. But for the audience, if the man behind the curtain becomes visible, the illusion is broken and the suspension of disbelief vanishes.

Highly skilled actors operate at a level where an audience never sees our skills at work, and if our skills are invisible to them, then we've gotten it right.

SET STRIKE

SET STRIKE

When the performances have ended, when the theater no longer rings with the applause of satisfied patrons, and when the cast party is over, we have a custom in the world of theater known as set strike. Here, we dismantle the set, storing what might be used again and discarding what won't be used again...or what we have no room to store. Costumes and props are put away, and the theater is rendered a blank canvas for whatever is next.

In the world of amateur theater – high school, college, and community – typically everyone is required to assist in this process. Obviously, it's a very practical process, but it's also a symbolic one as well. The staging of plays, you see, is an ephemeral art form, unlike paintings, for instance. The production of a play, as I hope I have shown, has a very clear beginning and ending.

So, there's something a little sad about set strike. But, as the saying goes, "nothing lasts forever." Even if we loved the experience of being a high school or college student, these experiences must come to an end. Like graduation, set strike marks a profound ending.

The beauty of set strike is it brings closure to what is almost always a meaningful experience. Since entering the professional world of theater, Mia has performed in several summer productions at her alma mater, Muhlenberg College, which utilized a combination of college students and professionals. Her director didn't require the equity actors in the show to assist with set strike, but Mia explains that she chose to help anyway. Given her life in the theater, she chose to lend a hand in bringing these productions to their conclusion, a meaningful ritual that she viewed as a vital part of the overall process.

In our lives as creators of theater, there would eventually come an ending – a set strike if you will. That ending, in 2019, was our retirement.

How do we sum up forty-three years in the theater? How do we understand the "why" of such a commitment? It's a question that's hard – perhaps impossible – to answer. Was it love? Well, yes – in 1973 I fell in love with an art form and a mega-talented girl, both in one magical summer. And while that sounds like a fairy tale, it's a bit too simplistic to explain the next four decades.

A realization I eventually had about myself, about ourselves, by the time we opened Center Stage twenty-nine years into our directing journey is that we are *artists*, something I was hesitant to call myself way back when I was in my late twenties and deciding what I might want to do to support our family instead of being a teacher.

Everyone involved in bringing a play to the stage should consider himself an artist. In order to motivate and inspire our casts to fully immerse themselves in their roles, I would give examples of great musicians in the world of classical, jazz, and rock music – people like Itzhak Perlman, Wynton Marsalis, or Eric Clapton.

"When Itzhak Perlman performs, he isn't playing the violin," I would explain. "He *is* the violin. Just bring up a video on YouTube and study these people, and you'll see what I mean."

Applying that concept to ourselves, I eventually came to realize that theater was more than something we did and more than something we loved (even though we *did* love it). It was something we *were*!

My mother, for instance, loved theater and loved music. Upon hearing favorite old songs, Mom would sit there listening and perhaps clap along or mouth the words. She was a lover of music, but not a musician and certainly not an artist. Artists don't simply love their art, they *are* their art.

I always enjoyed seeing live theater, but I loved directing plays much more. Would an artist, Picasso let's say, rather go to a museum or would he rather create a painting that might one day hang in a museum? The answer is obvious. The artist is a man of action, committed to his art form.

Mia recently described our life in the theater as "full immersion." It's true and had been true from the first play we directed. It was in this immersive world that our daughters grew up. Our life in the theater didn't end when we left rehearsal at the end of the night, but it extended into the remainder of the evening and into the next day and the next...and the next. In truth, the subject of our work in theater monopolized most conversations in our household.

LESSON:
The artist is a man of action, committed to his art form.

For Mia and her sister Gina, both professional actresses today, it remains that. Even between professional jobs, Mia is still fully immersed. Many of her friends in New York are actors, and their worlds revolve around what opportunities are available (or unavailable) to them, the rigorous process of auditioning, and discussing who is working and not working.

Gina, as a voice actor, feels she auditions approximately eight thousand times a year. Think of it! If you do the math, that's twenty auditions a day if she takes no days off – and she very seldom takes a day off. She may be auditioning at eleven in the morning or at eleven at night.

This was our daughters' life growing up in the Scarpa home,

and for better or worse, it prepared them for a future I can only describe as karmic.

Someone recently asked Mia if theater brings her happiness. The question made her realize that theater, for her, has very little to do with being happy or unhappy. Not for the artist it doesn't. It simply isn't always wine and roses. Did painting make van Gogh happy? Did composing music bring Beethoven happiness? Did acting, singing, and dancing make Judy Garland happy? There is strong evidence which suggests the contrary. Still, some inner drive compelled these artists and so many others to persevere in their art.

Contemplating the question, Mia asked the person, "Does being married always make you happy? Do your children always make you happy?" The answer, if we're honest with ourselves, is that sometimes our spouses and children bring us happiness and, at other times, they do not. Often enough – quite the opposite of happiness, in fact. That's how it was for Fran and me in the theater. And that's how it still is for our daughters. But happiness or not, often in life, we have certain proclivities that compel us onward.

Was our life in the theater the fulfillment of a dream? While the idea of fulfilling one's dreams is a romantic notion that may appeal to many people – as a family, we have a different perspective. I offer that a dream is something that we do at night while sleeping. In most cases, the fulfillment of what many people call a dream is unlikely.

Were directing plays and opening our own theater the fulfillment of our dreams? When we opened our doors at Center Stage in 2005, I might have thought so, but I would learn otherwise.

I offer, instead, the concept of fulfilling a goal. A goal is an *achievable end result* given a host of realistic factors. Personally, I grew up loving the game of basketball. But no amount of dreaming was going to land me a career in professional basketball. I possessed neither the physical attributes nor the skill required.

To open a full-time theater, talent, time, diligence, and financial resources are necessary requirements. Center Stage would not exist today if we didn't possess all of these, but let me just cite one.

Without the proper finances, it couldn't have happened. We needed to either have or raise the money to launch the theater. In our case, as stated, we made the choice to open a loan against the equity in our home.

I remember a guy I had known long ago coming to Center Stage for a show, and afterwards, he said to me, "This is great. You're living your dream, right?" I forgot how I responded, but I remember thinking, *This is no dream. It's the result of investing a lot of money and even more blood, sweat, and tears.* I felt that in a very visceral way. And to be honest, I also recall that at the time of this interaction, I felt anything but happy with our life at Center Stage. I thought, *Dreams, if they exist, wouldn't be this painful.*

And for Gina and Mia, earning an income as a voiceover artist and as a stage actress has nothing to do with dreams and everything to do with talent, persistence, hard work, and sacrifice.

Early in this volume, I explained that I often joked that our commitment to theater was an illness. It's not far from the truth. We have to ask ourselves, I think, if any compulsion is good for our health. This compulsion I speak of is *not* something I would recommend to anyone. And I don't feel that all theater people have it. In fact, in thinking about it, I was only able to think of a half dozen people we've known personally who lived the life of "full immersion" that we have, but I know dozens and dozens of people who *do* theater and who *love* theater but who haven't made it their whole world. They are probably the smart ones. I suppose each person who is involved in the world of theater would have to answer that question for themselves.

I recently read a captivating theatrical memoir, *Public/Private: My Life with Joe Papp at The Public Theater* by Gail Merrifield Papp, wife of the legendary producer/director, and I thought to myself, *On a smaller scale, this was our life*. Now, I don't claim to be Joseph Papp, who was truly an inspiring pioneer in the world of New York theater – but on a smaller scale, our life in little Shelton, Connecticut had many parallels.

This subject of full immersion brings back a favorite memory. We have a close friend who did some sewing for us behind the scenes. She was a seamstress who had once owned a curtain business. Upon arriving to show me a curtain she had made for a scene in *Les Misérables* for us, she paused before speaking to me, taking in all of the activity that was happening around us – several dozen volunteers hammering and drilling and painting and hanging lighting instruments on lifts. Finally, she shrugged and said, "How do you do this?" and then, after a short pause, with a look of utter bewilderment, she added, "*Why* do you do this?"

It's a fun story that we occasionally tell, but I understood her point. Why would anyone ever do what we did? Not because of a dream and not because of love alone. For us, as Mia said, it was about "full immersion." It wasn't about wanting to do theater but about *needing* to do it. One thing is for certain, full immersion is the only way we knew how to do theater.

It's not even something a person decides. It just is.

So, what drove us, you might ask. It's a question almost too complex to answer. One answer is the impact it had on the people within our reach – the actors, the volunteers, and the audiences. As we saw how it made life better for the kids and adults who performed in our shows as well as the many thousands of people who attended our productions, we forged ahead again and again. It was our art form and our contribution to society.

We have many notebooks and scrapbooks where cast members wrote us beautiful notes. I remember times, especially in our early days of directing, when Fran and I sat in bed at two in the morning reading notes in journals given to us by our casts where each person expressed what the experience had meant to them. As we read, we cried, not only because of the beautiful sentiments expressed but also, I think, from the sheer physical and emotional exhaustion of mounting a production and having it now be over. For us, and perhaps for any creator, mounting a play was an emotionally draining experience.

Even today, people who appeared in our plays twenty and thirty and forty years ago partly attribute who they became to their experience of being in our productions. While a fraction of those whom we directed attempted to make a go of the professional theater, the vast majority would, understandably, go into other fields. On so many closing nights, as performers graduated out of our high school drama club or the Youth CONNection, I would talk about how this might very likely be their last night ever on the stage...about how, in all likelihood, they would be too busy with future careers, marriages, and perhaps parenthood to act in plays. I recall looking into the faces of these graduates and seeing eyes filling up with tears because they knew what I was saying was true. They and I both knew deep within our hearts that, as John Lennon said, "Life is what happens to us while we are making other plans." But in that time and place, for what, in retrospect, might have felt like a mere moment in time, they got to perform on the stage and have an experience unlike anything they would ever have again.

We in the Scarpa family don't think there's any activity that benefits kids more than the theater. And that has absolutely nothing to do with the unlikelihood that they'll someday have a professional career. For *everyone*, no matter what their level of talent, innumerable skills and lessons are learned, lasting friendships are formed, and great memories are created that will last a lifetime. One person who performed in our shows recently shared about his experience: "It's amazing what this 'hobby' of ours gives back." Another offered, "I think (whether you intended it or not) we learned lessons in accountability, trust, and reliance."

Yes, we were keenly aware that the young people we directed were learning daily lessons about life at rehearsal that they would find invaluable to their future, whatever it might be. To use one last sports analogy, there is a story of famed Indiana University basketball coach, Bobby Knight, a man who was quite a powerful presence. Legend has it that he wanted to know which professors were teaching his players more than he was – because he wanted to meet those people and commend them. I can relate!

Like Bobby Knight, we knew that our actors gained many lessons in the theater. With the popularity of social media today, I recently happened across a meme floating around the internet with the words: *Theater teaches us to*...and then it goes on to illustrate a multi-colored list of lessons: *respect others, experiment, start a dialogue, find our voices, make connections, self-evaluate, express ourselves, observe, value aesthetics, learn from our mistakes, embrace diversity, reflect on our work, envision solutions, persevere, break away from stereotypes, have an opinion, collaborate, see another point of view, appreciate beauty, imagine possibilities, innovate, create.*

As creators of theater, we certainly didn't invent any of these lessons. They are there, inherent in the art form, ready for the taking for those of us who choose to participate. If these lessons aren't learned, plays will never reach performance.

Our life in the theater was very much about the art form itself. It was about a box of scripts and musical scores arriving one day in a UPS box...about lumber being picked up or delivered...about the smell of sawdust and paint...about the right costumes being hunted down, fitted, and organized...about long hours of rehearsing harmonies, choreography, and scenes – and seven or eight weeks later having a beautiful play to share with our audiences. It was about impacting the lives of our cast members and volunteers and about making high quality entertainment accessible to the people of our community – entertainment that, for some, may not have been otherwise available because of their age or financial circumstances or commitments.

For me, it seriously boiled down to a commitment to that art form...to the *play*...to the author of the play...to the actors who would perform the play...to the wonderful volunteers who would assist us in bringing the play to our stage...and to the audiences we served who would enjoy seeing the play.

I suppose, in its simplest form, we can't help but get back to *love*. It may sound hackneyed to say this, but I think of the song from *A Chorus Line*, "What I Did for Love." In the song, the professional performers express the sacrifices they made for their passion...for their art. That was our life in the theater.

Our life on the stage was a matter of using every fiber of our being to bring a professional level of excellence to our work – inasmuch as it was within our means. In the process, there were high points and low points...victories and defeats...happiness and hardships...joy and pain – the full gamut that life has to offer.

Would we do it again? Most of it – yes...and maybe some of it – no.

Opening and running a full-time theater was more than we could have ever imagined. Being who we are, we allowed Center Stage to swallow us whole. I remember seeing and then buying a t-shirt years ago with the saying emblazoned on the front: *I can't! I have rehearsal!* It had always been true...but with Center Stage and our full commitment to and immersion in the business, it was truer than ever. When one play opened, we began rehearsals for the next one the following day. In the process, we had little if any time or energy to spend with friends and family outside of that world. Those who really loved us and cared about us understood, but it was a sacrifice to be sure.

There comes a time when working in a field of endeavor (even one you love), as in writing a book, that you know it's time to end the story. It's a matter of knowing when to call it quits. I felt it in 2012 when I retired from the world of education, and within a few years, Fran and I knew in our hearts we needed to retire from the theater. Really retire this time! As the Center Stage years progressed, we realized our house was becoming a refuge – a safe haven away from our lives as directors. We tried not to discuss our work in theater when we were at home, which wasn't always easy considering who we are. And our home itself, I'm sorry to say, had been a place, historically, we had managed to put on the back burner. Now it would become the most important place in our lives, as it should have been the whole time. Updating some furniture and adding photos, especially family photos, to the walls and the shelves and on the mantle over the fireplace suddenly took on new meaning. We would find that, after a very hectic life directing productions, we would cherish quiet nights in the warmth of our home.

At the time of our retirement in 2019, I thought I might like to direct one play a year going into the future. I quickly realized that I don't have the physical or emotional energy for it anymore. Especially the latter. The way I usually say it is, "I don't have the stomach for it." I mean that in relation to handling stress. Getting a play, especially a large scale musical, ready for an audience is a high pressure situation. I had the "stomach" for it for a very long time, but no more. It's an acceptance of the aging process.

I also realized that I have a lot of creativity left in the old tank...so I write. This book will be the fourth that I've written and published in less than six years. Not bad.

Of one thing there is no doubt. I got hooked on theater in 1973 because it's a wonderful art form that impacts and transforms people in multitudinous ways. To best understand why we spent forty-three years of our life immersed in theater, I feel it's important to define the art form, and so I bring this book to an end with a definition of sorts.

I recently happened upon a video where renowned Broadway actor André De Shields discussed the theater, in its perfection and imperfection, in the process defining it more beautifully than I could. His words:

The theater is life enhanced. The theater is church. The theater is temple. The theater is worship. The theater is community. The theater is a totally different experience than any other medium. The theater is culture. The theater is literacy. And no other place can you go for that kind of enlightenment...for that kind of education...for that kind of entertainment. It's real, therefore we make mistakes... therefore we fall on our faces and we pick ourselves up again...and we never have to apologize for it because we never pretend that we are offering you perfection. We're gonna grow old right in front of your eyes...we're gonna cry right in front of your eyes...we're gonna break down — we're gonna go crazy...we're gonna get fat...we're gonna get skinny...we're gonna get sick. We're gonna do whatever it takes to lighten your burden...to solve that problem that you brought to the theater...to resolve that crisis... to make sure you go home lighter than you did when you arrived...happier than you did... exhilarated!

THANK YOUS!

Unlike my previous books, which were works of fiction, I didn't need very much help from other people to assist me in bringing *Lessons from the Stage* to completion. There was no need for beta readers or consultants of any kind. After all, *Lessons from the Stage* simply chronicles the life I led with my wife and daughters starting with my first time in a play in 1973 and ending with Fran's and my retirement from the theater in 2019.

First, I want to thank our good friend Lee Coffin for writing the foreword to this book. Lee performed in our shows throughout all of high school and college, and for us, he beautifully represents the thousands of "kids" who passed through our doors over the course of forty-three years. Like Lee, they took the lessons they learned and applied them to other areas of their lives.

In relation to writing and publishing *Lessons*, as always my daughter Mia worked hand-in-hand with me as editor and publishing partner to bring this volume from conception to the printed page. Together, we worked in collaboration, discussing the life of our family in the theater at length and how to best tell our story. So, to Mia, I send a million thanks. Without her, there would be no Next Chapter Press and perhaps no books by Gary Scarpa.

I also want to express my most heartfelt thanks to my wife Fran who was my partner in this theatrical life beginning on a warm June afternoon when she called out to me, "Hey, Gar! Who're you having lunch with?" That fateful meeting in a college play led to a fulfilling life of marriage and family, happily.

For Mia and Gina, who grew up on the stage, there were many gifts as well as sacrifices. Their contribution to the Shelton

High School Drama Club and especially to the Youth CONNection and to Center Stage were immeasurable. I love them for sharing this crazy life with us. Even our grandson Michael, while never drawn to performance, did volunteer to be on our backstage crew several times, and he faced the challenges of being a member of the Scarpa family and our world. So to our "kids" – I extend my deepest gratitude and my eternal love!

Our life in the theater simply had an energy of its own, propelling us forward from the day we began directing. As the old Sinatra song suggests, we did what we had to do and saw it through without exemption.

Beyond my immediate family, I want to thank my extended family – the thousands of amazing people who assisted us in this theatrical life – the performers who shared their talent and graced our stage; the volunteers who built and painted scenery, altered and organized costumes, and gathered props; the musicians who played in our pit orchestras; the skilled technical personnel who enhanced our shows with light and sound; and the dozens of thousands who bought tickets to our productions through the years. They were all a vital part of our experience and success, and without giving people like them, there would be no such thing as theater.

Finally, *Lessons from the Stage* is my best attempt to honor the theater, what it meant to us Scarpas, and what I believe it means to countless other people who have the good fortune to love theater and keep it alive. I hope you enjoy my book!

www.ingramcontent.com/pod-product-compliance
Ingram Content Group UK Ltd.
Pitfield, Milton Keynes, MK11 3LW, UK
UKHW041631190726
13854UKWH00006B/2436

9 781736 514658